TALES OF CRIMES PAST

TALES OF CRIMES PAST
A Casebook of Crime in Colonial India

SUNIL NAIR

First published in 2022 by Hachette India
(Registered name: Hachette Book Publishing India Pvt. Ltd)
An Hachette UK company
www.hachetteindia.com

1

Text copyright © 2022 Sunil Nair

Sunil Nair asserts the moral right to be identified as the author of this work.

All rights reserved. No part of the publication may be reproduced, stored in a retrieval system (including but not limited to computers, disks, external drives, electronic or digital devices, e-readers, websites), or transmitted in any form or by any means (including but not limited to cyclostyling, photocopying, docutech or other reprographic reproductions, mechanical, recording, electronic, digital versions) without the prior written permission of the publisher, nor be otherwise circulated in any form of binding or cover other than that in which it is published and without a similar condition being imposed on the subsequent purchaser.

The views and opinions expressed in this book are the author's own and the facts are as reported by him. The publishers are not in any way liable for the same. While the stories are based on the author's personal research and other published materials, some events, conversations and details have been altered or dramatized for narrative purposes. Sources have been referenced and quotes acknowledged to the best of the author's ability. Any inadvertent omissions brought to our attention in writing will be remedied in future editions.

Subsequent edition/reprint specifications may be subject to change, including but not limited to cover or inside finishes, paper, text colour, and/or colour sections.

ISBN 978-93-93701-26-8

Hachette Book Publishing India Pvt. Ltd
4th & 5th Floors, Corporate Centre
Plot No. 94, Sector 44, Gurugram – 122003, India

Typeset in Adobe Garamond Pro 11.5/13.8
by Manmohan Kumar, Delhi

Printed and bound in India
by Manipal Technologies Limited, Manipal

To my late mother Subhadra,
who fostered in me a love of books and reading,
thus ensuring I would never be lonely.

Contents

Introduction   xi

1. In Bad Taste: The Baroda Poisoning Case   1
2. Royal Folly: The Malabar Hill Murder   21
3. Murder, They Wrote: The Fullam–Clark Affair   41
4. Plague Take You: The Pakur Murder Case   64
5. Blood on the Tracks: A Murder on the GIP Railway   79
6. In Durance Vile: Death in a Bombay Brothel   99
7. Death in the Hills: An Unsolved Murder in Burma   110
8. Sultana: The Life and Legend of India's Favourite *Daku*   124
9. Deceive and Choke: The Cult of the Strangler   138
10. A Never-Ending Headache: Dacoity in the Raj   163
11. Unpalatable Crimes: The Menace of the Professional Poisoner   179
12. Crooks on the Line: The Railway Thieves   192

Acknowledgements   208
Endnotes   210
Other Works Consulted   221

Introduction

THE IDEA FOR THIS BOOK CAME SOME YEARS AGO FROM A colleague at Reuters who suggested that I put what I call my 'useless knowledge' and fascination for all things colonial and criminal to good use by writing a book on the subject. I had, not uncharacteristically, been boasting to her about my collection of books on crime when she came up with the idea. It seemed a daunting task at first, and so, being not overtly fond of hard work, I put it on my 'to do' list – a convenient way of putting off things I never mean to get down to. The COVID-19 pandemic, however, changed everything. Stuck at home all day with not much to do, and being prodded by the *memsaab* and a few friends to 'stop cribbing and write a book', I decided to give it a go.

Crime in colonial India has always been a subject dear to my heart, and I had unwittingly amassed quite a bit of literature on the subject. I thought a crime aficionado would probably get a good night's sleep if I were to recount some of the crimes I'd read about. I have, therefore, chosen to narrate some of my favourite tales of crime in British India and write about the people who committed them. A couple of them are well-known, but most, I believe, are pretty obscure. So much so that I was a little sad on finding that not one of my several Bengali friends in the media had ever heard of the infamous Pakur case that shook up Calcutta in the early 1930s. Equally, not many who I thought were hooked to the non-fiction crime genre seemed to know about the Bawla case or the notorious (in its time) Agra Double Murder.

Colonial India was home to an interesting and diverse array of criminals and deviants – including some that were very unusual and specific to the country. Policing, as we know it, and the 'rule of law', as we now understand it, were just about getting a foothold in the subcontinent in the early decades of the nineteenth century. The unsettled state of the country in the wide hiatus between the disintegration of the Mughal Empire and the consolidation of British rule in India put security of life and limb at risk. From lawless bands of freebooters to the semi-organized bands of *Pindari* marauders, and the roving gangs of thugs and dacoits which preyed on rich and poor alike, no man's life was worth much outside the security of his home or town/village. Even the worthy Charles Metcalfe, a future governor-general of India, was once set upon by a gang of robbers in north India on his way to Bharatpur in the early 1800s. His palanquin-bearers took to their heels and Metcalfe had to fight for his life, sword in hand. He saw the robbers off, but was left bruised and bleeding, and staggered to a nearby stream to wash his wounds. When he came back, he found his bearers calmly sitting around the palanquin – smoking!

Thugs and dacoits, professional poisoners and criminal tribes, child-lifters and cattle-rustlers, coiners and forgers, not to mention the rapacious village money lender and *daroga* – the field of colonial criminal enterprise is vast and varied. But my compass here is a little narrow. I merely wish to introduce the reader to a few remarkable crimes and criminals. The last four stories in the book (on thugs, dacoits, poisoners and railway thieves) do not deal with specific cases, but shine a spotlight on certain classes of criminals who led the police a merry dance in their time, and whose activities could probably never be entirely brought to a close.

One element about crime and criminals has always held an abiding fascination for me: the possibility, and the likelihood of escape or redemption after the deed is done. Not all crimes are found out, and retribution and justice do not necessarily follow. Scores of thugs and poisoners escaped the noose for want of hard evidence, and many a scoundrel saved his skin by turning 'approver' and betraying his comrades. The benefit of royal descent and the dictates of realpolitik ensured that titled maharajas were not very much inconvenienced by verdicts passed on them. Col. Morshead's killer in Burma was never identified and brought to book, and it was almost a century later that the researches of a western journalist in present-day Myanmar helped shed some light on the mystery.

Not all criminals meet what society deems their 'deserved' end. This is as true today as it was in colonial times. Harry Roberts, the prime accused in the famous Shepherd's Bush murders in England, where three policemen were shot dead in 1966, walked out of prison in 2014 after serving a total of 48 years, disappointing the many who had hoped to see him hang, or at the least die behind bars. Ronnie Biggs, who took part in the Great Train Robbery of 1963, escaped from the UK to live out most of his life as a fugitive in Brazil, before finally coming back to London where he died in 2013. Fowzi Nejad, sent to prison for his role in the Iranian Embassy siege in London in 1980, lives in the UK on state benefits. Back home, the protagonist in the famous Nanavati murder case of 1959, Commander Kawas Nanavati, was released from prison after a few years, and moved to Canada with his family to live a quiet life, before passing away in 2003. The young couple accused of murder in the famous Alavandar case in Madras in 1952 served time in prison and came out to set up a successful business in Kerala, raise a family, and lead a full life. The juvenile accused in the infamous Nirbhaya gang rape and murder is today a free man, simply because he was a 'minor' when the crime was committed. The wheels of justice indeed grind slowly, but not always exceedingly fine.

The certainty of punishment is probably much higher today than in colonial times due to advances in science, forensics and technology. However, on the whole, I have found colonial justice to be speedier. Most trials took place within months of the crime, sentences were quickly handed out and the accused punished. Where trials were delayed and prolonged, as in the Pakur case, the perpetrators benefitted, being sentenced to life imprisonment instead of stepping up to the gallows.

Traditionally, and according to a Persian couplet, crime was thought to be instigated by a desire for either of three things: *zan, zar, zameen* (women, gold, land). Not necessarily, I have found, for not all crimes are planned, and malice is not always a forethought. A mistaken sense of grievance, an error of judgement or a fit of uncontrollable rage, and sometimes simply being in the wrong place at the wrong time could set the stage for an atrocious crime.

In the end, criminals are only human, and their stories are our stories – the reflections (if sometimes perverse) of our suppressed wants, unmet desires or uncontrollable urges. I do not claim to have any specialized knowledge of crime or criminals, and have not dug too deep into the social/cultural/economic or moral aspects of the subject. This is by no means an academic book. I have, however, referred to contemporary/original sources and authoritative published works wherever possible, given the constraints of time and space, and the restrictions imposed on travel by the pandemic while this book was being written.

If the reader finds these tales as much a joy to read as they were a pleasure for me to write, I would be amply rewarded.

Sunil Nair

1

In Bad Taste
The Baroda Poisoning Case

THE 14TH OF JANUARY, 1875, SHOULD HAVE PASSED AS AN unremarkable winter's day for the good citizens of Baroda. But it was not to be. The city was restive and an ugly rumour was afloat: their ruler, Malharrao Gaekwar, had apparently been arrested and was in the custody of British troops, and the state would now be annexed. This was not strictly true, but a momentous, if egregious, event had in fact occurred earlier that day. By an order issued by the Viceroy and Governor-General of India Lord Northbrook earlier that day, the maharaja of the princely state of Baroda had been suspended from power and placed under 'honourable surveillance'[1] for allegedly attempting to poison the British Resident, Colonel Robert Phayre.

This was an unprecedented occurrence. No ruling Indian prince had been treated in this fashion ever since the last Mughal emperor, Bahadur Shah Zafar, had been deprived of the imperial throne of Delhi for his alleged role in the rebellion of 1857. And it was all the more shocking, since Queen Victoria's proclamation of 1858 had guaranteed that the rights, dignity and honour of India's native princes would be scrupulously upheld.

Meanwhile, Malharrao offered no resistance, and the British took care to see that no indignity was offered to his royal person. He was driven in the Resident's carriage to the house of the Residency doctor, with a guard of the British troops in place. Damodar Pant, private secretary to the Gaekwar, was also detained on suspicion of having helped in the poisoning as he tried to leave the city that evening.

The day passed peacefully. Reports had reached Bombay that trouble could be expected in Baroda, but the British were prepared. Four companies of the 7th Fusiliers and 120 men and six guns of the Royal Artillery had been dispatched to the state a day earlier. General Devine, the commander of the Gaekwar's army, had been told that he would be held accountable for the conduct of the state's troops, and he kept them well in hand. Arrears of pay amounting to ₹80,000 was disbursed among the men, and probably served to win them over. Col (later Sir) Lewis Pelley, the recently appointed special commissioner of Baroda, called a meeting of the leading men of Baroda that day and assured them that an annexation of the state was not on the cards, and that the British had only temporarily assumed control of Baroda pending an enquiry.

But why had matters come to such a pass?

By all accounts, Malharrao Gaekwar was not someone who could be held up as a model of virtuous kingship. The list of misdemeanours attributed to him by H.L. Adam in his account of the case in *The Indian Criminal* is long and colourful. Malharrao's first attempt to gain the royal *gaddi* was not without blemish. In his thirties, he was arrested as a suspect in the attempted assassination of his elder brother Khanderao, who was the ruler then. The evidence of the European soldier, who Malharrao had allegedly induced to shoot Khanderao, was not very reliable and the then British Resident was not convinced of Malharrao's guilt, but Khanderao still managed to send him to prison on that charge.

There was certainly no love lost between the brothers – Khanderao, too, was suspected of having made attempts on Malharrao's life by means of sorcery, human sacrifices and poison.[2] Always suspicious, Khanderao had four men cruelly put to death for allegedly associating with Malharrao while the latter was in prison. While one was hanged and another beheaded, a third was trampled to death by an elephant and the last blown from the mouth of a cannon.³

While Khanderao's actions were unlikely to have found favour with the British, he still held a trump card. He had stood by the British during the troubles of 1857, and the government acknowledged that but for Khanderao's loyalty, its hold on the whole of western India would have been compromised. As a reward, the British remitted the fine of ₹3,00,000 that had been imposed on his predecessor Sayajirrao II to pay for the maintenance of the Gujarat Irregular Horse. More importantly, he was also granted the insignia of royalty and the right to adopt an heir, with the *sanad* granting the latter use of the title 'His Highness the Maharaja Gaekwar of Baroda' for the first time.

Khanderao died in 1870 without a male heir, and without having adopted anyone to succeed him. Malharrao was, therefore, next in line to the throne, but Khanderao's wife Jamnabai declared herself pregnant, and so Malharrao had to be content with the regency, pending the arrival of the young widow's child. Malharrao tried to thwart a possible succession by a male child by questioning the genuineness of Jamnabai's pregnancy, and failing in this, by questioning the legitimacy of the unborn child. The maharani, knowing fully well that her brother-in-law was a man utterly lacking in scruple, refused to eat any food in the palace unless it was cooked by her own servants for fear of being poisoned. She also convinced the Resident to allow her to stay in the Residency during her confinement.

In the event, Malharrao need not have worried. Jamnabai gave birth to a daughter, and Malharrao finally found himself on the throne as the eleventh maharaja of Baroda. The *gaddi* now secure, he embarked on a career of villainy. Among the first of his victims was Khanderao's former diwan, Bhau Scindhia, on whose instigation Malharrao had been thrown into prison. Bhau Scindhia now found himself behind bars and attempts were apparently made to poison him. When this failed, he was placed in a torture machine called a *sikunja* and slowly squeezed to death. Others who were thought to be hostile to Malharrao were also done away with by means of poison.[4]

He also emptied out the state's coffers, splurging in time-honoured princely style on gems and women. While Khanderao, who was also a profligate spender of state revenues, had ordered two guns to be cast in silver, Malharrao went one up and ordered two guns to be made in gold. His favourites ran an extortion racket at the Baroda court to which he turned a blind eye. As per Adam's account, any girl whose beauty appealed to him was almost certain to be kidnapped by his minions. Indeed, the woman who now shared his bed as the maharani was allegedly another man's wife. His ministers and subjects despaired of him, and appeals were made to the British government to step in.[5]

Enter Col Robert Phayre. Deputed to Baroda as the new Resident, Phayre was not the best choice for the role of troubleshooter. An old-school type and something of a martinet, he could not have been the ideal candidate to knock sense into someone given to unbridled licence. The hard-bitten Phayre was a typical child of the Empire, with a long record of fighting in the wars that created it. Commissioned into the 25th Bombay Native Infantry of the Honourable East India Company in 1839, he served in the First Afghan War and was wounded in the Battle of Meeanee. During the Mutiny of 1857, he had served as the quartermaster general to the Bombay Army, for which he was commended by Sir Hugh Rose, the commander of the Central India Field Force. In 1868, he took part in the Abyssinia Expedition and was again mentioned in dispatches. This last service gained him an appointment as aide-de-camp (ADC) to Queen Victoria and he was also made a Companion of the Bath.

To no one's surprise, given his temperament, he did not get on well with Malharrao. Instructed to get things in hand, the crusty colonel was not pleased by what he saw in Baroda where he arrived early in March 1873. Barely had he been four days in the city, when he heard that Malharrao had had eight men flogged in the streets for allegedly poisoning one of his servants. Accordingly, his dispatches to the government about the Gaekwar's doings were quite alarming, if not exaggerated. His charges against the Gaekwar seemingly ran the entire gamut of abuses. The state treasury was being depleted by the maharaja and his favourites, extortion and oppression were rife, and the Gaekwar was seemingly addicted to numerous vices. The viceroy, while not pleased with Phayre's reports, also realized that his man in Baroda was not the kind of person to win friends and influence people, and was probably overstating things. The matter was, however, a serious one and could not be set aside, and Lord Northbrook, therefore, ordered an inquiry into the affairs of Baroda.

The First Baroda Commission, headed by Sir Richard Meade, then chief commissioner of Mysore, arrived at Baroda in November 1873. The five-member committee – which also included an Indian, Nawab Faiz Ali Khan Bahadur, the prime minister of Jaipur state – was to inquire carefully into the specific charges made by Col Phayre, and also into the charge of general maladministration.

In all fairness, since the government did not wish to be seen as interfering unduly in the affairs of a princely state, the Commission was asked to be 'careful to give no encouragement to frivolous or vexatious complaints, and their inquiries should be conducted not so much with the view of the redress of individual grievances, as for the purpose of ascertaining whether such general maladministration exists as to call for the further interference of the British Government'.[6]

The Commission examined over 200 witnesses, inquiring into 13 cases of complaints by British subjects, 65 complaints of general misgovernment by Baroda subjects, and 14 miscellaneous complaints, before submitting its report in March 1874.

The inquiry found that there was some truth in Phayre's claims. While the charges of oppression put forward by British subjects was found to be exaggerated, it could not be denied that the agricultural classes had reason to be aggrieved due to the oppressive levies made on them. Arbitrary proceedings had been instituted against bankers and other wealthy persons not in favour with the Gaekwar. More seriously, respectable married and unmarried women had been seized for compulsory service in the palace, and female prisoners in jails had been subjected to corporeal punishment. The report also found the state's officials to be largely unfit to hold responsible posts and castigated the chief minister, describing him as a 'man of evil repute'.[7]

That the state was badly administered was obvious, and a remedy was essential. The report recommended appointing a new minister of 'special administrative experience' to aid Malharrao in running the affairs of Baroda. It also added that the new minister should be 'supported by the Resident, and not be liable to removal without the special orders of the British Government, and he should have power to eliminate and dismiss incompetent or unfit officials and appoint others in their place'.[8]

And so the Gaekwar got away with, what was at best, an admonitory rap on the knuckles. Lord Northbrook also sent an official dispatch to Malharrao in July 1874 allowing him a period of 17 months (till the end of December 1975) to introduce reforms in the state.

Lord Northbrook's response may have seemed inadequate and short-sighted, but he probably felt that Phayre was also part of the problem. Phayre, for his part, could not have been delighted by Northbrook's efforts. But under the existing system, the viceroy could not be seen to be treading too hard on the Gaekwar's toes. Princely India was not administered like British India, and what went on within the boundary of a prince's dominions was none of the business of the Paramount power. While the viceroy could chastise, he had to be careful not to appear too harsh on a ruler without just cause. The British government was attentive not to antagonize the princely states too much after the events of 1857. Lord Dalhousie's famous Doctrine of Lapse, which had led to several princely states falling under British vassalage, was touted as one of the reasons behind the mutiny that had erupted only a decade ago. During that upheaval, most of the princely states either sat on the fence while some tacitly or actively helped the British. So, the British let them be.

However, purporting to be a benevolent force, the government appointed Residents or Political Agents (in charge of an 'Agency' comprising several small states) to the princely states to guide and advise them on running their states in keeping with modern notions of administration. It was a mutually beneficial relationship. The princes retained most of their privileges, did not have to worry about external threats from other powers, and were largely left to indulge their passions – as long as there were no overt excesses. The British Government, for its part, found loyal allies and partners for their idea of the empire and imperial progress. In a majority of states, the Resident and the maharaja, nawab or holder of the princely title got along well. As John Gunther puts it in his chapter on the maharajas in *Inside Asia,* the most important part of a Resident's job was what he (it was always a 'he') did not do.[9] The Residents were, in a sense, honoured guests, and in theory employed a light touch to get things done. That was the plan. But it was not always a success and sometimes could be an unmitigated disaster. In the event of a great crisis, to quote Gunther again 'the British Raj can do anything it likes'.[10]

A Resident had a small secretariat to help him in guiding the affairs of the state. Besides a small staff of clerks and other administrative officials, there would be a Residency or Agency surgeon and often a military advisor to assist with the training and management of troops in large states that had their own contingent of Indian State Forces. One of the most important roles of a Resident was advising the government on the succession of a ruler, and he could quickly find himself persona non grata in a state with a disputed line of succession. Rulers, therefore, were careful to keep to the right side of the Resident, who also had to be something of a diplomat. But sometimes things did not work out as planned and mutual antagonisms were not infrequent – with often unfortunate consequences.

While undoubtedly an imposing figure in a princely state, the Resident or Political Agent unsurprisingly also attracted a lot of hostility and resentment, which often bubbled over into acts of violence. For instance, Charles Burton, Political Agent to the Kotah Residency, was killed along with his two sons in October 1857 at the height of the mutiny.[11] Major R.L. Bazalgette, Political Agent to the Orissa States, was beaten to death by a mob in 1939 during internal disturbances in Ranpur State.[12] Frank Grimwood, Political Agent to the Manipur court, was killed during a minor uprising in 1891. While it did not have any real bearing on his murder, it later came out that he had not conducted himself with the high standard expected of someone in his position and had been consorting with the daughter of a former chief minister of the state while his wife was away in Shillong.[13] In what was probably a first, Lancelot Williams, the Political Agent in Bhopal, was once slapped in public by a teenage Sikander Begum, later to become the formidable ruler of Bhopal, for apparently playfully touching her earring.[14]

So, coming back to our errant protagonist, a chastised but hardly repentant Malharrao was not to be cowed, and he surely resented what he thought was needless meddling into his affairs. He did try to improve matters though, or gave the impression of attempting to do so, by appointing, Dadabhai Naoroji,[15] a man of exceptional credentials, as Diwan. This was probably Dadabhai's first venture into administration and realpolitik, and he tried hard to clean up the Augean stable. However, caught between an interfering Resident and an incorrigible royal, he could not achieve much and resigned.

The princely misdemeanours seemingly continued, but Malharrao now had a larger and more serious grouse. The British had refused to accept Laxmibai, a woman who was now staying with Malharrao as his wife, as the legitimate maharani and his offspring from that union as his legitimate heir. The lady's antecedents were, to say the least, questionable, and she was also apparently married to another man. Phayre was strenuously opposed to any such recognition, further queering the pitch for the succession.

Matters had thus came to a head when, on 2 November 1974, Phayre sent a damning report to the Bombay Government (which had oversight on Baroda) outlining further misdeeds by the now-furious ruler and the parlous position of the state. On the same day, Malharrao, too, wrote to the viceroy seeking Phayre's dismissal on grounds of being prejudiced against him and his officials. He was not getting a fair hearing, the Gaekwar complained. Phayre further aggravated matters on 5 November by privately ticking off the Gaekwar for the alleged attempts of his agents to bribe officials in Bombay for securing the recognition of Laxmibai's child as the legitimate heir.

Northbrook, one imagines, can't have relished the position he found himself in. Recognizing that matters in Baroda could not be brought to a satisfactory close while Phayre was in place, he sought the easy way out. He simply replaced Phayre, and named Col Lewis Pelly as the Agent to the governor-general and special commissioner of Baroda.

But that was not to be the end of the affair. To everyone's surprise, before the despatch recalling him arrived in Baroda, Phayre shot off a telegram on 9 November to the governor of Bombay, claiming an attempt on his life. The servants in the Residency, he said, had attempted to kill him that morning by lacing his *sherbet* (fruit juice) with poison.

This was, as all the parties involved were aware, a damning allegation, and one that could not be made or taken lightly. The British Resident in a princely state was the representative of the Queen Empress, and an attempt on his life amounted to treason – a serious charge indeed, and one that could have grave consequences for the ruler in question.

The news sent everyone – not least the British Government – into a tizzy. The newspapers made the most of it. Rumour and innuendo, fact and fiction combined to whip up passions and sides were taken. The viceroy was in a difficult position, and to the rulers of other princely states it would have sounded a bit ominous. A charge of treason against one of their kind could possibly endanger their position too. A battle royale seemed in the offing.

When crisis broke, Col (later Sir) Lewis Pelly, who was Agent to the governor-general in Rajputana, arrived at the Baroda Residency on 30 November 1874. Another soldier of the East India Company's (EIC's) Bombay Army, Pelly was seconded to the Foreign Department early in his career, serving in what came to be known later as the Indian Political Service. As a young man in his 20s, Pelly had served as assistant to the British Resident at the court of Baroda. While his latest appointment must have brought back fond memories of his time in the state, he is unlikely to have relished the position he now found himself in.

A police inquiry was ordered into the attempted poisoning and the Bombay police took over the case. Mr (later Sir) Frank Souter, superintendent of the Bombay Police, and Khan Bahadur Akbar Ali, head of the city's detective force, arrived in Baroda with their team to undertake the investigation. The police questioned the servants in the Residency and others who might be connected with the crime in any way, employing methods that, it was said, were not always above board and in keeping with the usual line of police investigations in India.

At the end of December, Pelly informed the governor of Bombay that Souter's investigations in Baroda had uncovered information that seemed to suggest that Malharrao had in fact instigated the attempted poisoning. The advocate general of Bombay then gave his considered opinion that a strong prima facie case of abetment of an attempt to murder had been made out against the Gaekwar. Northbrook, on being informed, issued a proclamation on 14 January 1875 that 'evidence has been adduced to the effect that His Highness Malhar Rao Gaekwar instigated the said attempt to administer poison to Colonel Phayre'. Because 'to instigate such attempt would be a high crime against Her Majesty the Queen, and a breach of loyalty to the Crown under which Malhar Rao Gaekwar is recognized as Ruler of the Baroda State' and also 'an act of hostility' against the British Government, it was necessary to suspend him from power in order to 'inquire into the truth' of the charge.[16]

The 'suspension' was an attempt to give an impression of British fair play – that Malharrao would have the opportunity of defending himself before any judgement was passed. Northbrook determined that the best way to do this was through a public trial that would be in the nature of an Inquiry Commission, with witnesses being called to give evidence and allowing cross-examination as in any criminal case, but without a judge or jury to pronounce a verdict. The Gaekwar's guilt or otherwise would be decided by a Committee composed equally of native and British officials. This seemed to be a fair, if rather unusual, proceeding given the rather special features of the case. The princely states were not pleased to see one of their number thus humiliated, but were conciliated by the argument that the Gaekwar would receive a fair trial, with two of his own peers – the Maharajas of Gwalior and Jaipur – on the commission along with Sir Dinkar Rao as the third Indian member.

The Commission was headed, just as the earlier one had been, by Sir Richard Meade with Sir Philip Melville and Sir Richard Couch (then chief justice of Bengal) as the other British representatives. Mr Scoble, the advocate general of Bombay, assisted by Mr J. Inverarity, would conduct the case against the Gaekwar.

Given the serious nature of the charge against him, Malharrao was advised to obtain a leading counsel from England. A famous English lawyer, Harry Hawkins, was first offered the brief, but he declined. Malharrao then obtained the services of Serjeant William Ballantine, a well-known London lawyer known to take up unpopular cases, and something of a character himself. Ballantine became a serjeant-at-law in 1856, which entitled him to wear the white coif or cap of that rank, and had made his name in England as a formidable criminal lawyer. He was part of the prosecution team that sent Franz Müller, a German tailor convicted for the first-ever train murder in London in 1864, to the gallows. Possessed of a violent temper and known for bullying witnesses in the dock, Ballantine had a reputation for being a verdict getter.[17]

He is said to have been paid a fee of £5,000 and a refresher of £100 a day for his services. On arrival in Bombay, he was instructed in the case by Mr Jefferson of Jefferson & Payne Solicitors, before proceeding to Baroda, where the trial was to be held. His arrival was eagerly awaited and all the principal stations between Grant Road and Baroda were thronged with people eager to catch a glimpse of the famous barrister as his train passed through. A reception committee comprising nobles and high officials was also assembled at Baroda to greet the man who had come all the way from England to defend the Gaekwar.

Legal luminaries came from all over India and Britain, drawn by the high degree of interest in the case, to witness the show in February 1875. British court reporters were drawn from the usual ranks used by the newspapers to report legal proceedings, which meant that the trial was being observed by men who were trained and practising lawyers and able to take an informed view of the proceedings

The Commission began proceedings on 23 February 1875 in open court, as in any common public trial. The three-week-long drama was however imbued with a sense of the comic from the start. The trial was conducted primarily in English and while two interpreters, Mr James Flynn and Mr Nowrozjee Furdoonjee, were on hand to provide assistance, it was not clear if the mainly native witnesses understood any of the proceedings. As the natives were familiar only with either Marathi or Gujarati, it was also difficult to explain the precepts and finer nuances of British law that were put forward in arguments to the non-English or limited-English speakers.

There were mainly two charges preferred against Malharrao. The minor charge was that he had tried to bribe the Resident's servants to find out the goings-on in the Residency, which led up to the more serious charge that this information was used to plan an attempt on Phayre's life at the instigation of the Gaekwar.[18]

The prosecution case was that, on 9 November 1874 Phayre returned from his morning ride, and partook of a glass of pomelo (grapefruit) juice that was kept ready for him as usual on his dressing-table. On swallowing a draught or two and finding it somewhat bitter, he threw away the contents, with the result that only a little sediment remained in the glass. This sediment, along with such adulterated stuff as could be scooped up from the rubbish on which it had been thrown, was sent to the Chemical Analyser, and the presence of some poison was detected.

It was Phayre's contention that the Gaekwar was behind the poisoning. This was allegedly done by mixing arsenic and diamond dust with the pomelo juice or sherbet, which as the Residency servants were aware, he was in habit of taking every morning. It must be mentioned that the use of poison to get rid of enemies or rivals was quite common in India, the usual and cheapest method being the use of the datura seed. Diamond dust or ground glass was also used, and often led to an excruciatingly painful death.

It came out at the trial that Ameena, the ayah at the Residency, and Rowjee Rama, Phayre's personal servant, along with Jagga the *punkah-wallah*, had been making visits to the Gaekwar's palace around the time of the setting up of the first commission of enquiry and were in the pay of the Gaekwar. A couple of goldsmiths testified that Rowjee had gold and silver ornaments made to the value of upwards of ₹500 – all of which he punctually paid, apparently from the money he received from the Gaekwar for providing inside information on the Residency.

The prosecution produced notes, apparently written by Ameena, Rowjee and Jagga about life in the Residency, which it claimed were passed on to the Gaekwar. The implication was that the Gaekwar had inside information about the goings-on in the Residency, allowing him to carry out his plan. Scoble took the view that the tampering with the servants was linked to the murder charge. Rowjee, whose duty was to bring the pomelo juice, was the prime suspect who had mixed the arsenic and diamond dust with the juice. On being taken into custody on 22 December, seven grains of arsenic had been found concealed in his stomach belt.

Dr Seward, the Residency surgeon, and Dr Gray, the chemical analyser to the Bombay government, gave evidence that poison had been found in Phayre's sherbet, and the prosecution called Rowjee and the Gaekwar's servant Nursoo to prove that it was placed there at the instigation of the accused. Rowjee deposed that the Gaekwar had offered him and Nursoo a lakh rupees each to put poison in the colonel's food. As they could not get at the food, it was decided to poison the sherbet, and the Gaekwar sent Nursoo a packet of poison, part of which was put into the glass of pomelo juice by Rowjee on 9 November.

Khan Bahadur Akbar Ali of the Bombay Police told the court that he had found the remaining packet of poison in Rowjee's belt, where the latter seemed to have unaccountably forgotten it. On promise of a pardon, Rowjee had then confessed that he had administered the poison at the behest and instigation of the Gaekwar. Nursoo, too, turned approver and corroborated Rowjee's statement.

The Gaekwar's private secretary, Damodar Pant, also gave evidence against his master, and confessed to have falsified the account books to hide the purchase of diamonds and arsenic. He also claimed that during a carriage ride after the failed poisoning attempt, Malharrao had admitted to the plot, but had threatened him to keep quiet. The ayah, Ameena, also confessed to having being asked by the Gaekwar for help in getting rid of the Resident by means of poison.

There was one more person involved: Pedro de Souza, deposed to having been 25 years in Col Phayre's service, with 15 years as his butler. According to Rowjee, Pedro too had visited the Gaekwar, who had given him a packet to put into the sahib's food.

Pedro had refused for fear of being implicated if the Resident died suddenly. The Gaekwar, Rowjee said, had then assured him that nothing would happen suddenly and that Phayre would only die after two or three months. The two had then left the palace with the package.

Mr Crawley Boevey, who had been assistant Resident at Baroda (and was in fact Phayre's son-in-law), confirmed that the ayah had been 'absent' from the Residency on some occasions (though he could not be specific on dates) and afterwards he heard her confess that she had visited the palace. While this by itself could not amount to much, the implication was that Ameena was an abetter in the plot.

Ballantine, known to be a formidable cross-examiner, would not let the prosecution arguments pass lightly. He cast serious doubts on Ameena's claims of being prompted by the Gaekwar to poison the Resident, and at times the heated exchanges between the two, conducted in languages that neither understood and which could only have added to the confusion arising from translation, provided much laughter and served to lighten the mood of the proceedings.

Rowjee, under Ballantine's forceful questioning, revealed that despite claiming to being bribed, he had never asked or received money for the attempted poisoning. He said that as the attempt had been a failure he did not want to claim money for a job that was not done. On being asked by Ballantine whether he lied on occasion, Rowjee's retort was that he only did it 'because people were after him' – something which brought up questions on the means employed by the police to force a confession.

Boevey, too, came in for some harsh questioning about a supposed purchase of arsenic and copper by or on his behalf by his servants. Apparently, rumours had being doing the rounds of the bazaars that some of Boevey's servants had bought arsenic and copper in his name, ostensibly to poison rats. There was also proof of this, it was said, in the shopkeepers' books. The assistant Resident emphatically denied this. This line of questioning was, however, not intended to impute that Boevey had anything to do with the poisoning, but to make the point that if some kind of poison was actually within the Residency, there was no need for Rowjee and Nursoo to go to the palace to obtain it.

Ballantine also tried to undermine the testimony of the doctors, questioning the quality and genuineness of the sediment that was produced for examination, given the highly insecure condition in which the sediment was preserved.

However, the biggest disaster for the prosecution case was Phayre himself who, in a fit of righteous indignation, tried to shout down Ballantine. The Resident proved to be an extremely unsatisfactory witness. On being asked why he threw away the contents of the glass if he believed that it contained poison, instead of preserving it, he said he did it because otherwise he might have been tempted to drink more!

Ballantine did his job well. He convincingly argued that the evidence presented and the testimony of witnesses on which the prosecution had based its case did not amount to the standards of proof required for an unequivocal conviction. He also cast doubts in the manner in which the police went about collecting their evidence, which would not have surprised anyone with experience of police investigations in India. He also cast aspersions on Sir Frank Souter and the police officials under him but the advocate general would have none of it, reminding the lawyer that Sir Frank was a 'gentleman of honour' and it did not behove the defence to suggest that he was engaged with his subordinates in a vile conspiracy for ruining the Gaekwar.[19]

Aside from all this, a curious, if somewhat farcical, incident occurred during the trial. Malharrao's servant Nursoo used to be taken out into the compound of the courthouse for his mid-day meals, attended by two policemen. One day, in an apparent fit of remorse for having given evidence against his master 'whose salt he had eaten', he threw himself into the well. He was promptly fished out and brought back to court. Ballantine could not let this pass without comment. Referring to the old saying, that truth is to be found at the bottom of a well, Ballantine said Nursoo had thrown himself into the well to find out the truth, which he had not found so far, and failing to find it at the bottom of the well, had come up destitute of the truth, as ever.

It was suggested by the defence that the case against the Gaekwar was concocted by his enemies. From the total absence of motive, the suspicious circumstances surrounding the case, the methods employed by the police to collect evidence and coerce witnesses, and the unsatisfactory nature of the evidence itself, Ballantine contented that no case could lie against the Gaekwar.

The trial finally concluded on 17 March 1875, with over 50 witnesses being examined, and the verdict of the commissioners was eagerly awaited. If Lord Northbrook had hoped for a unanimous decision, he was bound to be disappointed. The Commission was split down the middle. The native commissioners sent in separate reports, but their substance was the same – the evidence against the Gaekwar was insufficient to warrant a conviction. However, the three British Commissioners in their joint report said all the charges had been proved and found against Malharrao.

This put the viceroy in a difficult position. There were howls of protest by the British press against what they saw as a farcical trial and the Home Government back in Britain was also none too pleased about the way affairs had turned out. It was clear that a charge of treason against the Gaekwar would not hold ground. Also, a lot of princely feathers were being ruffled in India, and while the support of the princely order for the Crown was never in doubt, both the Home Government and the viceroy veered to the opinion that some middle ground would have to be found.

As the British could not put him away on the unsustainable charge of treason, it was decided that the Gaekwar would be deposed for 'notorious misconduct' and 'gross mismanagement' of his state.[20] He would be deprived of his throne, and a successor would be installed.

The proclamation deposing the Gaekwar was announced on 19 April, and Malharrao was quite upset when he heard the news. He protested, but to no avail and even his request that Jayajirao, his son by Laxmibai, should succeed him was refused. Three days after he was officially deposed, he was sent off by train into genteel pensioned exile in Madras.[21] He spent his last days there at Doveton House (now Women's Christian College) and died in 1882, aged 51.

News of the maharaja's deposition prompted some disturbances in Baroda city. The shops were closed and some people turned out on the streets with sticks and stones. The assistant Resident, Captain Jackson, was assaulted but managed to get away after shooting one of his attackers dead. General Devine, the head of the state troops, was also assaulted. For the most part however the state was quiet and serious trouble was averted.

The Gaekwar's hangers-on made a last desperate attempt to have things their way. Aided by loyal elements in the Palace Guard, they installed Laxmibai's son on the throne, apparently with the blessings of the senior maharani, Mahalsabai. It all came to naught though, and the still-born rebellion was aborted by the arrival of a squadron of British troops at the gates. Both maharanis and the would-be prince were put on a train and shipped out from Baroda into dignified oblivion.[22]

While there were other contenders to the throne, the British government decided that Gopalrao, a 12-year-old boy from one of the cadet branches of the royal family, would be Malharrao's successor. Maharani Jamnabai, the widow of Khanderao, formally adopted him as her son on 27 May 1875, after which he was duly installed on the throne. Sir Richard Meade, who had succeeded Pelly as Resident of Baroda at the conclusion of the trial, was in attendance when the young prince held his first durbar as Sayajirao Gaekwar III on 16 June 1875. Being a minor, Sayajirao reigned under a Council of Regency until he came of age, and was invested with full powers on 28 December 1881.

Malharrao's fate did unnerve the princely states, for it was now clear that they held their *gaddis* at the pleasure of the sovereign. These princely fears were soon assuaged however by the visit of the Prince of Wales in October 1875. A liberal dispensation of honours, decorations, medals, and other trappings during the Prince's visits to his various vassal states soon put paid to any remaining feelings of discontent. Malharrao would not be the last Indian king to be deposed, but the ruling princes were probably mollified by the knowledge that the wrath of the British sovereign would not be visited upon them as long as they stayed in line.

Sayajirao III had a long and prosperous reign until 1939. He was a reformer, and Baroda became one of the most progressive of Indian princely states under his administration. However, possessing an independent mind, his relations with the British were not always pleasant. At the Delhi Durbar of 1911, he famously turned his back and walked away after making only a perfunctory bow to the King-Emperor. It was also said that he walked away laughing, which did nothing to endear him to the British. However, they seemed to have forgiven him, for he was made a Grand Commander of the Indian Empire (GCIE) in 1919.

Col Phayre went back to military service and fought in the Second Afghan War of 1878–80, for which he was made a Knight Commander of the Order of the Bath (KCB) and received a vote of thanks from the Parliament. On retirement from the army, he took an active part in religious and philanthropic activities, authoring several books and pamphlets. Phayre died at his home in St. George's Square, Pimlico, London, on 28 January 1897.

Ballantine's magnificent defence of the Gaekwar won praise from all quarters, not just in Baroda and Bombay. A special *garba* song was composed and recited in his honour at Baroda. In Bombay, an address signed by some 1,500 worthy citizens was presented to him praising the competence, courage and independence with which he had conducted the defence. He was given a great send-off on his departure to England, and the crowd at the docks was so thick that his carriage could barely progress.

In the early 1880s, Ballantine hung up his lawyer's robes in order to write and travel, publishing several volumes of reminiscences. His interest in the theatre and journalism made him a familiar sight around London. Although he was recognized as an incisive cross-examiner, Ballantine was not regarded by his peers as being a model legal mind. The *Law Times*, in his obituary, stated that Ballantine 'left behind him scarcely any lesson, even in his own poor biography, which the rising generation could profitably learn'. Ballantine died at Margate on 9 January 1887, aged 75. He had lived a bohemian life and, though he earned very large sums during his career, died in penury.

2

Royal Folly
The Malabar Hill Murder

ON THE BALMY EVENING OF 12 JANUARY 1925, THE PEACEFUL environs of Malabar Hill, one of the smartest addresses in Bombay (now Mumbai), witnessed an unusually violent affray. It was around 7.30 p.m., and a few people were strolling around 'taking the air' (literally, *hawa khana*). Twilight had just set in and all was tranquil when a red Maxwell car rear-ended a black Studebaker that had driven up Little Gibbs Road towards the Hanging Gardens. In the back seat of the latter vehicle were a young woman named Mumtaz, her lover Abdul Kadir Bawla, and his secretary. As the passers-by watched, no doubt in some amazement and growing alarm, a group of six or seven men jumped out of the Maxwell, which the driver had brought to a stop a little ahead. A road rage incident seemed to be developing as the men began abusing the occupants of the Studebaker. One of the men then fired a shot at Bawla, who was sitting in the middle, while another opened the door and attacked the woman with a knife. The would-be abductors then tried to drag Mumtaz, her face streaming blood, into their vehicle. Then, the unexpected happened. To the amazement of the onlookers (none of whom had tried to intervene) another car drove up and four proverbial knights in shining armour jumped out to her rescue.[1]

These turned out to be English military officers on their way back to the Taj Mahal Hotel where they were staying. They'd had a few rounds of golf at the Willingdon Sports Club and were on the way back to Colaba when they had taken a wrong turn, arriving at the scene just in time. They now became unwitting – if not unwilling – actors in this fast-unfolding drama. Lieutenant John Saegert, an officer of the Royal Engineers who had been driving, rushed towards the men attacking the woman and was shot at, but grappled with them despite being hit on the shoulder. His companions Lt Francis Batley, Lt Maxwell Stephen and Col Charles Vickery also waded in and a violent scuffle ensued. Batley, an officer of the 1/7th Gurkhas, and the only one in the rescue party armed with a golf club, managed to carry the girl to the safety of their own car. Two of the assailants tried to get at the woman again, who was now sitting in the backseat, but Saegert charged at them and pulled them off. In doing so he was attacked with a kukri. Another man attempted to fire at him again, but the officer wrested the pistol away. His fellow officers then overpowered the man, while the remainder of the gang jumped into their car and sped away. None of the bystanders ventured to help. A European couple who happened to be passing by called the police. The woman and the injured men were taken to hospital. The police recovered a kukri, a jack-knife and a pistol from the scene of the crime.

The sole casualty was the man in the back seat at whom the first shot had been fired. Abdul Kadir Bawla, a well-heeled city businessman and member of the Bombay Municipal Corporation, was taken to the Sir J.J. Hospital where he died early the next day. The secretary, K.N. Mathews, who had been picked up by the couple at the Chowpatty sea face on their way to Malabar Hill, had jumped out of the door on the other side while the assault was underway. He took one of the bullets meant for his master on his arm, and had the misfortune to have it amputated.

And who was this Mumtaz in whose defence a few quarts of blood were shed on a Bombay street? Mumtaz Begum, as the newspapers revealed next day, was a Muslim dancing girl and former mistress of Tukojirao Holkar III, the maharaja of Indore. She had run away from her royal patron who quite simply wanted her back.[2]

The newspapers had a field day as a sordid tale of unrequited passion, concubinage, intimidation and murder were splashed on the front pages. When the case came up for trial, Mumtaz testified as a witness (in Urdu) and the somewhat salacious details of her unhappy life were made known to an incredulous public. The prurient element in the story kept it alive for a long time, making the Bawla Murder Case one of the most famous trails ever in the courts of pre-Independence India.

Mumtaz had been introduced into the Holkar court as a child-singer when she was about 12 years old by her mother. Wazir Begum had also been a famous singer in her prime and the child was merely following the family tradition. The family hailed from Amritsar but seemed to have moved around the country in search of patrons. Mumtaz had studied music and dancing at Hyderabad for a couple of years before she was brought to Indore by her mother and presented at the Indore durbar. The family made use of the young girl's talents and good looks by introducing her to men who quickly became besotted with her – a trend that would continue even after this infamous affair. Initially, Mumtaz would just sing for the maharaja but as she attained puberty and bloomed into a beautiful woman, she also shared his private apartments. She was accommodated in a separate bungalow in the palace compound along with her family and some servants. As a member of the Indore *zenana*, Mumtaz was now in purdah and, according to the mother's testimony, was always kept under guard.

Tukojirao was seemingly obsessed with Mumtaz and would not allow her any freedom. In April 1919, they had moved to Bombay for a while where Mumtaz and her mother were housed in a bungalow on Nepean Sea Road by the maharaja, who occupied a suite at the Taj Mahal Hotel. Soon after, on the pretext of taking her out to a movie show with the maharaja, Shankarrao, an official of the Indore durbar, took her to Victoria Terminus and put her on a train to Indore against her wishes. Wazir Begum then filed a complaint with the commissioner of police of Bombay, saying that her daughter was a minor and was being held against her will. Shankarrao was arrested, but as the mother could produce no evidence of her daughter's age, the case was thrown out and Mumtaz remained in the Indore *zenana*.

In May 1921, Mumtaz went on a trip to England under the alias Kamalabai, along with the senior maharani and some other Indore officials. The assumed name may have been a ploy by the maharaja to pass Mumtaz off as his wife, and she was brought to Bombay ahead of her journey. Wazir Begum, on getting to know of this, again complained to the police that her daughter was being forcibly confined. Mumtaz was then traced to a steamer that was about to depart for England, but on being questioned by the police, she said she was travelling of her own free will. The maharaja was not present, having left for England some weeks previously along with the junior maharani. Testifying before the court, Mumtaz said it had been a good opportunity to escape, but she feared for her life and had been tutored on what to say to the police on pain of death.

Mumtaz returned from England in December and was taken to Indore. Nearly a year later she became pregnant. After several entreaties, her family, including her step-father Mohamad Ali, was called to Indore during her confinement and lived with her under guard. Eventually, Mumtaz delivered a baby girl, who died under circumstances that were not entirely clear. The nurses simply reported to the family that the child was dead. Mumtaz, however, was convinced that the child had been killed by the nurses, a charge later refuted by the defence, contending that the girl had been stillborn. With the death of her child, something seemed to have snapped and an anguished Mumtaz decided to leave the maharaja's household. This was easier said than done. Tukojirao would not let her go.

Earlier, in the first three years when she was his mistress, Mumtaz told the court, Tukojirao treated her fairly well. She had the use of a car and a house of her own, and while she was not paid anything, her mother was given a regular salary. He did give her some jewellery, but this was part of the Indore state treasury and was soon taken away. However, Tukojirao's ardour cooled off over time, and he began to treat her badly. He was still very possessive about her though, and would not allow her any freedom. She made attempts to contact the police and seek help but was always thwarted.

In March 1924, the family accompanied Tukojirao to Bhanpura (in Madhya Pradesh, then part of the Central Provinces) on a hunting trip. Here he seems to have relented and told Mumtaz that she could leave if she wished. However, he did not give any orders to this effect and the mother and daughter were forced by a Mr Sule, a minion of the Indore household, to stay put. They were then ordered to go to Mussoorie and on the way there, at Delhi, Wazir Begum sent telegrams to the commissioner of police, Delhi, and the viceroy seeking assistance, but no redress was forthcoming. The family then moved to Amritsar, but were tracked down there by Shri Ram Shambu Dayal, the maharaja's head servant, and threatened with dire consequences if they did not return to Indore. Distraught and fearing for their lives, the women hired two Gurkha guards to watch over their house and also acquired a car and a driver to get around. The mother also wrote to the deputy commissioner of Amritsar for assistance, but her petition seems to have never reached him.

At Amritsar, however, things took a curious turn. According to Wazir Begum's testimony, the family became acquainted with a Delhi-based shawl merchant called Biharilal through their driver. Biharilal, on being informed of their plight, offered to help. He suggested they move to Bombay where one of his brothers was a barrister and would assist them in filing a suit against the maharaja. They could stay at the barrister's bungalow at Andheri, he proposed, and also offered the services of his servant Ramlal who would accompany them. The family agreed and, arriving at Bombay's Victoria Terminus on 18 June 1924, were met by Bulaquidas, also one of Biharilal's brothers, and taken to a bungalow in Versova.

The bungalow was located at a very lonely spot, and the family felt ill at ease there. Wise in the ways of the world, the women realized that all was probably not as it seemed. Convinced that they had been lured into a trap, and fearing an attempt on their lives, they left the bungalow within a day or two and moved to Hakim Buildings in Madanpura in the bustling Muslim quarter of the city. In their besieged state of mind, the crowded lanes and bylanes peopled by their co-religionists may have seemed to offer some security against possible assault or abduction. Before leaving the bungalow they also met Mr Fuller, the superintendent of police at Parel, who also advised them to move – but he does not seem to have done anything further.

Bulaquidas tried his best to dissuade them, but gave in as the family were now determined to move. He, however, sent his servant Ramlal to stay with them. Some days later, on 25 June, Bulaquidas showed up at Hakim Buildings and spent the night there along with Ramlal. The next day Mumtaz's stepfather filed a complaint with the police accusing Bulaquidas and Ramlal of stealing his money and documents while he had stepped out for his morning namaz.

Ramlal now confessed that he was part of a gang led by Shri Ram Shambu Dayal who had been ordered to bring Mumtaz back to Indore or cut off her nose, and do away with Wazir Begum and her husband. Biharilal and Bulaquidas were also part of the conspiracy. Biharilal, it turned out, was not a shawl merchant but an accountant of the Indore durbar. Wazir Begum's sister Nathubai was also in on the plan and had been recruited to provide information on the family's plans and whereabouts.

Shri Ram was arrested and confessed to have acted on the orders of his Highness but no action was taken against Tukojirao. Mumtaz's mother's petition to the Bombay police commissioner seeking protection from the maharaja was also not acted upon. Wazir Begum and her husband then moved again to Amritsar, where in November she wrote to the deputy commissioner, F.H. Puckle about her apprehensions that some mischief might be perpetrated against her family. Puckle was not sympathetic. 'Returned to the applicant. On the facts stated, there is no ground for taking any cognizance,' was the response from the deputy commissioner's office.[3]

Why had Mumtaz not followed her family to Amritsar? Sometime after her arrival in Bombay and before her mother's last missive to the authorities seeking help, Mumtaz had acquired a new lover. Abdul Kadir Bawla was introduced to Mumtaz by Allabux, her mother's cousin who was a taxi-driver in Bombay. Bawla was hopelessly smitten by her charms. He lavished gifts and jewellery on her and also provided her a house to live in. By Mumtaz's own account, Bawla was a generous lover, giving her an allowance of ₹1,000 a month besides clothes and other necessities. According to the testimony of her aunt, Bawla could not bear to be away from Mumtaz. The inseparable couple went on several excursions outside Bombay, and Bawla even took her to the Poona races. She finally came to live with him in his house at Chowpatty and was very happy there. She was also pregnant, and it is not unreasonable to assume that she hoped to become his wife one day. But that was not to be.

Less than a week after Puckle's refusal to intervene, Bawla was shot dead and Mumtaz's sorry tale, which the authorities had so callously disregarded and tried to sweep under the bureaucratic carpet, was out in full public view.

The police moved quickly and inquires were instituted in Bombay, Hyderabad, Amritsar and Indore, suspects rounded up and interrogated, and nine men were sent up for trial. All the accused had connections to Indore, and most were members of the State Forces and the Police. This created some problems of jurisdiction as they were subjects of the State of the Indore while the crime had been committed in British India, but the necessary extradition warrants were soon obtained and legal proceedings got underway. The accused were charged with entering into criminal conspiracy to kidnap Mumtaz Begum out of British India, for causing her grievous hurt in the attempt to kidnap, and with the murder of Bawla.[4]

The case of the *Emperor vs Shafi Ahmed Nabi Ahmed* that began on 27 April 1925 at the High Court of Judicature at Bombay had a matinee opening of sorts. It has a stellar cast. The eminent Mr (later Sir) Jamshedji Kanga, advocate general of Bombay led for the crown, assisted by Mr Kenneth Kemp (later a judge of the Bombay High Court). Mr Kurshed Framji, a well-known Bombay lawyer and a friend of Bawla, represented Mumtaz. The defence had a number of legal luminaries, led by Mr J.M. Sengupta of the Calcutta Bar, who appeared for the main accused Shafi Ahmed, along with Mr Nadkarni. The formidable Mohamed Ali Jinnah, one of the country's top-notch lawyers, appeared for accused number 9, Anandrao Phanse (adjutant general of the Indore State Forces), who was alleged to have organized the plot, under the orders of Tukojirao. The other seven accused were defended by Mr S.G. Velinkar of Bombay. Justice (later Sir) Lewis Crump, a career-civil servant with wide experience on the bench, presided and a special jury was appointed. A huge crowd turned up to watch the proceedings and special arrangements had to be made to regulate entry into the courtroom.

As the trial unfolded, a diabolical plot hatched by an obsessed prince to secure a woman whose affections he had lost was laid bare. Tukojirao soon found himself in a very nasty spot as the wires buzzed between Government House in Bombay and the viceroy's office in Delhi, but he was never directly implicated or charged in connection with the crime. It would, however, cost him his crown.

Mumtaz had become a celebrity overnight. She testified in Urdu (She could not speak English, but could speak a little Marathi) and, for one who had always led a mostly secluded and sheltered life, acquitted herself well. The scars on her forehead plainly visible for all to see, Mumtaz gathered sympathizers within and outside the courtroom. Holding her own against the battery of lawyers arrayed against her, she endured the most severe cross-examination for two days with considerable elan. To one who had done time in the Indore durbar, intrigue and innuendo were not unfamiliar, and she may well have silently revelled in the courtroom drama.

The plot to kidnap Mumtaz had been organized almost six months earlier in Indore and Bombay, where Tukojirao (and other Indian royals) had several residences. It was in one of these, Aurora House, that the conspirators had planned the abduction. The red Maxwell car had been purchased for ₹16,000 in October 1924, especially for this purpose. Mumtaz's uncle Allabux appeared to have been a not-so-unwilling member of the conspiracy. In his testimony, he said that he had been told by a friend that the maharaja wanted to see him, and later Tukojirao's ADC Zakaullah had invited him to Aurora House where he met some of the accused. On being told that the watchman at Bawla's house in Tardeo had also been bribed to leave the back door open at a convenient time, Allabux said he had informed Bawla and the watchman had been dismissed.

Tukojirao's men seemed to have bribed, threatened, or cajoled most of the people around Mumtaz who kept them informed about her movements. Two of the accused had even followed the couple to Lonavala, and stayed at a hotel in Poona during this time. On the day of the outrage, the accused men had followed Bawla all over the city and the Maxwell had been seen near Crawford Market at 6.15 p.m. and then later at the Phirozshah Mehta Gardens on Malabar Hill. There were two drivers in the car, one of whom was to have driven Bawla's car away to another spot after disabling all the passengers.

The English officers, hailed for rescuing a damsel in distress, testified in a packed courtroom that included many ladies. Besides being the main witnesses for the prosecution, they were also participants in the affair. Their gallant conduct was commented upon by both the defence and the prosecution.

The actions of Lt Saegert, who was shot at and wounded, are best described in his own words and are probably a fairly accurate record of what transpired. They had, Saegert said, driven up Ridge Road, when he

> ...saw two cars draw up to the right side of the road. Just as we came round the corner about 30 yards away we saw some figures getting out of the leading car and then we saw some flashes. Directly after the flashes, there were loud screams from the second car. The flashes were the flashes of a pistol. I did not hear the report. When I heard the screams, I stopped the car and we all got out... When I got to the car I saw three man trying to drag a woman out of the car and two men standing level with the chauffer's seat... three men were threatening the woman with knives and she had already been cut with the knife. I shouted and ran up when one of the two men near the chauffer's seat turned round and fired at me with a pistol on the right shoulder and the other man stabbed me with a knife as I ran past. I pulled off two of the men who were attacking the woman and threw them into the road... As I closed with the man who first fired at me, I heard loud screams from the direction of my car. I left the man who was attacking me and turned around and now two men were again attacking the woman. I went back and called out these people and we fought together and as we fought we got round to the front of my car.[5]

One of these men had a large knife or Kukri and I took it away from him.

Lt Batley, who had carried Mumtaz to Saegert's car, told the court: 'She was bleeding profusely and there were three cuts on her forehead. I put her into our own car, put her out of the way of the struggle.'[6]

He also related how his fellow officers had helped him secure Shafi Ahmed and hand him over to the police. His wounds were then bound up and he then went up to look at the other wounded man who was now lying on the road, and who he later learned was Mr Bawla. He was then taken to St. George's Hospital where he was admitted for treatment for 10 days.

Lt Batley and Col Vickery also corroborated his statement and also described their own role in the rescue. Saegert and Batley also described the faces of their assailants and how they had later identified them in a police line-up at Indore.

The statements of the accused were peppered with what were obviously bare-faced lies. The testimony of accused number 1, Shafi Ahmed Nabi Ahmed, a Risaldar of the Indore Mounted Police and the sole member of the gang to be captured on the spot, would test the credulousness of even the most fair-minded judge. He said he had arrived from Indore a few days prior to the attack to meet one of his friends, who was a fruit-seller. He had gone to the Hanging Gardens for a view of the sunset, and on hearing the woman's screams had rushed to help. He was taking her away from the man who had seized her when the Europeans intervened. They had assaulted him and a knife that he had in fact snatched from the real offender was taken away. He had been injured in the affray and was taken to hospital. Sometime later, Inspector Jeffreys of the Bombay Police had shown him four or five men from Indore and asked him implicate them. He had told the Inspector that he was innocent. Asked by the judge why Mumtaz would want to implicate an innocent bystander, he replied he did not know why! Asked to account for the ₹2,000 (a substantial amount in 1925) that were found on his person when he was arrested, he said it had been given to him by his uncle as he was soon to marry his cousin.

Accused number 2, Pushpasheel Ponde, an ADC at the Indore durbar, was a relative of Anandrao Phanse, the ninth accused. He denied having ever been a party to the plot or having been to Aurora House. Evidence had been submitted to prove that Ponde had stayed in Poona while following the couple to Lonavala, and had met Shafi Ahmed and Phanse there. The red car had been seen outside the hotel two days prior to the murder. He denied having received any telegrams from Phanse during his stay at Poona. He said he had been there to join a college, and had not been in Bombay on the day of the murder. He admitted that he had accompanied Phanse to buy the car, but was told that the Maxwell was for Phanse's personal use. It was a coincidence that he and Phanse had been at Poona and Bombay at the same time. He had never used a pistol in his life.

Bahadurshah Mahomedshah, accused number 3, who allegedly drove the red Maxwell on the day of the crime, said he had resigned as a motor driver for the Indore State and had never been to Bombay. His brother Akbar Shah was accused number 4 and said he was in no way involved.

Shamrao Dighe, accused number 5, was a captain of the Indore Air Forces. He denied having ever been to Bombay and said he had been wrongly identified by an English officer as he was the only clean-shaven man in the identity parade. The injuries on his person were sustained after a fall from his bicycle and the cut on his fingers were caused by a kite-string when he was flying kites.

Accused number 6, Mumtaz Mahomed, was a sub-inspector in the Indore Police Crime Investigation Department (CID). He, too, denied having been to Bombay and said he had been all the while in Indore looking after his son who was unwell.

Abdul Latif Moyuddin, a motor-car driver from Indore and the accused number 7, also said he had never left the city during the period in question. He had bought a new car at an auction and had been busy tinkering with it. The injuries on his foot were due to shoe bite, he said.

Karamatkhan Nizamatkhan, a pay sergeant in the Indore State Imperial Service Lancers was accused number 8, and apparently received gunshot wounds in the scuffle. He, too, denied any role in the affair and said he had been out hunting that day, when he accidently shot himself in the leg. He also injured his hands and shoulder when he fell down after being hit.

Finally, Anandrao Phanse, adjutant general of the Indore State Forces, said he was not involved in any plot to kidnap Mumtaz. According to him, Mumtaz had agreed in October to come to Indore with him, and he had purchased a car on her instructions to take her back. Phanse said she had done this after an appeal by Shankarrao, a minister in the Indore household, who had been put under arrest for no fault of his after Mumtaz had left the maharaja. Referring to her throughout his statement as Kamalabai Sahiba, Phanse said he had never intended to take Mumtaz back to Indore by unlawful means.

The testimony of the various witnesses and the accused was followed with great interest in the country and even abroad. It was also reported at the other end of the world. The *New York Times* of 14 January had carried a single-column report describing the assault under the headline 'Slain by Bombay Thugs; Leading Moslem Shot and His Companions Are Injured.'

The *Times of India*, being a Bombay-based newspaper, led the coverage, devoting considerable space to the trial, which did not sit well with the accused. Mohammad Ali Jinnah was incensed from the comments made by the newspaper on the nature of evidence even as the trial was underway and moved an application for process against the paper for contempt of court. He said the comments were unfavourable to the defence and would prejudice the jury and interfere with the course of justice.

Justice Crump, admitting that while some the comments could be viewed as objectionable, said he could not see how it interfered with the due course of justice.

Jinnah demanded that the *Times of India* correspondent be called to the court to explain its remarks on the case. Justice Crump said he would think the matter over and pass orders in due course but then seems to have let it pass, and no action was taken on the matter.[7]

The defence lawyers faced an uphill task. Faced with the very detailed statements of the British military officers, there was not much that could be laid in favour of the accused. It was suggested that Bawla had pulled out a pistol and that the accused had fired in self-defence but that argument did not hold. It was proved that while Bawla did possess a licensed revolver – and one was in fact produced before the court – he was not carrying it on his person when he was assaulted. Forensic tests also revealed, if indeed there had been any doubt, that the bullets fired at Lt Saegert and Bawla came from the two pistols recovered from the assailants.

The defence, fully aware that they were fighting a lost cause, also put up the implausible argument that Mumtaz had been willing to go back to the maharaja, but had been restrained by Bawla. It was a feeble defence and got nowhere. The suggestion was untenable as Mumtaz had called out for help and tried to get away from her assailants, and had also been maliciously wounded in the attack. The prosecution also countered with evidence given by Mumtaz's counsel K.F. Nariman, who deposed that he had been consulted by Mumtaz a few months before the attempted kidnapping and had told him that she would rather drown herself than go back to Tukojirao.

During the proceedings, Mumtaz's counsel also informed the court that the Indore durbar had sought an extradition warrant against Mumtaz on a charge of stealing jewellery that belonged to the Indore State, but the agent to the governor-general in central India had refused to sanction it. Mumtaz, in her defence, said the jewellery in question did not come from Indore at all but was family property and had been given to her great-grandmother by Maharaja Ranjit Singh of Amritsar (the reasons for which were not stated).

A curious fact about the case was the absence of any direct motive for the accused to attack Mumtaz. To the layman following the case and indeed the newspapers, the attack on Mumtaz was motivated purely by jealously. It was difficult to believe that Tukojirao was driven by lust or passion after having had her for a decade. If she had once been beautiful, no trace of it now remained. Those who saw her in court were not captivated by her looks. It had to be wounded pride. The fact that all the conspirators were from Indore weighed against Tukojirao. As none of them had any personal reason to abduct or attack her, it was thought that they could have acted only on orders from the king though this was never proved.

The attempt to disfigure Mumtaz did not sit well with those who followed the case and cast Tukojirao in very bad light. It was not clear whether the assailants had tried to cut off her nose – an archaic method of revenge often employed by thwarted suitors in certain parts of the subcontinent – but deep gashes had been inflicted on her forehead, and Tukojirao became a diabolical villain in the frenzied newspaper coverage of the event. He was also vilified in the press for allegedly ill-treating his first wife, the senior Maharani Chandravati Bai.

Finally, after nearly a month, when both prosecution and defence had concluded their arguments, Justice Crump summed up the case for the jury, going over the specific legal points on which they were to base their verdict. The summing-up itself was a masterly feat – covering 145 typed folio pages – and when it concluded no one in the court with a smattering of legal knowledge could have been left in any doubt about the outcome.

The jury deliberated for just over an hour before returning their verdict. On 23 May 1925, a little over four months after the dastardly attack, seven of the accused were found guilty while two – Mumtaz Mohamed and Karamat Khan – were unanimously acquitted. Justice Crump accepted the verdict and Shafi Ahmed, Pushpasheel Ponde, and Shamrao Dighe were sentenced to hang. The other four accused were sentenced to transportation for life.

Jinnah earned his very considerable fees (his standard fee in the 1930s was said to be ₹1,500 per day), saving his client Anandrao Phanse from the hangman's noose. Apart from the charge of conspiracy, Phanse was found guilty of abetment of murder, which carried the death sentence. The judge, however, admitted Jinnah's argument that Phanse had been away from the scene of the actual murder and the abetment charge against him could not hold. Phanse was accordingly sentenced to transportation for life. Jinnah made a strong appeal for a lesser sentence, and while the adjutant general did not oppose the plea and the judge also seemed sympathetic, there were only two possible punishments for abetment from a legal standpoint – death or transportation for life – and his plea was rejected.

Expectedly, the verdict was challenged and an appeal was made to the Privy Council. Sir John Simon (of 'Simon Go Back' fame), one of the best lawyers in England, appeared for the appellants, but his arguments failed to influence their Lordships and the appeal was dismissed.

For the men who had put their lives on the line to gratify a ruler's whim, it was the end of the road. On 19 November 1925, Risaldar Shafi Ahmed and Captain Shamrao Dighe, both young men in their twenties, were hanged. Pushpasheel Ponde, the third accused to be sentenced to death, cheated the hangman. He apparently became insane after the sentencing and was kept under observation at Poona Jail. His later fate is not known.

And what of the man who pulled the puppet strings? Tukojirao Holkar found himself in very hot water over the murder. The maharaja's culpability could not be denied, but how close he was to the conspiracy could not be conclusively established.

The story was keenly followed to its conclusion by newspapers in the empire's colonies and across the English-speaking world and created quite a sensation, which the British Government could have done without. The political fallout of the affair had to be kept in mind, for Indore was no two-bit princely fief. Entitled to a 19-gun salute, it was one of the principal states of central India and part of the fabled and once-powerful Maratha Confederacy that held sway over much of India following the disintegration of the Mughal Empire and before the consolidation of British rule in India. The Holkars had always been a force to reckon with, and their relations with the British had not always been smooth. Tukojirao's father, Shivajirao Holkar, had been forced to abdicate in 1903 and Tukojirao being a minor had ruled under a council of regency before he came to the throne at the age of 21 in 1911, when he also attended the coronation of King George V. In keeping with those of his ilk, he exhibited a fondness for jewellery. A story goes that, just before the outbreak of the Great War (World War I), he was in Paris and visited the famous jewellers, Chaumet, where he spied a pair of diamonds that came from the Golconda mines near Hyderabad. Each diamond was 46 carats and he bought them all, adding to an already burgeoning collection.[8] An otherwise model prince with modern ideas, he had invited the Scottish town planner Patrick Geddes to prepare a master plan for Indore city in 1917. His loyalty to the empire was beyond doubt and during the Great War, he had given ₹1 lakh towards the war effort and was created a Knight GCIE in 1918. Hitherto, he had given his imperial masters no trouble.

But the Malabar Hill affair could not be brushed aside. Indeed even before the case came to trial, R.I.R. Glancy, the Agent to the governor-general in central India, wrote to the viceroy about the options available to the Government of India.

The colonial government by now had plenty of experience in dealing with wayward princelings. This was not the first time that princely passion had caused embarrassment to the Sovereign and dealing with raging hormones was seemingly an unspoken part of a viceroy's responsibilities. Indeed, just a few years earlier, the heir-apparent to the throne of Kashmir, Hari Singh, had got himself into a pickle over a woman. On a visit to England, he was introduced by a British army officer to a woman of easy virtue whose husband blackmailed the prince after catching him in flagrante delicto. It was of course a classic entrapment, masterminded by the British officer. Young Hari Singh was told that a scandal would cost him the succession to the Kashmir *gaddi* and he was made to hand over cheques to the order of £300,000 to the crooks. Alas, the whole affair became public anyway when the blackmailers fell out and one of the men took the Midland Bank to court for paying £150,000 to the wrong person. The

British were thoroughly embarrassed, and while the prince was only named in the case as 'Mr A', his identity was never really a secret. The prince got off lightly though he came in for a good bit of ribbing and was thereafter often referred to as 'Mr A'. To his credit, Hari Singh took it sportingly and the affair did not do his career any harm and he acceded to the throne in 1925.[9]

Tukojirao was not so lucky. A commission of inquiry by his peers or a possible deposition seemed to be the only way out. The maharaja, however, would not go quietly and did not consider himself answerable to the Government of India. In his opinion, echoed by many of his fellow rulers, his obligations according to the treaty by which his family ruled over the state were to the English Crown, and not to the Government of India and he could not be bound by and subject to the orders of its courts. In the end, after a lot of wrangling, Tukojirao was persuaded by the viceroy to abdicate. This he very reluctantly did on 26 February 1926, and his only son, 21-year-old Yashwantrao, succeeded to the *gaddi*.

Mumtaz recovered from her wounds, and delivered Bawla's child, a girl. Bawla reportedly left a fortune of ₹40 lakh on this death and Mumtaz benefitted from a substantial bequest. If she mourned Bawla's passing, it was not for long. Just over a year after her harrowing ordeal, she married Abdul Rehman, the son of a rich businessman from Karachi, and had two children with him. The marriage did not last and the couple divorced in 1929, it was said, on the insistence of Rehman's father. Mumtaz then left Karachi and apparently moved back to Bombay, but nothing is known of her life since. Her story has fascinated many across the years and has been told in quite a few books, often inaccurately. John Gunther, in his widely acclaimed *Inside Asia*, included a paragraph about the story but got the details wrong, when he wrote that Mumtaz was 'abducted by a rich and madly infatuated Bombay merchant'.[10] Her tale was also told on celluloid in 1925 with the release of, a silent and now forgotten film, *Kulinkanta*.

No traces remain of the Bawla family, which was once quite well known in the Memon community of Bombay in the 1920s. It was said they had sworn to avenge Bawla's murder and had hired a contract killer from Bombay to eliminate Holkar. The movement of suspicious elements in Indore, especially Pathans, was monitored and the maharaja's security was beefed up. However, nothing came of this supposed threat and it may well have been based on hearsay. The family is thought to have moved to Pakistan after the partition of India. Some trace of the Bawlas does linger in Bombay though. The Bawla Masjid, said to be built by the family, still stands on N.M. Joshi Marg, Lower Parel, and is the second largest mosque in Mumbai.

John Saegert, the Scotsman who played such a key role in rescuing Mumtaz, was just 24 years old at the time of the murder. He served with the Royal Engineers and went on to a distinguished career in the army. When the Second World War broke out, Saegert became the first officer commanding No. 9 Commando Group in 1940. He was later captured, and died in Toronto in 1946 as a result of his imprisonment. He was awarded the Distinguished Service Order.

Col Charles Vickery had seen action on many fronts before that fateful evening on Malabar Hill. He served in the Boer War in South Africa, and was a member Royal Artillery in the First World War when he was posted to the Middle East. In 1920, Vickery was appointed the British Agent in Jeddah, and played a role in the rise of Ibn Saud, the first monarch of the Kingdom of Saudi Arabia. He left the army in 1935 and contested unsuccessfully as a Tory candidate in the UK general election. He became a county council member in Durham, and wrote frequently on military affairs.

Among those arrayed on the side of the defence, it was Jinnah who probably left the most lasting impact on both Indian history and geography. The Bombay lawyer and one-time champion of Hindu-Muslim unity would, in time, espouse the cause of a separate state for Muslims in the subcontinent and leave India in 1947 having more or less single-handedly created the state of Pakistan, where he died a few years later.

Tukojirao Holkar probably had the last laugh in the Bawla affair. He was not away from the spotlight for long. Only 36 when he forfeited the throne, the ex-maharaja did not allow the discomfiture of his abdication, humiliating as it was, to dampen his spirits. Always something of a bon vivant, Tukojirao retained his zest for the good life and moved on to other conquests. He travelled abroad a great deal after his abdication and met Nancy Miller, an American of mixed French and Swiss ancestry, at a casino in Switzerland. He fell in love with her and they were married on 17 March 1928. Nancy Miller converted to Hinduism and was named Sharmishta Devi. The union was by all accounts a happy one and the couple lived in style, having a lively social life, entertaining and travelling between India, the US, and Europe. Tukojirao lived to the grand old age of 88, dying at his home in Paris in 1978, a full five decades after the infamous affair at Malabar Hill that had so transformed his life.

3

Murder, They Wrote
The Fullam-Clark Affair

INSPECTOR SMITH OF THE RESERVE POLICE FORCE KNEW A LIAR when he saw one. And Lt Henry Clark – who had come into the Agra Cantonment police station earlier that day to report a murderous attack on his wife during a robbery at his house – had just lied through his teeth. Clark said he'd been at the Agra Railway Station a little before midnight to meet a friend named 'Mr Joikim' who was travelling to Bombay just about the time when his wife was assaulted. It had not occurred to Clark that Agra was not a stop on the Delhi–Bombay line – but Smith let it pass. Then, when pressed a little, Clark said his friend's name was Menzies. That was another blatant lie – a desperate attempt to create an alibi. And in doing so, he only succeeded in securing the noose that was slowly tightening around his neck.

In the early hours of that Monday morning, 18 November 1912, Clark had turned up at the police station and told Head Constable Safdar Hussain that his wife Louisa had been assaulted in her bedroom around midnight by a gang of burglars and left badly wounded. His teenage daughter Maud, who was asleep on another bed in the same room, had survived unscathed.

The police arrived at a crime scene that was bloody enough. Mrs Clark's skull had been fractured and her head cut open by powerful blows, possibly from a sword or a similar sharp weapon.

Her assailant had also slashed at her body quite a few times, leaving many deep wounds. Part of the little finger of her left hand, sliced off as the unfortunate woman raised her arms to ward off the blows, lay beside her on the pillow, caked in blood.

Louisa Clark was lucky to have survived. Her daughter Maud, who had woken up to see a man standing beside her bed with a stick raised above his head, had jumped out of bed and run screaming out of the room. The robbers had then panicked and scattered. The terror-stricken girl had then come back into the room to help her mother, and bandaged her wounds.

Curiously, the family dog – a bull terrier named Julie – had not intervened, and had not even barked, while his mistress was being attacked. The verandah doors which gave access to the house were closed. However, a glass pane on one of the door panels was broken. One of the murderers could have easily put an arm in and pulled back the bolt that secured the door. Still, one did not have to be a policeman to suspect that this could very well have been an 'inside' job.

Clark had arrived home about half an hour after the attack. After looking at his wife, and seemingly being none too distressed, he had gone around the other rooms to see if anything had been stolen. The robbers did not appear to have taken anything of value. However, a bedsheet from Clark's bed was inexplicably missing. Why would the robbers take away a bedsheet?

Unfortunately, Mrs Clark succumbed to her wounds later that day, and what initially looked like a case of attempted robbery with violence now drew a charge of murder.

Inspector Smith was unimpressed by Clark's explanations. The good doctor was no paragon of virtue – indeed he was notorious for being involved in a long-running affair with an Anglo-Indian woman called Augusta Fullam, whose husband had conveniently passed away a year ago. Smith decided to call on the woman – *cherchez la femme*!

A brief interview with Mrs Fullam was enough to nail Clark's lie. Yes, she told Smith, Clark did tell her that he would be going to the Agra Railway Station that fateful night to meet a friend who was en route to Bombay – a Mr Joikim. Clark had instructed the woman well-enough, and she played her part, but the man himself had lost his nerve and changed the story.

Incidentally, the mythical Menzies that Clark was supposed to have been meeting was probably a piper by that name with the Cameroon Highlanders who was a champion draughts player with whom Clark had communicated with a few years ago. However, Menzies had left for England in 1908, and it is not known why Clark came up with his name. On being informed that no Delhi–Bombay train stopped at Agra, Clark offered a weak defence saying he had made a mistake and that Menzies was going from Allahabad to Bombay. The explanation fooled no one and Clark was formally arrested and charged with the murder of his wife.

However, the matter did not rest there. While the police were certain of Clark's guilt, the involvement of the widow Fullam could not be ruled out. Mr Horace Williamson – the superintendent of police, Agra – felt a deeper probe would be in order, and Inspector Smith was directed to conduct a thorough search of the Fullam residence. Accordingly, on 19 November, a little after Mrs Clark had been buried in the cantonment cemetery, Smith knocked on the doors of the Fullam bungalow. Mrs Fullam was not inclined to cooperate, but there wasn't much she could do when the inspector produced a search warrant.

Smith was well aware of the gossip surrounding Fullam and Clark by now and this, one assumes, provided an added impetus to the investigators to unearth any evidence that might nail the couple. Legend has it that Inspector Smith stumbled upon a tin trunk under Mrs Fullam's bed by chance. He had been sitting on the bed when his foot stuck the trunk, or so the story goes. It is most likely that a routine search brought forth the trunk. Surely, a police team searching the room of a woman who was probably guilty of a murder would be unlikely to have omitted to look under her bed.

In any case, the trunk was found, with Augusta protesting all the while that it did not belong to her, and that it was in fact Clark's – which it actually was. She claimed not to have the key, and so Smith decided to force the lock. Inside were several bundles of old letters, all tied up with string or ribbons. One look at Mrs Fullam's flustered face was enough to convince Smith that he had found the goods. He officially impounded the trunk and, after sending for a padlock to secure it, had it sent to the government treasury for safe-keeping until Superintendent Williamson could look at it.

The next morning, on 20 August, Williamson began to study the contents of the box. He probably guessed that these were love letters, but otherwise could not have had any idea of what they contained. Patiently, opening one bunch after another, he read each of the letters – and there were nearly 400 of them! The missives, so foolishly stored away by the besotted Mrs Fullam, unravelled a nauseating tale of illicit love and callous, cold-blooded murder. They also blew the lid on what turned out to be one of the great scandals of early twentieth century British India.

Not only had the duo plotted to get rid of Mrs Clark, they had also done away with Mr Fullam a year earlier by means of poison. Williamson now had on his hands not just a single murder inquiry, but two! The sordid details of the plotting and planning, the subterfuge and the betrayal, were all laid out in the little pieces of slowly yellowing paper. Their revelation in the days to come – involving as they did a white man and an Anglo-Indian woman – caused a minor tut-tutting storm in the staid circles of British-Indian society. Completely forgotten today, the Fullam–Clark murder had achieved notoriety in its time as the 'Agra Double Murder'.

But coming back to the story and its dramatis personae...

Augusta Fairfield Fullam came from a family that had roots in India that went back nearly a century. Her father was a river pilot in the Bengal Pilot Service, which he had joined in the 1860s when the service was open only to Europeans. Augusta was the first of two daughters born to Mary Augusta by her second marriage. There was some Indian blood in the family, and so they belonged to a class of people in British-India known as Eurasians, and later as Anglo-Indians. Not top-drawer folk, but still very respectable, though one would not expect them to socialize with the *pucca* white memsahibs who had, by the opening years of the twentieth century, drawn very clear social lines that were fraught to cross.

Augusta, a vivacious and attractive woman who had been married when barely out of her teens, was in her mid-thirties when she met the handsome Lt Henry Lovell William Clark, a doctor in the Indian Subordinate Medical Service, sometime in 1909 in Meerut. Well-read, fond of poetry, and a passionate woman by all accounts, she fell hopelessly in love with the 42-year-old Clark.

Clark was also married, but conveniently for both parties, had a reputation as a ladies' man. Born to English parents in Calcutta, he claimed to come from a distinguished family with roots back in England. Augusta, who was a bit of a social butterfly, would have been impressed by the pedigree.

Augusta's husband Edward Fullam, then 44, was a deputy examiner in the Military Accounts Department, and was known to the Clark family. Edward was a family man – decent, quiet, religious, and devoted to his wife and three children. It may have been the difference in their ages or their varied temperaments, but Augusta could not find happiness with the slightly dour, conformist Edward.

Clark couldn't have been more different. He possessed a violent temper, and could be abusive. He had four children, three boys and a girl, none of whom seemed to have liked their father. He was also a philanderer, which led to many domestic quarrels. Clark could not abide his wife – who was 10 years older to him – and was known to have referred to her as a 'd——d swine'[1].

The long-suffering Mrs Louisa Clark was a model wife and mother. A gentle, well-bred woman, she had been a nurse at the Calcutta Medical College when she first met the much-younger Clark. If there had been any love in the marriage it did not last long, and within a few years Louisa had settled down to an unhappy domestic existence. Well aware of her husband's philandering and dishonest nature, she tried to make the most of a bad marriage. Their domestic troubles were not hidden from the children, who were devoted to her, and Maud often contemptuously referred to the woman who had stolen their father's affections as 'the wonderful Mrs Fullam'. When asked at the trial whether her mother had been jealous of Augusta, Maud replied that 'she had nothing to be jealous of'.[2]

Henry Clark and Augusta Fullam were blind to the world. The infatuated Augusta was a prolific correspondent, pouring her heart out to her new-found love in missives that were liberally peppered with terms of endearment and affection (my *buchha*, my lovey *buchha*, my own *buchha* darling, my one and only love, my king, and so on) that led to suppressed chuckles and sniggers when the contents of her love notes became public knowledge. But the contents of those letters were also deadly, for they dealt with the best means of getting rid of their respective spouses without causing any suspicion. Frantic notes went back and forth between the lovers as both Edward and Louisa stubbornly refused to die.

Edward Fullam, cuckold though he was, does not seem to have objected strongly to his wife's doings. Maybe he had just given up on her, or had become resigned to his fate. But he was no fool, and surely would have had some inkling that his wife and her lover were plotting to do away with him, as his health slowly deteriorated under the influence of medicines and potions that Clark very kindly administered to him after he repeatedly fell ill as a result of his wife's cooking.

Edward though had surely trusted Clark not too long ago. Clark had attended the birth of the Fullam's last child, a girl named Myrtle, in January 1910. It had been a difficult birth, but the child had been delivered safely, and Edward believed that Clark had saved his wife and child. Given the circumstances, the paternity of the child may have been in doubt, but Edward does not seem to have been concerned. He had another reason to trust Clark. Both were Freemasons and belonged to the same Lodge in Meerut. It may not have initially occurred to the upright and honest Edward that his Lodge-fellow was well capable of coveting a brother mason's wife.

Though born and brought up in the country, the hot weather of upper India did not suit Edward and he was constantly ill. Augusta tried to help, with medicine offered by Clark, but Edward's condition only grew worse. No surprise there, for they were slow-poisoning him. In July 1911, Edward went down with what was thought to be heat stroke, probably after consuming Clark's concoctions, and had to be admitted to a hospital in Meerut. He was discharged on 14 August, but had to be readmitted after a few days at home. He had taken ill again after Augusta, according to the testimony of her 9-year-old daughter Kathleen, put some 'medicine' into his tea, causing a burning sensation in his throat and tongue. Augusta had become a little nervous and worried by this time, as her letters revealed, and may have suffered pangs of guilt, but steeled herself and carried on.

In early September 1911, the medical board found Edward, who was still in hospital, unfit to continue in office and incapable of carrying on his work. He would therefore be retired on pension, the board decided. This no doubt came as a shock to the Fullams, but they were offered free transport on a troopship to England, and Edward did consider the idea for some time. An alarmed Augusta soon talked him out of it, with some help from Clark, who made visits to the hospital and convinced Edward to stay on in India. Clark, who was staying in Agra with his family at this time, suggested that the Fullams move there and promised to help them find a house. The blandishments and cajolery worked, and in the end Edward made up his mind to retire to Agra. It was a fateful decision.

Earlier, the family had considered Bangalore, with its mild, cool climate, as a possible retirement spot for Edward who, it must be remembered, could not stand the heat of the plains. However, nothing came of it. Vague plans were also made to temporarily move to the hills of Dehradun to allow Edward to recover his health. Also, Edward's brother William, who lived in Dehradun, was unwell and thought to be on his deathbed, and Edward wished to see him for what would possibly be the last time. However, William died before the planned move and so the trip to the hills never materialized. In Edward's debilitated state, going back to the heat of Agra did not make sense, and the senior doctor at the hospital, a Major Palmer, later expressed surprise at the change of plan as he had thought the family was moving to Dehradun. So, Edward's decision to move to Agra came in for much comment later, when the facts of his death became known. According to his Orderly Gunner Dixon, who later gave evidence at the trial, Edward had told him that he was unwilling to go to Agra as he feared he would be poisoned by Clark. And yet in the end, he seems to have allowed himself to be persuaded. Maybe he had a death wish. Given his frail health and the mental agony that he was now undergoing, it may have seemed the easy way out. Edward, unlike his wife, had never possessed a strong mind.

On 8 October, a Sunday, the Fullams moved to a small bungalow on Metcalfe Road in Agra which Clark had helped them find. Edward was still quite weak and took straight to his bed. He did not know it then, but he had just another day to live. On the evening of 10 October, Clark visited the house. It was a hot day and Edward was seated outside in the garden having dinner, while Augusta and Clark were in the dining room with the children. Augusta, who had brought him some soup and meat from the kitchen, seems to have poisoned her husband yet again, for Edward soon got up and went to lie down in his room. He then vomited and called out. Clark now went into Edward's bedroom while Augusta conspicuously stayed away. He then sent Edward's bearer Gurbaksh, who was in the room, to look for a doctor who lived near the Agra Club, but he could not give the bearer the name of the doctor.

Then, as Kathleen watched from her room (where she could see what was happening in her father's bedroom), Clark injected Edward thrice with a syringe – in the arm, chest, and shoulder. The girl had been sent to bed by her mother, but had gone in to see her father a few minutes earlier, when Edward told her, 'I'm going. Be a good girl and God will bless you.' Kathleen asked if he wished to see her mother, but he replied that he did not. 'No. Don't call her. I don't want her'.[3] He then closed his eyes and lay back, and the girl then went back to her room, from where she saw her father draw his last breath.

As the poison took effect, Kathleen heard a gurgling sound emanating from Edward's throat. The helpless little girl again went up to stand beside her father. In a few moments, all was quiet. Clark came into observe what had happened, and checked Edward's pulse. Seemingly oblivious to Kathleen's presence, he went into the dining room where Augusta waited, and uttered a single word 'Gone!'

And with that he was out of the house, cycling away into the night. There was work to be done! As he pedalled to the Agra Club, Clark came upon the bearer, who he then ordered to go back to the house, saying 'the sahib is dead'. Coming back to the bungalow, Gurbaksh found his master lying dead and Augusta sitting quietly in the dining room.

Meanwhile, Clark went into the club, where he found a senior doctor of the Agra Hospital, Capt. J.S. Dunne of the Royal Army Medical Corps (RAMC) having dinner. Calling him out on to the verandah, Clark asked Dunne to accompany him to visit a friend who was quite ill. He did not say that Edward was dead. Dunne called for his bicycle and the two men quickly cycled to Metcalfe Road.

Capt. Dunne, faced with Clark's corpse, naturally said it was now too late, and promptly went back to the club. Bizarre to relate, Augusta and Kathleen then went to sleep in one of the spare beds in Edward's room while Clark rested on another. He needed a good night's sleep as there were things to be arranged the next day.

The next morning, Clark asked Dunne if he would provide a death certificate for the body he had seen the night before. Dunne refused outright saying he could not do so as he was not aware of the man's illness and the reason for his death. Edward found a way around this. He had thought it out earlier. As a surgeon, he was empowered to write out a death certificate, but it had to be counter-signed by another medical officer. Would Dunne oblige? Dunne raised no objection to this, and so what would have otherwise been a medico-legal hurdle was eliminated. Officially, according to his death certificate, Edward Fullam who had been 'suffering from general paralysis for the past three months, had a relapse and died from heart failure at 9.20 p.m. on the 10th October, 1911'. The certificate bore the signature of H.L.W. Clark, Assistant Surgeon, ISMD (Indian Subordinate Medical Department) and was countersigned by J.S. Dunne, Captain, RAMC. Edward could now be safely confined to his grave.

At 5 p.m. on the evening of 11 October 1911, Edward was laid to rest in the Agra Cantonment Cemetery. His body would lie there undisturbed, until it was disinterred 14 months later to seek evidence of poisoning. Kathleen was forbidden by her mother to speak about her father's death. The girl, dutifully quiet, kept her peace and held her tongue – until her day in court.

Life for Augusta continued as before, though she had to move into a smaller house as her finances were none too strong. Clark visited his mistress every day, oblivious to all the gossip and finger-pointing that could not be avoided after Edward's death. The unrepentant and now merry widow, relieved of her husband, lavished her love on the unscrupulous Lothario. Her letters became more effusive and sentimental – in fact their contents would make the reader cringe even in our permissive times; in their day, they would have been positively scandalous.

It is not known what Clark thought about her ardent outpourings on paper, but he kept all her letters safely stored in the dispatch box, which he deposited in Augusta's house. He was known to be a coarse fellow and not the kind who set store by mushy love-letters, but he did not get rid of them as he should have – and thus sealed his doom.

There was still one more minor irritant that Clark needed to get rid of – his wife Louisa. He quickly set about this, but his wife was too smart for him. She might have guessed that her husband and his lover were involved in Edward's untimely death, and that she was next in line.

Clark had been attempting to get Louisa out of the way much before Edward Fullam was in his grave. One day in early April 1911, Clark had attempted to poison his wife with arsenic, but foolishly tried to enlist the aid of an unwilling house help. Calling him into his room, Clark gave his servant Bibu a packet containing some powder (it was a purgative, he said) and asked him to add it to the *memsaab*'s tea for three successive days, after which he would be given a reward of ₹50. He also told Bibu he would be strangled if he mentioned this to anyone. Bibu smelt a rat and refused. Later, when Clark had left the room, the servant called Mrs Clark and gave her the packet (which Clark had not taken away) in the presence of her son Harry, explaining why it had been given to him. By coincidence, Clark's junior in the medical service, Assistant Surgeon Linton, happened to be in the house that evening and Harry gave him the packet, asking him to examine its contents. Linton took away the packet, and told Harry the next day that it contained a 'slow poison' but did not reveal what it was. The powder was in fact a compound of arsenic, and Linton – who like almost everyone within the Clarks' circle knew of his affair with Mrs Fullam – probably guessed to what use the powder would be put to. However, he was subordinate to Clark in the service and so held his tongue. Meanwhile, the hapless Bibu ran away to his home in Delhi.

Warned by Bibu, Mrs Clark was now on her guard. Intent on doing away with his wife, Clark introduced another servant into the house in early May 1911. This was Buddhu, who was actually a hospital servant working under him, but now doubled as a table servant at his house. Wasting no time, Mrs Fullam herself took matters in hand and offered Buddhu ₹50 if he gave Mrs Clark a powder to put in her food. Buddhu refused.

Augusta and Henry were now running grave risks in trying to get a servant to do away with a family member. Servants in English and Anglo-Indian households were always kept at arm's length. There was an unwritten but strict code governing the master–servant relationship. While a servant of long standing could be deemed loyal and trustworthy, he could never be a confidant. So, by asking a house servant to poison the master or lady of the house, Augusta and Henry were putting themselves in a very vulnerable position indeed – if not just doing something obviously foolish.

But the lovers were desperate – and yet another attempt was made. In April 1912, according to his testimony at the trail, Buddhu was given some powdered glass by Clark to put in his wife's food. He again refused, saying it would not work as the powder was very thick and could not be mixed with anything without arousing suspicion. Buddhu had his position in the hospital where he had worked for 18 years to think of and did not want to get into any trouble that might cost him a decent job. A furious Clark swore at him, and took the powdered glass away.

The harassed Buddhu, at this time, was also making a bit of money on the side – Mrs Clark was paying him an extra six rupees every month, probably in the hope that it would prevent any attempts at poisoning that her husband might try to execute through his servants. Buddhu, quite naturally, would not have been too keen to do away with a golden goose.

Thwarted repeatedly, Clark now changed tack. He threatened to have Buddhu expelled from the hospital unless he agreed to put some 'medicine' in the memsahib's tea. Buddhu now had little choice. His job at the hospital was much more important than the extra six rupees a month. He agreed to do Clark's bidding, but very cunningly, so as not to get into any trouble himself, poured only a little bit of the poison into Mrs Clark's morning tea. The lady obligingly vomited it out and was very sick. She wasn't fooled. 'Your father is trying to poison – me,' she told her daughter Maud.[4]

Clark then tried to get Buddhu dismissed from the hospital for alleged incompetence, but he appealed to Louisa who promptly supported him. She sent two applications on his behalf to senior Medical Department officials, both at Meerut and Agra, vouching for his services and good conduct, and Buddhu was allowed to continue at the hospital. Although Buddhu was released from his duties at the Clark household for a while, he was reinstated after about a month.

In July, Buddhu made yet another half-hearted attempt to shorten Louisa's life. Mrs Clark became violently sick after consuming two spoons of pulao at dinner. Also present at the table that day was Assistant Surgeon White of the ISMD, who was being considered as a possible suitor for Maud. White worked under Clark, who was not present that evening. Excusing herself, Louisa rushed to the bathroom and vomited. She complained of severe pain in her stomach, and White gave her some brandy to relieve the pain. She vomited several times that night, but survived.

Buddhu was now in disgrace and shunted back to the hospital. Again, he had not put a sufficient amount of poison in the food to dispose of his mistress. Clark was understandably furious, but there was not much he could do about it except giving the incompetent poisoner the cold shoulder.

Louisa recovered after a while and went to live with her son Harry in Meerut, taking a much-needed break from her husband's increasingly desperate and brazen poisoning schemes. She would have known by now that her husband would stop at nothing to get rid of her. Clark did not even come back home in the evenings now, and usually had his dinner with Mrs Fullam. Louisa also confided her fears in a letter written to one of her sisters in Calcutta, saying it would probably be best to separate from Clark once Maud was married, and live with Harry in Meerut as she could no longer trust her husband.

Edward, though, was not one to give up easily, and he knew his wife was aware of who was behind all her recent bouts of ill health. He feared that she might go to the police with her suspicions, and that would never do. If the police got hold of Buddhu, all that would be needed were a few blows from an iron-shod lathi for the truth to come out. Desperate situations called for desperate measures, he decided. A direct attack was now called for.

When Mrs Clark arrived back home on 14 November, Buddhu had resigned and departed from the house. He had, in fact, now been tasked with carrying out a physical attack on Louisa, and seems to have reasoned that it would be better to not be part of the household when this happened. Clark had instructed him to get hold of some *badmash*es from the bazaar to do the deed. Mrs Clark was to be killed in the house, but it should look like an attempted robbery gone wrong. Clark would be away from home and try to establish an alibi. He seems to have left the details to the incompetent Buddhu. The price for the foul deed was a paltry ₹100 which was to be provided by Mrs Fullam.

They could not risk getting professional killers or dacoits to stage an attack. So Buddhu had to do his best. He seems to have somehow given Clark the impression that he was well acquainted with the underworld of Agra. The four men he finally got together to do the deed were not the common riff-raff of the bazaar, but not hardened criminals either: Sukkha, 20, was a *darzi* or tailor who had a shop in Lalkurti Bazaar; Budhha, 23, was a *banjar* or pedlar who frequented the Sadar Bazaar; Ramlal, also from Sadar Bazaar, was a 22-year-old greengrocer from a well-to-do farming family; Mohan, 22, also known as 'City Man', was a *bharbhoonja* or corn-parcher from Chakkipet, Agra.

Of these, only the last two had any police record. Ramlal had once been detained by the police for the alleged murder of a money-lender, but was not convicted. Mohan had a previous conviction for theft, for which he had been whipped with a rattan cane. He was well-known to the police and was thought to be something of a hard nut to crack.

Given their antecedents, it was doubtful if the four young men could be trusted with a serious criminal enterprise, but Buddhu had decided that they were good enough for the job. The sum offered, when split five ways, was quite insignificant. The men were quite sore about it and bullied Buddhu, and in turn Clark, to cough up some more.

The plan, as conceived by the mastermind Clark, was quite amateurish. The men were to break into the bungalow around midnight while Clark was away, enter Louisa's bedroom, and bash her head in. It was not quite clear what was to be done about Maud, who would also be sleeping in the same room, and conceivably very likely to wake up while her mother's skull was being cracked open. Clark was certain he did not want Maud harmed in any way. The plotters seem to have completely disregarded the dog, Julie, who could be expected to create a ruckus. If one went by the dictum that well-begun was half-done, it was not a very propitious start.

On the evening of Sunday, 10 November – the day chosen for the murder – Kathleen Fullam saw Clark, who was in the house as usual with her mother, let in two men into the dining room. The men were natives, and one of them was Buddhu, who she knew as someone who had often come to the house earlier with medicines and letters from Clark. The other man she did not know, but would later identify as Sukkha. She could hear them talking and the late-night visitors were demanding money, which Clark refused to give, saying they had been paid earlier. 'This is the last time we will ask you for money,' one of them said. 'If you give it to us tonight, it will all be finished tomorrow.'[5] Mrs Fullam then came into the bedroom, not knowing that her daughter was watching, and took some money from the cash box and went out, presumably to hand it over to the two men. The natives then departed, climbing onto a tree in the compound and jumping out over the wall. An unusual exit, and one that only deepened Kathleen's suspicion that something diabolical was underway.

Clark left the Fullam residence sometime after 10 p.m. He had to set up his alibi at the Agra Railway Station for the time when his house was to be robbed and his wife killed. But before that he had one last meeting at the hospital with Buddha and Sukkha to make sure that the deed would be done that night. The would-be murderers now tried to arm-twist him for a bit of cash, and with only hours to go before the final act, Clark could not take chances. Some money changed hands.

As planned, Clark turned up at the Agra Railway Station sometime around 11.30 p.m., and sat in the Station Master's room. He knew he had to be seen to be present at the station and spoke to Assistant Station Master D.F. Menzies. He was waiting to meet a friend who would be arriving shortly on the Delhi mail train, he told the railway official.

In the Clark household, all was quiet. The man of the house had left that evening at about 6 p.m., and both Louisa and Maud knew that he would be at Mrs Fullam's where he usually dined these days. Before leaving that evening, however, he told his family to be careful as he had received his pay, which was in the house, and that there were burglars about. It was a very uncharacteristic remark, and one that Maud clearly remembered later.

The house was not really secure. The main door into the hall from the verandah was never bolted or locked. This was to allow Clark to enter without waking up the house after he returned late every night from his assignations with Augusta. There were two outer entrances into the verandah, which gave access to the interior of the house. One of these door panels had a missing pane, and all one had to do to enter was to put his hand in and slip the bolt. Still, mother and daughter were quite secure as long as the bull-terrier was out on patrol. Something the robbers had completely failed to consider.

One can only imagine Clark's impotent rage when he returned shortly after midnight – having seen off the mail train on which there was no one to receive – to find the would-be assassins loitering around the compound, their task unfinished. They would not go in because of the dog, which had barked a few times, driving them back into the shadows. Clark said he would soon fix that. That Clark had forgotten about the dog seems inexplicable, but he had probably told Buddhu that the dog would be locked up in one of the rooms, or it may have slipped his mind altogether in the excitement of finally seeing his plans coming to fruition.

Striding into the house, Clark picked Julie up and locked her in an outhouse in the compound, and cycled away some distance down the road to wait. The *badmash*es then tip-toed into the darkened house, trying to locate Louisa's bedroom. A visibly nervous Buddhu now wanted to call the whole thing off. There was not much light and they could not make out the memsahib from the miss-sahib – and Clark had said that Maud should not be harmed. And what if Maud recognized him? Ramlal, who was made of sterner stuff (he was after all a one-time murder-accused) then grabbed a sheet off Clark's bed and wound it around the frightened Buddhu's head. Now no one could recognize him! To work, then.

Entering the room, Buddhu, by now probably regretting having allowed Clark to talk him into this hazardous enterprise, held aloft a lantern he had taken from Clark's bedroom, providing his accomplices enough light to make sure of their victim. It is not conclusively known who stuck the fatal blows, but it may have been Mohan, the hardened offender. Sukkha and Ramlal were also thought to have rained blows on the woman with their lathis. Maud was lucky to have escaped as, despite all that Buddhu later said about the girl not being a target, the other men would not have wanted to leave behind any witnesses and may well have bludgeoned her to death had she not bolted out the room screaming. As the assassins scooted, Buddhu threw the bedsheet into one of the boxrooms, where it was later found by Maud.

Clark now entered for the final act. Just a little before 1 a.m., 30 minutes after the attack, he called from the verandah to be let in as the door was bolted. At Louisa's bedside, he tried to speak to his now unconscious wife. No reply. He then went around the house to see if anything had been taken. Nothing seemed to have been stolen – only the bedsheet in his room was missing.

He then enquired about the dog, and seemed concerned by its absence. Making an excuse to go out to see if any of the chickens had been taken from the hen-coop, he quickly scooped up Julie from the outhouse and quietly slipped in with the terrier through the bathroom door at the back. When Maud told him that the dog had not given any warning about the intruders, Clark said he would get rid of Julie.

Maud may have had her suspicious about Clark having something to do with the happenings that night, and pointedly asked her father why he was back so late this night, when he otherwise came in much earlier. Clark quickly gave out his story about having gone to meet a friend at the railway station, but did not say who it was.

Uncharacteristically for a doctor (and a surgeon at that) whose wife was lying with her bloody head patched up with makeshift bandages, Clark had still not attempted to tend to Louisa's horrific wounds. He instead went out to seek help and sent in two of his subordinate doctors, who did the best they could, cleaning and bandaging the unfortunate woman's head.

Clark then, strictly following established procedure, went to inform his commanding medical officer about the incident. Before that, however, he went to meet Augusta. 'Thieves broke into my house and nearly killed my wife,' he announced.[6] Augusta, who may have been worried about the 'nearly' asked what the 'damage' was, and he replied, 'Her head is cut open and the brain is exposed.'[7] Kathleen, who had woken up when Clark knocked on the door, was standing beside her mother, quietly watching this charade. Clark had a glass of water and went off. Augusta then went back to her bed. She seemed calm, but would certainly have been concerned. Had that fool Buddhu bungled it again?

After meeting his commanding officer, Clark went to Laurie's Hotel and roused Major G. Buchanan of the RAMC, and after informing him that his wife had been attacked in their bungalow, he asked Buchanan to accompany him to the police station. When the two men got back to the house with Head Constable Safdar Hussain, Louisa was still unconscious and blood was again seeping through the newly applied bandages. Later he went back to the police station to file an official report.

Inspector Smith arrived to find that Louisa had still not been moved from the blood-soaked bed. It was a sickening sight. The poor woman was clearly beyond help and only uttered a few words in Smith's hearing. 'Someone came to my bed last night…' She couldn't say more, and gurgling sounds came from her throat. She died that afternoon.

Smith was no fool. Experience and instinct told him that Clark was behind the murder. He took down a statement in writing from the bereaved husband but it wasn't convincing. Smith refused to fall for the 'friend on the train' story.

Superintendent Williamson more or less figured out the two murder plots as he went through the letters in the dispatch box. Also tucked away among the letters was another crucial piece of evidence that would hang Clark – a pencilled draft of the fake death certificate meant for Edward Fullam. All that was needed was to join the dots. Routine police work.

Augusta and Clark were arrested. Defiant and not a bit contrite, they refuted all the charges against them. Edward Fullam's body was exhumed and sent for a belated post-mortem to the Agra Civil Hospital. The doctor who conducted the forensic examination found the state of preservation of the intestines, liver, diaphragm and heart to be consistent with the injection of poison, specifically arsenic.

Buddhu was also arrested and, feckless rogue that he was, quickly agreed to turn approver. He sang long and hard and implicated everyone – his four accomplices, Augusta and Clark. The four *badmash*es made a run for it, but were soon apprehended. Mohan, the last to be taken – from a train in Gwalior – had a ₹500 reward on his head. Buddhu had implicated him as the man who had struck Mrs Clark with a short sword, thus sealing his fate and effectively sending him to the gallows.

Augusta and Clark had their day in the Allahabad High Court. There were two separate trials. The first, for the murder of Edward Fullam, was held on 23 February 1913, with a European jury in place, a privilege the accused could claim as British-European subjects. Only Clark strictly qualified on this count, but as Augusta was a co-accused charged with the same offence she was also given the benefit of a European jury. The trial took only three days but the courtroom was packed for the hearings and special arrangements had to be made to accommodate the crowd that trooped in to see the two defendants. It wasn't every day that a *gora sahib* and *gora mem* stood in the dock for murdering their spouses.

It was also remarkable that the children of both defendants gave evidence against their parents. Kathleen's testimony detailing how Clark had administered the poison to her father while her mother stood by chilled the hearts of all who were in the courtroom that day.

Clark would have been in no doubt as to where the jury's sympathy lay, and the little girl's words had finally sealed his doom. Still, unprincipled scoundrel though he was, he tried to save Augusta. She was not really aware of what the powders and medicines he gave her to administer to her contained, he said, and he was the only one who was responsible for Fullam's death. In a strange attempt at defending his actions, he also said that after moving to Agra, Fullam was in very poor health and that he had in fact given him the fateful dose to put him out of his misery! The jury was not impressed.

The British and Anglo-Indian community, one assumes, was also none too pleased. All the sermonizing and moralizing about Christian values could not hold water when two representatives of the ruling race were found to be faithless to their troth, and had betrayed the most sacred of institutions, marriage and family. Even though this was not the prim Victorian age, and the Edwardian era that had just passed was a moment for letting some of their hair down (just like the late King had done back home), this was India and here the white man was judged by a higher standard and was seen to be morally superior to the native. Venerable greybeards shook their heads in the clubs and the *memsaabs* felt they could not look their servants in the face. Just what did Fullam and Clark think they were doing? And whatever would the natives think?

The two principal protagonists obviously did not give a fig about what society thought. Augusta Fullam now turned on her lover and said she had no intention of killing her husband and that Clark had led her up to it. She was also by now pregnant with Clark's child and knew that she could therefore not be hanged – the law, as it existed then, would not allow it. However, both were convicted but Augusta's sentencing was postponed given her condition.

The second trial, for the murder of Mrs Clark, was postponed a few times and finally took place on 13 March. The four principal accused – Sukkha, Buddha, Ramlal and Mohan – were on trial for the murder of Mrs Clark. Being Indians, they should have been tried in the Sessions Court, but were also tried in the High Court in an unusual legal proceeding, along with Mrs Fullam and Mr Clark, who were charged with abetting the crime. The hired native assassins pleaded not guilty. They were nowhere near the scene of the crime on the night in question, they argued.

Their lawyers said that the police had extorted confessions from them by torture. This was standard procedure for the defence in Indian courts, but it did not convince the judge.

Buddha, Sukkha, and Mohan were pronounced guilty and sentenced to hang, but Ramlal's lawyer managed to convince a majority of the jury that no real case could be made out against him as none of the witnesses produced by the prosecution could actually shake his alibi. The idea of a retrial for Ramlal was mooted, but then discarded on a legal technicality and he was acquitted. Buddhu, having turned approver and ratted on his comrades, escaped punishment. Clark and Augusta pleaded guilty and were sentenced to death, in both cases. Mrs Fullam's sentence was, as per the law, commuted to transportation for life.

On 26 March 1913, Henry Clark was hanged in the Naini District Jail. By all accounts, he walked up to the gallows and went to his death without flinching. His body was later buried in the Allahabad Cantonment Cemetery where the Garrison chaplain read the funeral service. A handful of friends, his brother and his three children were in attendance. Clark had apparently asked to see Augusta for one last time, and as a condemned man this would have been granted, but she refused to see him.

Augusta had contemplated an appeal to the Privy Council in England, but later dropped the idea as it was unlikely to succeed. Unlike Indians, for whom transportation for life meant a trip to the Andaman Islands, Augusta was held in Naini jail.

True to form, Augusta managed to charm the English staff at the jail who found her a delightful woman, full of grace and charm. A senior matron at the female ward described her as 'a good lady and gentle... an English lady and not an Anglo-Indian, and by no means a wicked woman'.[8] The English jailor, Col Hudson of the Indian Medical Service, was won over by his new prisoner and was all praise for her. He is said to have remarked that he could not understand how a woman with so sweet a nature could have committed the crime of which she was found guilty.

Augusta gave birth to a baby boy in the jail, on 28 July 1913. She nursed the child devotedly, but was not fated to live her life out and see him grow up. Worn out by the debilitating summer heat of the plains, she died of heat-stroke on 28 May 1914 at the prison hospital, aged 38, and was buried at the Muir Road Cemetery at Allahabad. The star-crossed woman had survived her lover by just over a year.

And what of the other unwitting (and unwilling) actors in this drama?

Augusta's child with Clark was brought up in an orphanage, and did well for himself in later life. He joined the merchant marine and went on to become a captain, commanding merchant convoys to England during the Second World War. His ship was torpedoed by a Japanese submarine but he survived and went on to marry and settle down in Sydney where he set up a paint-manufacturing business.

Kathleen, too, despite her difficult and unhappy childhood, settled into a life of quiet domesticity after marrying an Englishman in India. Myrtle, the Fullam's last child (of doubtful paternity) was adopted, trained to be a nurse and later moved to England.

4

Plague Take You
The Pakur Murder Case

IT WAS A WINTER'S DAY IN 1933, AND THE IMPOSING BRICK-and-iron pile of Howrah Railway Station was packed with the usual Calcutta crowd. The press of humanity on this day, 23 November, was probably no different from any other as the great and the good of Bengal elbowed and shoved their way into the station as lustily as the *hoi polloi* of this great city on the banks of the Hooghly.

No one paid much attention to a party of well-dressed men and women as they entered the portals of one of the busiest railway stations in British India. Their dress and deportment would have immediately singled them out as members of the *bhadralok*, which they were. Heading the group was Amarendra Chandra Pandey, a young zamindar making a journey to his ancestral home at Pakur after an unscheduled visit to the city. Also in the party were his widowed aunt Surjabatidevi, his sister Bonobala, and his deceased half-sister's daughter Anima. A male relative and a friend had also come to see them off. However, there was an unexpected – and not welcome – addition to the group. This was Amarendra's older half-brother, Benoyendra, whose presence at the station was unexpected – and rather unusual – as the brothers were not on the best of terms.

As the group moved in through the booking area of the station, Amarendra suddenly winced as a short, dark man clad in *khaddar* (homespun cloth) brushed past him. Crying out that he had been pricked, and visibly in pain, Amarendra rolled up his right sleeve to examine his arm to reveal a tiny puncture, and oozing out of it was a colourless liquid. The offending man was nowhere in sight.

The women, for reasons that would be apparent later, were at once alarmed and not a little solicitous. They asked him to cancel the trip and see a doctor immediately. Only one from the group seemed unconcerned. Laughing off the women's pleas, Benoyendra grabbed his brother's arm and massaged the area round the puncture in an apparent bid to provide some relief. It was nothing, he insisted. Amarendra, whatever his misgivings and probably feeling a little foolish over all the fuss being made on what seemed to be just a harmless pinprick, decided to continue on his journey. And so, deaf to the pleadings of his companions, he boarded the train and made for his home, well over 250 km away, the journey filled with the women's entreaties to turn back to Calcutta immediately and see a doctor.

A day after his arrival at Pakur, Amarendra fell sick, and finally agreed to go back to Calcutta for a medical examination, giving in to his anxious relatives. Back in the city on 29 November, the family rented a house and a reputed doctor, Nalini Ranjan Sengupta, was summoned. Noting the mark of a hypodermic needle on Amarendra's right deltoid, he advised a blood culture. Amarendra agreed, and this was done by Dr Santosh Kumar Gupta and the sample was sent off to a laboratory.

But the young zamindar would not live to learn the outcome of the test. Days after providing the blood sample, Amarendra took to his bed with a very high fever. Soon, his tongue turned black and he developed a swelling on his face, groin and armpits. Now mortally sick and visibly sinking, he never recovered and passed away on 4 December, two weeks after the encounter with his unknown nemesis at Howrah. His relatives, anxious and alarmed at this turn of events, would have been naive not to have suspected that something was amiss. However, there wasn't much they could do just then. The result of the blood test was also yet to arrive.

Meanwhile, the body had to be cremated. An otherwise irresponsible Benoyendra took charge of the arrangements with alacrity. If any thought was given to informing the police and conducting an autopsy, given the rather unusual circumstances in which the death occurred, it was not acted upon. The family was a reputed one and despite their misgivings and perhaps with the best of intentions, did not want any untoward publicity. An obliging doctor known to Benoyendra wrote out a death certificate that claimed Amarendra had died from sepsis pneumonia. Amarendra's body was then consigned to the flames. It was later said that Benoyendra had also bribed the registrar at the cremation ghat, but no evidence to support this was ever produced at the subsequent trial.

Amarendra's blood culture report came in a day later. Its findings stunned his family and friends. The blood sample, the report said, contained *Pasteurella pestis*, the deadly plague bacteria. One can only imagine the fear and consternation that this would have generated. Surely, there must be a mistake? How could Amarendra have contracted the deadly scourge? And then the scene at the railway station played out in their minds all over again. The family was now convinced that the seemingly accidental prick on his arm by the stranger at Howrah was responsible for Amarendra's death. But who would want him out of the way? There was only one suspect. Amarendra's friends and family were now quite certain that there had been foul play, and that Benoyendra had a hand it. It could not be otherwise, for there was a long history of acrimony between the two.

The Pakur Raj zamindari, a sizeable and wealthy estate in pre-Independence days, was not in Bengal but in what was then Bihar and is now the state of Jharkhand. The head of the family, Pratapendra Chandra Pandey, had married twice – in hindsight, the cause of many a dispute among step-siblings. He had succeeded to the zamindari of Pakur on the death of his elder brother who had died young and childless, leaving behind his widow, Surjabatidevi. The vast family property was equally divided between Pratapendra and Surjabati, and there appears to have been no heartburn or dispute over the settlement.

Pratapendra had four children: Benoyendra and his sister Kananbala, from the first marriage, and Amarendra and Bonobala, from the second. Amarendra was the youngest in the family and, as his mother had passed away within weeks of his birth, he was brought up by his aunt. Surjabati was fond of her youngest nephew and lavished all her love and attention on the child. The Pakur estate brought in well over a lakh rupees each year (a sizeable sum in the 1920s) and Pratapendra's large family was brought up in comfortable circumstances.

When Pratapendra passed away in 1929, his share of the family property was divided equally between his two male descendants, Benoyendra and Amarendra. The two brothers were also revisionary heirs to their aunt. There was a slight hitch, though. While Benoyendra was then 27, the younger Amarendra was only 16 and not of age to inherit. The elder sibling was therefore entrusted with Amarendra's share of the property, which was to be handed over to his younger half-brother when he turned 18. It was all done in good faith, but anyone acquainted with the family would have been naive to assume that Benoyendra would simply hand over a lucrative estate to his half-brother on a platter.

Benoyendra could be best described as dissolute. The access to easy money and the wrong kind of companions only served to inflame this trait. Alcohol and women were among his chief vices. He also frequented what are delicately known as houses of ill-repute, and was even said to have travelled to Bombay to savour the fast life. More seriously – and this was a very sore point with a family that had a reputation to uphold – he had taken up with (or was taken in by) a dancing girl named Balikabala, thus dragging the fair name of the Pakur Raj zamindari in the mud of Bengal. Not the most upstanding of young men, certainly, and not one the bhadralok would be disposed to view with anything approaching favour!

Amarendra, to the delight and relief of his family and its well-wishes, was cast in an entirely different mould. By all accounts an affable, if serious-minded, young man, he was the antithesis of his step-brother. He possessed none of his elder brother's vices and seemed keen on obtaining an education. After completing his matriculation, Amarendra went on to join the Patna College for his BA degree. The education was easily funded by the family's substantial income, but Benoyendra always seemed to display a marked reluctance to part with his brother's share of it, and often delayed sending him money for his college fees and other expenses. Amarendra, even while in his teens, was mature and canny enough to realize that it would not be easy to get his brother to part with his share of the money. Thus, as soon as he reached the age of maturity in 1931, Amarendra officially began proceedings to obtain possession of his share of the family property.

In this he was encouraged by his doting aunt. Surjabati, well aware of her elder nephew's wayward ways, strongly advised Amarendra to demand and take possession of his rightful share at the earliest. Benoyendra, naturally, was not too pleased with this, but there was not much he could do. The terms of the will were clear and unambiguous, and so very reluctantly he agreed to hand over what was his brother's due. But the whole episode was marked by bitterness and recrimination. It was not a good augury of things to come – while Amarendra had gained his inheritance, he had also made a dangerous enemy. And, as the events that transpired would show, one with fiendish cunning.

As it subsequently came out at his trial, a discomfited Benoyendra had begun toying with the idea of getting rid of his half-brother for over two years before the actual murder. In this he was aided by his friend Dr Taranath Bhattacharjee, who was an even blacker sheep than Benoyendra. Taranath, who had been introduced to him by the dancing girl Balikabala, had apparently been sponging off Benoyendra, and the loss of a good chunk of the latter's income possibly had a bearing on his riotous lifestyle as well. It was Taranath, a microbiologist by profession, who suggested that it would be best if Amarendra were to die of natural causes, ideally of a malevolent disease. It is thought that the plague that had ravaged parts of Bihar in the 1920s gave Taranath the idea of using the plague bacilli to achieve this end. Accordingly, he tried to obtain a quantity of plague culture.

This was easier said than done, but Taranath was nothing if not resourceful. Given his medical background, he was aware that the only place in India where plague bacilli was being cultured, and from where he could obtain a sample, was the reputed Haffkine Institute in Bombay. He must have been in an even greater hurry to get rid of Amarendra than his stepbrother, for on 12 May 1932, he sent an express prepaid telegram to the Haffkine Institute seeking samples of virulent plague culture, ostensibly for laboratory work.

Named after the microbiologist Waldemar Haffkine, a Russian Jew who first introduced cholera and plague vaccines into India in the 1890s, the institute was at the forefront of research into infectious diseases in the country. Established in 1899, and located at Parel in central Bombay (where it still stands), it was one of the few places where plague culture could be obtained on request. The institute also supplied cultures to government institutions and research bodies if approved by the proper authority. Under no circumstances would the institute ever consent to send plague cultures to private bodies or individuals. The authorities at Haffkine were therefore not moved by Taranath's request, and the addition of the fictional Diploma of Tropical Medicine (DTM) to his name – to which he was not entitled – did not impress them either. They promptly replied that they could not comply with his request unless he obtained the permission of the surgeon general of Bengal.

Nothing daunted, Taranath changed tack and tried again. Later that month, he approached Dr Ukil of Calcutta and sought permission to work in his laboratory under his supervision, having somehow convinced him that he was on the verge of finding a cure for plague. It may be that Dr Ukil was a simpleton, or Taranath was just too glib-tongued, but Dr Ukil acceded to his request and managed to obtain a sample of plague culture from Dr Naidu at Haffkine. However, Dr Ukil did take all the necessary precautions and Taranath was not allowed to handle the culture independently. Eventually, attempts to subculture the strain proved futile and the strain had to be destroyed. Taranath then tried to persuade Dr Ukil to indent for a second strain, but he refused. But Taranath was not to be thwarted and managed to obtain some tetanus germs that he thought would do the trick. Duly armed with this, Benoyendra proceeded to his aunt's house in Deoghar, where Amarendra was then staying with Surjabatidevi during the Puja vacation of 1932. His arrival was unexpected and caused some surprise. Moreover, he had brought a stranger along, who he introduced as a compounder. Once settled in, Benoyendra suggested that Amarendra go out for a walk with him and his companion. Amarendra, probably not wanting to give offence, agreed to this, and as they walked around the estate, Benoyendra produced a pair of eyeglasses, or pince-nez, and suggested Amarendra try them on. The nosepiece of the eyeglass, it turned out, had been smeared with tetanus germs, and as Amarendra put it on, the elder brother helpfully jammed it down on his nose, piercing the skin. Amarendra's reaction at the time is not known, but there was nothing in Benoyendra's actions yet to arouse any suspicion, and he may well have shrugged it off.

Confident of their success, Benoyendra and his unknown companion departed for Calcutta, while Amarendra promptly fell ill within a few days. His face began to swell up and he had lost sensation around the nose. A local practitioner, Dr Saurendranath Mukherjee, diagnosed it as a tetanus infection and administered an anti-tetanus injection. Meanwhile a distraught Surjabati had telegraphed Benoyendra, asking him to send the family physician to Deoghar, which was only a few hours' drive from Pakur. Benoyendra promptly returned, but instead of the family doctor, was accompanied by Dr Taranath who he said was a trusted friend. Taranath suggested a shot of morphine as treatment. This was disputed by the local doctor who refused to oblige. Benoyendra then turned up with a Dr Durga Ratan Dhar, who proceeded to inject Amarendra with an unidentified 'serum' obtained from Calcutta. But Amarendra was still not getting any better and developed an abscess at the site of this injection. Benoyendra was soon back again, now with a Dr Shibapada Bhattacharya in tow. By this time, his relatives were thoroughly worried and suspicious of Benoyendra's 'doctors' and refused to allow them to treat him further. And so Amarendra survived.

Early in 1933, his relatives took him to Calcutta where he was attended by the illustrious Dr (Sir) Nil Ratan Sircar[1] under whose care and medication, Amarendra regained his health, though his heart was said to have been permanently damaged. The once active, healthy young man was now overcome by fatigue and bouts of dizziness. And so, after a few months in Calcutta, he went back to the family seat in Pakur.

For Benoyendra, it was back to square one. Egged on by the sinister Taranath, he then resolved to get his hands on some plague culture, come what may. On 30 April 1933, Benoyendra set out on a scouting expedition to Bombay in quest of the elusive plague culture. Staying at the Orient Hotel, he gave his address as Tagore Castle Lane, Calcutta, which was actually Taranath's residence. He also hired a guide, Ratan Salaria, to show him around the city. A *Times of India* directory helped him ascertain the names of doctors attached to the Haffkine Institute. Never short of ideas when it came to subterfuge, he sought out Dr Naidu, and holding out a letter of introduction from Taranath, said he was here to inquire on behalf of his friend, whether the institute would allow the use of its facilities to test to a possible drug for the plague. He was told this was impossible unless he had the permission of the institute's director. Needless to say, Benoyendra did not meet the gentleman concerned, and left for Calcutta on the same evening.

On 1 July, Benoyendra was back in Bombay. This time he stayed at the Sea View Hotel, again giving the same Tagore Castle Lane address and engaging the same guide. This time though he was more direct. He tried to bribe two veterinary surgeons – Dr Nagarajan and Dr Sathe – who were attached to the Haffkine Institute, to get him some plague culture. The two vets did not oblige but Nagarajan did tell him of an alternative source for the plague culture: The Arthur Road Hospital (now Kasturba Hospital for Infectious Diseases). It was the only place in Bombay where plague cases were then treated and where the culture was being made solely for supply to the Haffkine Institute. It must be kept in mind that, during this time, research into various aspects of plague was also being conducted at Kanbum Valley in the Madura (now Madurai) district of what was then the Madras Presidency, and there were also plague hospitals in Poona, Hyderabad, and Secunderabad. However, plague cultures were not being produced or available in any of these places.

So, having arrived there, Benoyendra met the hospital superintendent Dr Patel, and sought permission on behalf of his 'doctor friend' to work in his laboratory on his alleged plague cure. Dr Patel needed some convincing but eventually gave in, telling his assistant Dr Mehta that a Bengali doctor was expected to arrive soon at the hospital to carry on work on plague bacilli and to give him all the necessary facilities. At Benoyendra's request, Dr Mehta obtained Dr Patel's permission to indent for a single tube of live plague culture from Haffkine, pending the arrival of Dr Taranath who turned up on 7 July to carry on his 'work'. Meanwhile, the persistent Taranath had not stopped chipping away at Dr Ukil in Calcutta and had managed to obtain a letter of introduction addressed to the officer-in-charge of the Haffkine Institute with the request that Taranath as a bacteriologist might be granted facilities to experiment on the curative value of a likely drug for plague.

The conspirators stayed at the same hotel, Benoyendra as usual picking up the bill. They also purchased some white mice from a bird-seller in the city's Crawford Market. Taranath then got to work at the Arthur Road Hospital, testing the cultures he received from Dr Mehta on the mice, who soon died of plague. He was allowed to work freely in the laboratory, sometimes assisted by Dr Mehta, and was given access to all the necessary appliances. It was also noted that he brought with him a small bag containing instruments. On the evening of 12 July 1933, when an experiment on one of the mice was still incomplete, Taranath told Dr Mehta that he had to leave for Calcutta on some urgent business, but would be back shortly. He was never seen there again. The plague culture now in their possession, Benoyendra and Taranath left for Calcutta the same night.

With all the props for his nefarious scheme now in hand, Benoyendra tried to lure his intended victim back to Calcutta. He may have now been a little desperate, for he indulged in some very foolish antics that were later adduced as proof of his guilt and sealed his fate. On 18 November 1933, he tried to persuade Surjabatidevi to send a telegram summoning Amarendra from Pakur, but she refused outright. He then sent a fake telegram using her name with a message calling him urgently to Calcutta to discuss property-related matters. Only weeks ago, there had been a fallout between the brothers on a matter of withdrawal of cash assets related to their joint estate from banks. In October, a sum of ₹17,000 had been paid to the Pakur Court in respect of a compromise decree in favour of the joint estate, and Benoyendra had tried to withdraw the money. Amarendra had opposed this, and a petition of objection was filed, with the result that Benoyendra's order for withdrawal was rejected.

Amarendra, under the impression that this was the matter alluded to in the telegram, arrived in Calcutta on 19 November, only to find that he had been duped. Harsh words were employed and charges and counter-charges exchanged. The relations between the brothers, always strained, were now stretched to breaking point. The family, too, was worried. Benoyendra's actions were getting out of hand and they feared he would do his stepbrother some harm. For some time though, peace was restored, and it was decided that a decision on the settlement of claims to the joint estate would be made on a later date in Pakur.

While in the city, Amarendra went to the Purna Theatre one evening with five of his female relatives. Benoyendra, who had not been invited, turned up there, and it was later established that he was seen on the premises with a man whose description matched the man who would later inflict the fatal prick that killed Amarendra. The man may have been hired by Benoyendra to do the deed that evening, and was probably put off as Amarendra was surrounded by his relatives – but this is only conjecture.

Surjabatidevi and Amarendra decided to leave for Pakur on 26 November. Somehow, Benoyendra got wind of their plans and turned up at his aunt's house the evening before, and managed to confirm the time and date of their departure. He also said he would be at the station to see them off. Amarendra's fate had finally been sealed.

But so was Benoyendra's. His early clumsy attempts to harm his younger brother left no one in doubt as to who was responsible for Amarendra's death. Benoyendra had just been a little too clever and more than a little rash for his own good. And to imagine that no one would ask questions was a trifle foolish.

The blood culture report triggered a storm that would blow Benoyendra's cover. The presence of plague bacilli in the blood was a cause of great alarm, and the Calcutta civic authorities had to be informed. The doctors who heard about the case were also baffled. Tongues began to wag and discreet inquires were instituted. The director of the School of Tropical Medicine was consulted and made aware of the facts of the case and his opinion sought. The reply was unequivocal: yes, it was indeed possible to kill someone by injecting a dose of plague bacilli by means of a hypodermic syringe. The family was accordingly informed. Fully convinced now – if they ever had their doubts – that Amarendra had indeed been a victim of foul play, some of his relatives discussed the matter with a pleader known to the family in Pakur and decided to institute a police inquiry.

A petition was then presented to the Deputy Commissioner of Police at Calcutta by Amarendra's relative Kamala Prasad Pandey on 22 January 1934. The head of the detective branch, E.H. Le Brocq, Indian Police (Imperial Police or IP, the precursor to the Indian Police Service), was put in charge of the case, and a confidential inquiry was set in motion by Sub-Inspector Sarat Chandra Mitra. On 17 February, an FIR was lodged by Kamala Prasad Pandey at the Tollygunge Police Station against five persons: Benoyendra Chandra Pandey, Dr Taranath Bhattacharya, Dr Shibapada Bhattacharjee, Dr Durga Ratan Dhar, and the unidentified person who had injected the plague bacilli into Amarendra's arm at Howrah.

On learning of the FIR against him, Benoyendra tried to flee, but did not get far. He had been under police surveillance for some time and was picked up that very night from a train at Asansol Railway Station on his way to Bombay. Dr Taranath and Dr Dhar were arrested over the next two days. Dr Shibapada Bhattacharya managed to evade the police dragnet for nearly a month but was caught on 24 March. But the small dark man who committed the foul deed could not be found. Though Benoyendra admitted to having taken him to the Purna Theatre to identify his brother, he could not give any clue to his whereabouts. He set the police on a wild goose chase, giving false addresses to mislead them about the unknown stranger's supposed hideouts. In the end, his identity was never revealed and he escaped the vengeance of the law.

Benoyendra confessed to having hatched the plot to kill his brother since the time Amarendra had sought his share of the inheritance. Taranath had been a willing accomplice in this nefarious design. As it turned out, Taranath wasn't even a qualified doctor – merely a research assistant at the Calcutta Medical Supply Concern, a laboratory on Cornwallis Street. Apart from him, Dr Dhar and Dr Shibapada had been enticed with generous amounts of cash.

In the end, it was the same old sordid story of unmitigated greed. But the diabolical plot that Benoyendra and Taranath hatched pushed the story into the realms of the bizarre. Never in India was anyone known to have been killed by the injection of a dose of lethal bacteria. It was the first case of individual bioterrorism recorded in the country, and probably anywhere in the world.

The trial generated a lot of interest and saw the usual ups and downs. A total of 85 witnesses were called to testify, and over 300 exhibits introduced in evidence. Moreover, the police had done an admirable job of investigating a crime that spanned Pakur, Deogarh, Calcutta, and Bombay. Several strands of evidence had to be stitched together to put forward a prosecutable case. Justice Lort-Williams, in his judgement, described the case as being 'probably unique' in the annals of crime.[2]

Given the peculiar modus operandi of the crime, volumes of evidence were proffered by the medical experts. The defence put them through a severe cross-examination with a view of establishing the probability or possibility that the diagnosis that Amarendra died of plague was wrong. It was even suggested that the blood culture had been mixed up with that of some other person, or had been either accidentally or deliberately contaminated.

Amarendra, it was contended, could have contracted the plague either from his half-sister Kananbala, who allegedly died of mumps on 10 September 1933, or otherwise naturally from a flea-bite or some other source. Dr Nalini Ranjan Sengupta, who had examined Amarendra on 29 November and detected the mark of a hypodermic needle on the right deltoid of the deceased, refused to accept the defence suggestion that the mark which he saw was that of a flea- or insect-bite. Medical evidence was also produced before the court to show that plague culture could in fact be transported from Bombay to Calcutta and kept alive for a period of six months from July to the end of November, when the offence was actually perpetrated.

The accused tried to brazen it out. On his arrest, Taranath told Sub-Inspector Mitra that he had never been to Bombay all his life either alone or with Benoyendra. Insisting that he had no knowledge about the culturing of plague bacilli, he denied having ever approached any doctor for a letter of introduction. He admitted that he had known Benoyendra for three or four years. Later, while on bail, he went to the police and altered this statement, and admitted that he had been to Bombay, but not with Benoyendra. At the trial, he denied that he had known Benoyendra prior to September or October 1932.

Benoyendra admitted to having been to Bombay, but denied that Taranath had ever been with him there. He had visited the city with regard to a film venture, he said. However, the guide he had hired in Bombay put paid to all his lies, and was able to give the police precise details of all his movements. Further, and more incredibly, Benoyendra said he had never heard anything about Amarendra having been pricked by a stranger at Howrah Station. In the end, his fanciful claims did not wash with the jury. It took them just four hours to find Benoyendra and Taranath guilty of murder by a unanimous verdict. The sessions judge sentenced the two men to death.

The other two accused – Dr Durga Ratan Dhar, who administered the fake dose of anti-tetanus serum at Deoghar, and Dr Shibapada Bhattacharya, who provided the false death certificate – were acquitted for want of evidence and got off scot-free.

The defence immediately filed an appeal with the Calcutta High Court. A battery of eminent counsel led by N.K. Basu appeared for the accused, while the advocate general of Bengal represented the Crown. On 9 January 1936, Justice Lort-Williams and Justice Nasim Ali affirmed the lower court's decision, but given the inordinate length of time between the commission of the crime, the Sessions judgement and the final disposition of the appeal, set aside the death sentence. Instead, Benoyendra and Taranath were sentenced to transportation for life in the Andaman Islands.

Not much is known about what happened to them thereafter. According to published reports, Benoyendra was freed under a general amnesty when India became independent in 1947. But the long years in prison probably unhinged his mind and he is said to have become insane. There are unsubstantiated reports that he threatened his wife with a rifle on his return to Pakur and barricaded himself inside the house which was then stormed by the police and was killed in the ensuing shoot-out.

The devilish Taranath Bhattacharya's later fate is also unknown, but he is said to have gone mad while in the Andamans. Of the once famous Pakur Raj zamindari, nothing remains except the old Rajbari which still stands in the town.

5

Blood on the Tracks
A Murder on the GIP Railway

LATE IN THE EVENING OF 21 JULY 1931, GEORGE HEXT, A YOUNG British soldier, stepped into a first-class carriage of the Punjab Mail at Lahore Railway Station. Boasting of a single heavy passenger locomotive that hauled eight carriages, the Punjab Mail was an express service provided by the Great Indian Peninsula Railway (GIPR) and was very popular with British servicemen travelling to the Punjab and beyond to the North-West Frontier Province (now Khyber Pakhtunwala). Running daily between Bombay, Delhi and Lahore, it covered the 1500 kilometres between Bombay and Delhi in about 32 hours at an average speed of about 50 kilometre per hour. Beyond Delhi, the train ran on the tracks of the North Western Railway and terminated at Lahore, where the headquarters of the railway were also located. Those proceeding further, mostly military personnel heading for their depots, garrisons and regimental centres on the frontier, changed to narrow-gauge trains run by the North Western Railway, which deposited them at the railheads closest to their destination.[1]

George Hext was heading for Poona, a long way down in western India, to attend a Signals Course for young officers. The 22-year-old Hext came from a long line of servicemen. His father Major John Edward Hext had died prematurely at Rawalpindi in 1922 due to wounds sustained in the Mesopotamia campaign during the Great War. Born on 15 September 1908 at New Abbot in Devon, George was educated at Marlborough College before being selected for the Royal Military Academy at Sandhurst as a King's India Cadet in 1927. Passing out a year later, he was appointed to the Indian Army on 30 August 1928, and subsequently commissioned into the 2nd battalion of the 8th Punjab Regiment. Arriving in India on 5 October at Bombay, he reported to the 1st Battalion, Rifle Brigade, at Jullundur in the Punjab. This was standard practice for military officers starting out in India – newly commissioned officers destined for the British-Indian Army had to spend a year with a British Army unit before moving on to their allotted regiment.

His training completed, George formally joined his regiment on 10 October 1929 at Idak near Bannu on the North-West Frontier, south of the famed Khyber Pass. His battalion, the 2/8th, had seen service in Mesopotamia during the Great War (when its title was the 90th Punjabis) and also in the Third Afghan War of 1919. On arrival, George found his battalion engaged in peacetime duties and the young soldier's introduction to soldiering probably involved nothing more arduous than road-protection and garrison duties. George had his first taste of frontier warfare the following year as the battalion was called out to suppress one of the little wars that were always flaring up on the North-West Frontier, and was promoted to the rank of lieutenant in November 1930.

Early morning on Monday, 20 July 1931, George left Idak and travelled over 35 kilometres by a military lorry to Bannu along with his bearer and most likely with an armed escort as the trigger-happy Pathans could be counted on to take potshots at soldiers despite the cessation of hostilities. Boarding a narrow-gauge train of the North Western Railway at 1 in the afternoon, he travelled to Kalabagh on the left bank of the Indus, where he and his fellow companions took a ferry to Mari Indus on the east bank. Here they boarded a broad-gauge train at 7.35 p.m.

and arrived at Rawalpindi at 6.40 the next morning. The train to Lahore would not depart for another six hours and, like so many soldiers before him, George would have made use of the excellent facilities at Rawalpindi station for a welcome bath and a hearty breakfast.

At midday, the train pulled out and headed for Lahore, arriving at 7.55 p.m. on Tuesday, 21 July. Here he began the last stage of his journey on the Punjab Mail, which would shortly begin its return run to Bombay. He was joined in this compartment by Lieutenant Eric Sheehan of the 28th Field Regiment, Royal Artillery. The 25-year-old Sheehan was also attending the same Signals Course as George and one imagines that the two Englishmen found each other's company congenial and passed the time in easy, informal banter. Bluff, young men in the prime of their lives, they did not have the slightest hint of what fate had in store for them before they reached their journey's end. Just under an hour later, the train steamed out of Lahore and headed out into the hot night across the dry Punjab plains, arriving in Delhi at 7.30 a.m. on Wednesday, 22 July. After an hour and 15 minutes, it departed for its final destination south to Bombay, where it was due to arrive at 4.40 p.m. on Thursday.

However, on this occasion, when it pulled into the grand neo-gothic pile that was Bombay's Victoria Terminus Station, the Punjab Mail was several hours late and two of its first-class passengers were missing. In an act of appalling and pointless brutality, George Hext had been murdered on the train overnight while Eric Sheehan was badly wounded.

News of the attack caused a sensation. The Punjab Mail Murder, as the newspapers headlined it, caused a huge uproar and drew public attention in both India and England. The senseless murder of a young man in the prime of life – for no fault of his other than being in the wrong place at the wrong time – evoked both sympathy and anger. As it turned out, George was simply the unwitting victim of a robbery gone wrong. The perpetrators were young men of much the same age as him, and probably did not have murder on their minds when they entered his compartment. In fact, the leader of the gang, a young Indian named Yeshwant Singh, seemed to have been driven by a misplaced sense of patriotic zeal. The aborted robbery, according to him, was simply a means to obtain funds which he intended to put to use in the service of his country. He was simply trying to emulate other young men across India who, fired by revolutionary ardour, sought to overthrow the British Raj by violent means.

The decade following the end of the Great War was a time of great political ferment in India. Over a million Indians had responded to Britain's call to take up arms, and it was not unreasonable if they demanded the same freedom from foreign domination for themselves at the end of the war. The calls to overthrow British rule were loud and unceasing, and inspired a growing band of young men, many of them well born and educated, to take up arms against the foreign oppressor. The early 1930s saw an increase in the number of violent attacks on British officials, particularly in Punjab, the United Provinces, and Bengal. A large number of the victims were policemen who were seen as stooges of the British.

In April 1930, a band of young revolutionaries led by the legendary Surya Sen mounted a raid on the armoury of the Auxiliary Force India (AFI) at Chittagong and made away with some firearms and ammunition. The Police Lines and the European Club were also attacked. These raids were ultimately foiled and many of those involved were quickly run to ground, but the audacious attack sent shock waves across British India. In May 1930, Mr D.B. Murphy, assistant superintendent of police at Mardan in the North-West Frontier Province, was shot dead. A few months later in August, shots were fired at Francis J. Lowman (the inspector general of police in Bengal) and Mr Eric Hodson (the superintendent of police, Dacca) when they were visiting a colleague at the Dacca Medical Hospital. Lowman died on the spot while Hodson took a bullet in the shoulder. During the same month, in a very bold attack at Dalhousie Square in the heart of Calcutta, Commissioner of Police Sir Charles Tegart had a narrow escape when a bomb thrown at his car exploded harmlessly, missing its target by inches. In December, Lt Col Simpson, a former officer of the Indian Medical Service and the inspector general of prisons, Bengal, was shot dead in his office at the Writers' Building in Calcutta by three revolutionaries – who then went around the building shooting at other targets until they were finally cornered. In April of the next year, James Peddie, the district magistrate of Midnapore, was shot dead by a young man while attending a school exhibition. The Bombay Presidency, which over the years had produced a fair share of revolutionaries, was not quiet either. On 22 July, a day before George Hext was to meet his tragic end, Acting Governor of Bombay Sir John Ernest Hotson had a lucky escape after he was shot at by a student at Fergusson College in Poona. The bullet lodged itself in a notebook in his pocket.

George Hext would not be so lucky, but his killing was not in any way political, for he was too small a pawn on the chessboard of the empire. The murder was the unfortunate collateral damage of a plot gone horribly wrong. Three men were involved in the plan, though only two took part in the attempted robbery that ended in Hext's untimely death. The prime instigator, Yeshwant Singh, was one of the six sons of a postal overseer from Damoh in central India. The 31-year-old was employed at Bhusawal Station as a railway cabin man, a position procured for him by his uncle Gore Lal, a retired station master of the GIPR. The second man, 19-year-old Deo Narayan Tiwari, came from Khamgaon in the United Provinces. On the recommendation of his brother-in-law Ramprakash, he had found work as a labourer in the Carriage and Wagons department of the GIPR at Bhusawal Station. Dalpat, a Maratha in his early twenties, was the third of the trio and had been employed as a candidate cabman at Bhusawal Station for over a year until he was discharged in March 1931. A seemingly mild-mannered man, he had obviously been led by his two comrades, whose acquaintance he made while working at the station. Of the three, Yeshwant Singh was the more dominating type and the evidence given at their subsequent trial suggests that the other two were intimidated and carried along due to his blustering, forceful ways.

Yeshwant was possessed of a strong nationalist bent. While not formally a member of any organized political party or revolutionary outfit, he felt the need to contribute in some way to the freedom movement. He also seems to have been somewhat naive, for his basic plan to aid his motherland was to simply commit a robbery to obtain money and firearms, which could be put to good use in the revolutionary cause. That, after all, was what a lot of young men around the country were doing. His ideas on what do afterwards were somewhat vague and, unsurprisingly, did not enthuse either of his comrades (who were probably very alarmed at what he was leading them into), but he kept at it and in the end Deo Narayan agreed to go along, if a little reluctantly.

Sometime in June 1931, the two made a solemn plan to commit a robbery at the first suitable opportunity and oaths were sworn, supposedly on holy water taken from the Ganges (it actually came from the tap in the Bhusawal station yard). Unexpectedly, during the same month, Yeshwant's wife died, but the domestic tragedy did not undermine his revolutionary fervour in any way. If anything, he seemed even more determined. Deo Narayan, who had by now developed very cold feet, soon received a letter from Yeshwant reminding him of their promise, and the two agreed to execute their plan the following month. On 21 July 1931, both Yeshwant and Deo Narayan reported sick at Bhusawal Station, complaining of stomach ache, and received permission to return to their homes. That evening they contacted Dalpat and asked him to come to Yeshwant's house in Bhusawal. Not surprisingly, the weak-willed Dalpat was quickly cajoled or bullied into taking an oath on the 'Ganges water' and agreed to lend a hand in whatever venture his two companions had in mind.

The plan was simply to rob a first-class passenger within the confines of his carriage. It is difficult to know if any violence was intended but all three men carried weapons, probably to feel secure rather than with any intention to use them. Dalpat had hidden a safety razor within his clothes, while Deo Narayan carried a knife and Yeshwant had a crudely fashioned double-edged dagger. This last weapon was deadlier than it seemed. It had been made from the stump of a broken sword which Yeshwant had ground down and sharpened with a file. None of the men had any previous criminal record and they would have been understandably nervous; Dalpat very likely a little more than his companions.

To allay any suspicion, it was thought best to travel some distance beyond Bhusawal, where they were known and could be easily identified, and accordingly the three boarded the 5 Down to Itarsi a little way up the line, travelling ticketless in the third-class compartment. In the heaving, sweat-stained mass of humanity that crowded the carriage, they were unlikely to attract any particular attention. At Khandwa, the next stop, Yeshwant and Deo Narayan paced the length of the platform seeking a suitable victim but met with no success. The train finally reached Itarsi Junction at 4 a.m., and the three went to the waiting room for a few hours' rest. At daybreak, after tea and refreshments, they drifted aimlessly about the town trying to kill time till the evening. Soon tempers were fraught and Deo Narayan, not happy with the way things had turned out, quarrelled with Yeshwant. It was not a happy party that rushed to the station in the evening to avoid a heavy shower of rain. However, they soon patched up their differences and a transformed Deo Narayan now resolved to go ahead with the plan come what may. The 6 Up train, which would take them back to Bhusawal, was expected only sometime before midnight, and so the three men went off to sleep for a few hours in an empty carriage in the Itarsi marshalling yard.

At 11.30 p.m., the Punjab Mail rolled into the Itarsi Junction. This was the 6 'Up', which was actually going 'down' south to end its long journey at Bombay the next evening. The three men walked the length of the platform looking for a suitable victim and then climbed into a third-class compartment. A little past midnight, the train started again. Yeshwant and Deo Narayan had made up their minds to break into a first-class carriage, but Dalpat was not told about this. The two men had probably realized that the feckless Dalpat was unlikely to be of much help and decided to leave him out. When the train stopped for a few minutes at Khandwa, Yeshwant and Deo Narayan climbed onto the footboard of a first-class carriage and stood there in the dark holding on to the door handles while Dalpat was left behind. They travelled thus to the next station, Dongargaon, without being spotted. An agonized Dalpat had by now realized that his companions really meant to carry out their plan this very night. Thoroughly alarmed, he left the train and went to the waiting room at Dongargaon. Here, amazingly, given the peculiar situation he now found himself in, he went off to sleep. If it ever occurred to him to contact the railway staff and tell them what was likely to happen, he did not act upon it. Worried about saving his own skin, he probably hoped and prayed that his rash companions would not do anything that would implicate him as well.

By now, in the early hours of 23 July, George Hext was fast asleep on the lower berth of the sleeper compartment (coupe) of his first-class carriage. Equipped with two bunks, the compartment could be used as an ordinary living room during the day. It also boasted of a small bathroom, where passengers could beat the heat of the day with a cool shower before tumbling into their beds.

Eric Sheehan occupied the upper berth. There was, however, a third passenger that Deo Narayan and Yeshwant were unaware of when they chose this carriage for their misadventure. Fast asleep on the floor was Sheehan's cross-bred terrier Kim, who was attached by his leash to the bunk frame. All was dark and the two young officers slept peacefully as the train sped through the night at around 65 kilometres per hour. Outside, the two Indians clung to the swaying side of the train on the left hand side, smoke and steam rushing past them from the engine that was immediately ahead of the carriage, waiting for an opportune moment to set their desperate plan in motion.

It would be just as well to describe here the scene of the crime. The first-class carriage of the GIPR's Punjab Mail in which George travelled was largely identical in design to those favoured by railway companies all over India during the 1920s. The train's eight carriages were painted maroon and were of three types – mail, third-class passenger and upper-class passenger. The last was composed of second- and first-class compartments with four and two bunks, respectively. Being built for the broad-gauge network, the coach design allowed for a fair amount of space and comfort in the upper-class compartments. The carriages were of the non-corridor type and each compartment was equipped with a bathroom and toilet. The doors to the carriage opened inward, a feature that allowed the perpetrators to enter the coupe even while the train was in motion. The compartment may also have been a bit crowded with the soldiers' kits, boxes, and chests spread all around.

Unfortunately, as it turned out, the fan in the compartment was out of order. July nights were very hot, and so the Englishmen left the window open, bolting the door from the inside, and secured the window space with a venetian-style shutter. Some 10 minutes out of Dongargaon, Deo Narayan quietly forced the catch on the window shutter and reaching in through the window, withdrew the bolt, and opening the door climbed into the darkened compartment. Yeshwant, holding a torch, was right behind him. The duo probably meant to make a quick search of the compartment and withdraw quietly with whatever they could lay their hands on. They had not counted on the presence of the dog. Aroused from his sleep, the little terrier began to bark and Deo Narayan, bending down, promptly stabbed it with his knife. The commotion woke up George who started to sit up. Crouched beside the lower bunk clutching his home-made dagger, was Yeshwant Singh. Shining his torch on George's face, he began to furiously stab the Englishman who was now trying to get out of his bunk. Despite his hands being badly slashed as he tried to shield himself, George managed to stand up and grapple with Yeshwant. Deo Narayan, who had been trying to dispatch the dog with his knife, now turned to find George's back towards him. Lifting his arm, he plunged the knife into the right side of the officer's back. Completely severing a rib, the blade tore into George's lung, inflicting a fatal wound.

All this happened in the span of a few seconds, and Eric Sheehan was already fully awake. Looking down from the upper bunk at the struggling forms in the dim light of the torch, he realized what was happening and flung himself on Yeshwant without a moment's hesitation. This timely interruption allowed George to turn his attention to Deo Narayan. Despite his wounds and the heavy loss of blood, he managed to wrest the knife free from his attacker's grasp, while the unfortunate Deo Narayan had the ends of three of his fingers sliced off. One of these would be left behind on the floor of the blood soaked carriage, and in time would send him to the gallows.

Freeing himself from a rapidly weakening George, the panicky Deo Narayan dashed past the fighting forms of Eric Sheehan and Yeshwant Singh and swung out of the open carriage door. Staggering around the compartment, the badly wounded George tried to pull the communication cord but failed and collapsed on the floor.

Eric Sheehan, a big man weighing 89 kg, was now fighting for his life in the darkened compartment. He cried out to George to pull the communication cord, unaware in the darkness and confusion that his companion was bleeding to death on the floor, alongside his beloved terrier. By now, Eric had been badly slashed across his chest and was trying to take away the dagger from his assailant's grasp. Clutching the double-edged blade, the powerfully built Sheehan managed to break it off, leaving the handle in the Indian's hand, but also badly lacerated his own palm in the process. Reversing the blade, he now stuck it into the right side of Yeshwant's chest. The blade then fell from his hands to the floor. The two men were now hitting out madly at each other, tumbling all over the compartment in the dark. Finally, Sheehan managed to find the communication cord and pulled hard on it but the train did not stop. The chain was jammed!

At this moment, Yeshwant managed to free himself from the Englishman's grasp and made for the door. It had slammed shut after Deo Narayan's exit and so the bloody and bruised Yeshwant climbed out through the window. Sheehan and Hext were left alone in the compartment that was now awash with blood. Curiously, two other officers also heading for the Signals Course in Poona were travelling in the same carriage. Each of them occupied a single berth on either side of the compartment where the attack took place. One of them, Lt J.F. Williams-Wynn of the 5th Field Regiment Royal Artillery, had been awakened by the muffled shouts and screams, but assumed that it was an altercation between some Indian passengers and went back to sleep. Sometime later, after several attempts, Sheehan finally managed to pull the communication cord and the Punjab Mail came to a halt in the darkness between Dongargaon and Mandwa.

The guard, stepping down to investigate the reason for this emergency stop, probably got the shock of his life. Two Englishmen, bruised and bloodied in a first-class carriage, was the last thing he would have expected to see. The alarm being raised, Hext's bearer (who was probably in a second-class carriage), the train driver, and other passengers quickly gathered and together they tried to help the injured officers as best as they could. Roused by the commotion, Williams-Wynn too got out of his compartment and hastened to their aid. Williams-Wynn may have been stuck by a sense of guilt at not having acted sooner, but as his compartment was partitioned off there was not much he could have done, even if he had realized that two of his fellow officers were engaged in a life-and-death struggle just a few feet away. Sad to say, both George and Sheehan were armed, but could not reach for their weapons to defend themselves. Both officers carried service revolvers, but these were packed away in their baggage. Eric Sheehan always travelled with his 12-bore shotgun but this had been secured in its case and stowed in the luggage rack.

The train then moved on to Mandwa, where the telegraph operator sent messages further up the line to Burhanpur seeking medical and police assistance. At the Burhanpur Railway Station, an Indian doctor and a constable were waiting. They quickly jumped on board and the Punjab Mail resumed its journey as Dr Deshpande began a fruitless battle to save George Hext's life by administering whatever medical help he could in the moving train. At Bhusawal, a gaggle of officials stood in readiness as the train pulled in. The district medical officer, Dr Robertson, quickly took charge and the two men were rushed to the Railway Hospital.

For George Hext, it was the end of the road. Yeshwant's crude dagger had inflicted eleven terrible wounds on his upper body, puncturing the young officer's lungs and intestines. His palms and forearms had also been badly cut as he attempted to ward off the attack. However, it was Deo Narayan's knife that proved to be the most deadly – cutting entirely through a rib and penetrating the pleural cavity. But for this wound, which caused severe bleeding and trauma, the doctors might have had a hope of saving Hext's life. He died shortly after 3 p.m. at the Bhusawal Railway Hospital without regaining consciousness.

Eric Sheehan suffered several minor wounds, the worst being a knife thrust into the right side of his rib cage. He lost a great deal of blood but, being young and fit, made a quick recovery. After seven days at the Railway Hospital in Bhusawal and a further week at the British Military Hospital in Deolali, he was discharged and rejoined his regiment at Lahore. His gallant defence of George Hext won much deserved praise from his fellow officers and his providential escape was commented upon.

What no one, and not the least Eric Sheehan, could know was that this would not be the end of the story for him. A further sequel awaited.

When the Punjab Mail arrived at Bhusawal Station, the police carried out a thorough examination of the carriage and questioned the passengers and crew for a description of the men involved so that a search could be organized in the surrounding countryside into which the attackers had vanished. However, no description was forthcoming and even Eric Sheehan could not provide any clues as the attack had taken place in almost total darkness. The police did collect some evidence that Williams-Wynn had picked up from the floor of the compartment – a dagger blade and its handle, a knife, and a torch. Apart from these, a more macabre piece of evidence linking one of the perpetrators to the crime was found under George's bunk. It was the top phalange of a human finger which had been sliced off when George grabbed the knife from Deo Narayan's hand. Also found on his bunk was the book George had been reading before he lay down to sleep. Ironically enough, containing accounts of several remarkable murders with all their gory details, the book was titled *Great Stories of Real Life*.

From Sheehan's account of the struggle in the train, it was obvious to the police that both the attackers would have some injuries on their person and their clothes would be bloodstained. Local police detachments for miles around were alerted and asked to be on the lookout for possible suspects.

After their hurried departure from the compartment, Deo Narayan and Yeshwant had moved back to their former positions on the footboard of the carriage and clung to the door handles, awaiting a suitable opportunity to jump off. The train soon ran down a gradient, and as it slowed down at the bottom (as the chain had now been pulled) both men jumped off and entered the thick jungle all around. A brief conversation followed and they decided to split up in the hope of confusing any pursuers.

Dalpat, for his part, was far removed from these dramatic happenings. His slumbers at the Dongargaon Station waiting room were rudely interrupted by shouts from the station master's office. The official was talking on the telephone to his counterpart at another station up the line, and Dalpat heard him say that two first-class passengers in the Punjab Mail had been attacked by thieves. Quickly putting two and two together, Dalpat hid the safety razor in a stack of railway sleepers. At daybreak, he hitched a ride with the guard of a goods train back to Bhusawal. Though he had taken no part in the robbery, he must have been aware of what awaited him if either of his former companions were caught. Characteristically, he did nothing and stayed quietly at home for a few days before going to attend his aunt's funeral at a nearby village.

Meanwhile, the hunt was on. A party of gangmen informed the police near milestone 331 that a man dressed in a black coat and shorts with canvas shoes had been seen going towards Mandwa. Mr Edward, the deputy chief engineer of the GIPR, happened to be on an inspection tour in the area where the two men were expected to have jumped off the train and he put a gang of 50 trackmen at the disposal of the railway police to ferret out the suspects. The jungle in this part of central India was quite dense, comprising low, stunted trees and thorny bushes that afforded easy concealment to any fugitive. The search party was looking along the tracks when, near milestone 326, they sighted a man answering the description given by the gangmen limping along the permanent way. On being discovered, the man quickly ran down an embankment and disappeared into the jungle. Finally, after several hours and many miles of pursuit, an exhausted Deo Narayan was cornered and taken into custody. He had been resting in a shed, and moved away as he heard people approaching but was tackled by a labourer working in a field and captured.[2] The sliced-off fingers on his bloodstained hands were proof enough of his involvement. Later, the Central Provinces Police, which conducted the investigation into the murder, were able to match the phalange picked up on the train with one of his fingers.

Yeshwant Singh had been making his way through the jungle for many kilometres, doubling back and forth to confuse the pursuers he was sure would soon be on his trail, when he came across a small tribal settlement. Exhausted and thirsty, he stopped there for a brief rest and asked for water. Nobody there had heard of the murder yet, but his furtive looks and bloodstained clothes aroused suspicion and, while he was resting, word was quietly sent to the nearest Railway Police post about the suspicious stranger. A police party soon arrived and, in a little over nine hours after he had jumped off the train, Yeshwant was under arrest.

At Bhusawal, an otherwise sleepy town that seldom made the headlines, the local British community went into immediate mourning. The Bhusawal Contingent of the AFI mounted guard over Hext's body before being relieved by a detachment of the East Lancashire Regiment from the cantonment at Deolali. Hext's remains were taken to Bombay by the Nagpur Express and laid to rest the next day on 24 July at the Sewri Cemetery. A small detachment of the 4th Battalion, 8th Punjab Regiment representing his own battalion and a bearer party of the East Lancashires fired three volleys over the grave and their buglers sounded the Last Post. By a remarkable coincidence, the chief mourner happened to be Col W.M. Mcleod, the officer commanding Bombay District, who was Hext's uncle.

Under interrogation, Yeshwant and Deo Narayan soon revealed the details of their failed plan. Dalpat may have entertained the hope that his companions would choose not to disclose his role in the plot as he was not involved in the actual murder, but it was not to be and the police came knocking at his door in a few days. Naturally, the police sought a motive for what was viewed as an inexplicable crime. The accused were not hardened criminals and had no previous records. Their choice of victims was also surprising. If indeed a simple robbery had been attempted, it was unthinkable why someone would target a couple of soldiers who were unlikely to carry any money or valuables on their person, and would most likely be armed and able to defend themselves. In the prevailing political climate, and as the victim was an Englishman, the police then began to look for another motive. A search of Yeshwant's house revealed newspaper clippings from the nationalist press glorifying the actions of Bengali revolutionaries and publications of a similar nature. Photographs of prominent Indian political leaders who were then in the forefront of the fight against British rule were also found. The police also discovered a letter in Deo Narayan's home confirming Yeshwant's plan to keep their oath. While it was in all probability an attempted robbery gone wrong, the annual police report for the Central Provinces and Berar for 1931 noted that Yeshwant had been influenced by the revolutionary Bhagat Singh, who had been hanged earlier in March that year. The report also commended Railway Police Sub-Inspector Man Singh for his prompt action that led to the arrest of Hext's assailants.[3]

The case came up for trial before Mr F.J. Woodward presiding at the Court of Sessions in Nimar. Each of the three men was charged with 'conspiring together to further certain revolutionary activities by doing robbery and murder on running trains'.[4] In addition, Yeshwant and Deo Narayan were charged with 'murder by intentionally causing the death of Lieutenant Hext and the attempted murder of Lieutenant Sheehan'.[5] The three pleaded not guilty.

Besides the weapons employed in the deadly attack, 54 witnesses and 71 documents were produced before the court. The accused retracted the statements they had made earlier but their lawyers did not find it easy to mount a defence, given the evidence presented by the prosecution. The accused also made contradictory statements that cast doubts on whatever they said. Yeshwant Singh cooked up the most unlikely story to account for the attack on the two Englishmen. He said they had entered the first-class compartment under the mistaken impression that it was a third-class carriage as it was dark at Dongargaon. The officers were angry at the intrusion and abused them and attacked them with daggers. The Indians had merely attempted to defend themselves and in the process Hext had inadvertently lost his life. It did not sound very convincing.

The hapless Dalpat tried hard to disassociate himself from his companions. He took no part in the actual attack, he said, and had been forced into the venture by the other accused. However, what worked against him was his failure to inform the authorities at Dongargaon that a serious crime was about to be committed. His failure to surrender to the police also weighed heavily against him.

Deo Narayan, though initially a reluctant recruit, was damned by his subsequent actions. It was he who forced the catch on the window and entered the compartment first. It was with his knife that the dog was killed when it gave the alarm that aroused the two officers. Lastly, it was the fatal thrust of his knife into Hext's back that transformed a botched robbery into a murder. The violence of the wound inflicted on Hext's back did not suggest any reluctance or half-heartedness on the part of the accused.

Yeshwant was unrepentant – and even somewhat defiant – to the end. While awaiting his sentence, he wrote to his father saying he would 'laughingly go to the gallows' if sentenced to death, claiming that what he had done was the act of a brave man.[6] Urging him not to grieve, he begged for his father's forgiveness and ended his letter on a philosophical note that 'no man was mortal and all of us have to die someday'.[7]

On 21 September 1931, Yeshwant Singh and Deo Narayan were sentenced to death by hanging for the murder of George Hext and the attempted murder of Eric Sheehan. Dalpat was found guilty of conspiracy and sentenced to transportation for life. Judge Woodward did not spare the GIPR either, and the company was censured for poor maintenance of the communication chains in its carriages. The accused appealed their sentence, but could not get any relief. Yeshwant and Deo Narayan were hanged at Jabalpur Central Jail on 12 December 1931. The city observed a hartal following their execution.[8]

The story of the Punjab Mail murder was widely reported in the British and Indian press. Coming a day after the attack on Sir John Hotson in Poona, it drew both scathing comment and outrage. On 24 July, in the British House of Commons, Sir Stanley Baldwin sought further details about the attack from the Secretary of State for India. The secretary, Captain Wedgewood Benn, was not in possession of all the facts but informed the house that he would table it as soon as details were forthcoming. The House expressed its sorrow and condoled the death of the young officer.

George's fiancée Joan Simpson learned of his death from a newspaper. The Simpsons were out for a family outing in Plymouth when they heard the newsboys crying out about the death of a Devon man in India. Joan purchased a copy of the paper and her shock on reading about her future husband's murder can be imagined. The two were childhood sweethearts and both families had approved of the match. However, as George was very young and early marriages by army officers were frowned upon, the two had decided to wait for a few years till George had the required seniority and means to wed. In time, Joan reconciled herself to her loss and married an officer of the Royal Navy a few years later.

But this is not the end of this sorry tale of unexplained and egregious events. Eric Sheehan, who so fatefully escaped death on the Punjab Mail, went through another similar and entirely unexpected ordeal a few months later. In September, he had travelled to Nimar along with Hext's bearer to give evidence at the trail. A few days later he boarded a train for the return journey to Lahore. Travelling in a first-class coupe identical to the one in which he had been attacked some months before, he occupied the lower bunk – just as George Hext had in their last tragic ride. This time, however, he was taking no chances, and placed his service revolver under his pillow before he turned in for the night. The train stopped at a little wayside station just before daybreak, and Eric was fast asleep. Just as the train was pulling out, he was awakened by the sound of splintering wood. Sitting up with a start, he saw the dim figure of a man crouched beside his bunk. In the feeble glow of the lights outside, he saw that the man had smashed the slatted window shutters to gain entry. Scenes from his fateful journey in July flashed back in his head, and without a moment's hesitation Eric Sheehan pulled out the revolver and pumped two bullets into the intruder. Leaping to his feet, he pulled the communication card and the train came to a halt at the end of the platform. The injured man was moved out of the compartment, and expired shortly afterwards on the platform.

But the man Eric had shot and killed was not a thief. An educated 20-year-old Eurasian from a respectable family, the young man was merely trying to get a free ride back home and had broken into the compartment in the mistaken belief that it was unoccupied. Sheehan had shot and killed an innocent man who had the misfortune to enter a compartment that had been occupied by a passenger who had nearly lost his life a few months ago in similar circumstances. Worse, by another tragic coincidence, the young man was the brother of a soldier serving in Sheehan's own regiment. The officer's anguish may well be imagined and, to add to it, Sheehan was now charged with murder. It had all been a horrible mistake, but the law allowed for no other solution. Eric had fired deliberately, possibly with intent to kill, and the question of guilt could only be decided by a court. In November, Eric Sheehan stood trial for murder at Saugor in the Central Provinces. He pleaded not guilty, and his defence was brilliantly conducted by an Indian lawyer. In the end, as was largely expected, the court found in his favour and Eric was acquitted.

He soon returned to regimental duties at Lahore and, later in 1933, finally attended the Signals Course at Poona. During the Second World War, he served with the British Expeditionary

Force in France where he was wounded in action. He went on to have a successful military career before finally retiring as a lieutenant colonel in 1952.

George Hext and Eric Sheehan were not the last English officers to be attacked on a train in India. On the night of 20 June 1942, a train on the Kalka–Simla Railway came to an unexpected halt due to boulders lying on the tracks. Shots were fired into the train and two men, their faces muffled, entered one of the compartments and robbed the passengers of their wallets and handbags. Six people, including Major Carey-Grey, Wing-Commander Hogg and his son Lieutenant Hogg, Col Waller of Army Headquarters Simla, and a Mr Bolton and Mrs Trewby were killed in the attack. It was initially not clear whether the attack was planned by dacoits or by Indian revolutionaries targeting the British officers.

A year later, two brothers, Abdul Karim and Abdul Rahim – both employees of the North Western Railway – were found to be involved in the crime. The attack on the train had been planned as they wanted money to buy or abduct girls to get married. Abdul Karim was already married, and apparently committed suicide following a shoot-out after a police party tracked him down to his house in Bhatinda in November 1943. The younger brother, Abdul Rahim, was arrested at Dera Ismail Khan in the North-West Frontier Province sometime later. He was hanged in Ambala Jail in 1946.

6

In Durance Vile
Death in a Bombay Brothel

AROUND 10 P.M. ON 20 FEBRUARY 1917, HAVILDAR VITHOO Jagoji and Constable Badruddin Hassan of the Bombay Police were going down Hajam Lane near Duncan Street, which was then a not-very-respectable quarter of the city. The two men had just completed their shift and the walk home should have been uneventful unless, as sometimes happened, it was livened by the antics of an occasional drunkard stumbling home after a grog-soaked evening. This night, however, would turn out to be different as the policemen spotted a group of men carrying what seemed to be a body wrapped in a sheet out of a house. Another man, a few paces behind, appeared to be directing them. The house from which the men had just stepped out was known to be a brothel, but it was the furtive behaviour of the man in charge of the party that caught Jagoji's attention. The man turned on his heels as soon as he spotted the policemen, and began to walk in the opposite direction.

Their suspicions aroused, the policemen immediately apprehended the man and ordered the bearers to carry the corpse (for that was what it was) back into the building. Then they began questioning the man. Syed Mirza was known to the police as a brothel owner, one of several who ran many such establishments in the city's red light district of Kamathipura, and Jagoji, who lived in the nearby Two Tanks area, may well have been familiar with him.[1]

Mirza's answers were evasive. The girl, who was called Akootai, had died of venereal disease, he said. Jagoji was not convinced and he was marched off to the Maharbawdi Police Station for further questioning. Inspector Lewellyn O'Brien and Sub-Inspector Mahomed Khan then proceeded to Hajam Lane to conduct an inquiry. A cursory examination revealed a number of bruises on the woman's body, and the corpse was sent to the morgue for a post-mortem.

The story that emerged was shocking. Akootai had been beaten, starved and tortured for several days. The police surgeon, Arthur Powell, who examined the body of the unfortunate woman at the morgue a day later, stated in his deposition that her death had been caused by injuries sustained by the beating she had received from her tormentors. There were 18 large weals on her body caused by the blows of a cane or stick. There were several large bruises on her legs, thighs, arms, back and head. The fifth and sixth ribs on the right side had been broken by the blows inflicted on her body and had been the cause of her death.

But why was Akootai beaten to death? This is her story.[2]

Akootai (alias Taibai) was a Mahar and, according to a statement provided by her cousin Naikoo, came from Kolhapur State which lay to the south of what was then the Bombay Presidency. Her age is not given in the documents relating to the case but she was probably in her twenties like the other women in the brothel. Naikoo, a labourer employed in the Drainage Department of the Bombay municipality was not the most reliable of witnesses. Akootai, he said, was married, but he could not remember her husband's name! With Akootai not alive to contradict him, Naikoo could have been lying and may well have sold her to the brothel himself to clear an outstanding debt. This was quite a common practice, and men who found themselves in debt would sometimes sell their wives, daughters or other female relatives to pay off a brothel owner. Often, a destitute widow or a deserted wife would be enticed with offers of a job as a house maid or *ayah* and sold to a brothel. Occasionally, a woman would enter a brothel herself to pay off some debt or simply to make ends meet. Akootai's antecedents are not very clear, but she seems to have been in Mirza's keeping for some two years before her death.

Her lot cannot have been an easy one. Women did not enter the hellhole of Kamathipura in search of the good life. 'Kamathipura,' as Samuel Sheppard's excellent *Bombay Place-Names and Street-Names,* published in 1917, informs us, 'is commonly used to denote the prostitutes' quarter, and the same may be said of Grand Road and (Cursetji) Shuklaji Street, both of which connote a good deal more than geography.'

The brothel district of central Bombay, which had been in existence since the middle of the nineteenth century at least, also included a few other localities such as Foras Road, Bellasis Road, Falkland Road and Duncan Road. Writing in 1854, Michael Kirwan Joyce, late Bombay Police Force, informs us in his *An Exposure of the Haunts of Infamy and Dens of Vice in Bombay* that these houses of ill-repute were clustered 'about Dobee Tank, behind the County Jail, Lower and Upper Colaba, the Girgaum, Duncan, and Belassis Roads, and the main road reading to Parell'.

According to Joyce, many 'heinous crimes' were committed in these 'houses of debauchery. Many young girls are enticed away from their parents, guardians, and respectable homes, and received in these haunts of vice, while others traffic for the spoliation of female honour.' Men, too, were not entirely safe in these places and, unless careful, could find themselves robbed, assaulted, or worse, especially if under the influence of liquor.

An amazing variety of nationalities were represented in its insalubrious quarters. The white sailors coming off the ships in the nearby port could choose from Poles, Germans, Italians, French, Russians, Armenians, and Japanese. European-only brothels catering to white men were quite common and in the 1880s Shuklaji Street, where there were a number of these establishments, was also known as Safed Galli (white lane).

According to S.M. Edwardes, police commissioner of Bombay from 1909 to 1916 and author of *The Bombay City Police - A Historical Sketch 1672–1916* and *Crime in India*, there were some who believed that the European prostitutes provided an extremely essential service to white manhood and the empire. If they were to disappear, it was feared, white men would 'resort to Indian women' – something that 'could not be regarded with impunity by those responsible for the general welfare of India'. The colonial state had, therefore, established brothels for soldiers near their cantonments or regimental bazaars where the men could get some sexual release. These places were regulated and health checks were conducted to ensure that the women were not infected with venereal disease.

The European prostitutes, Edwardes informs us, usually came to India of their own free will after 'serving an apprenticeship' in Europe, Constantinople or Egypt, and while most of them lived and died in debt, some managed to save enough to take back to their own countries and lead comparatively respectable lives. However, the colonial administrators tried to ensure that no British woman indulged in such activities, and prostitutes from Britain were discouraged and liable to be deported if found practising the world's oldest profession in the empire's colonial outposts.

With the Indians though, it was a different story. The ordinary sex-starved Indian seeking a prostitute in Bombay, who could not savour the delights of white skin, had to make do with their brown-hued counterparts, and so he went looking for his wares in the 'cages' of Kamathipura. These were degrading affairs, the women sitting behind barred windows and doors, trying to catch the attention of the men passing by in the street. It is said that it was the police in the 1890s who insisted on the brothel-owners putting up metal bars on their establishments so as to prevent the men, often the worst scum of the city, from forcing themselves on the women. A good number of the men who visited these miserable hovels were labourers from the nearby docks and mill-workers who resided not far from the locality. They often came from the same social strata and background as the women whose companionship and favours they bought in exchange for a few *annas*. The name Kamathipura comes from 'Kamathi', denoting a class of labourers from the area of the southern Deccan and the Nizam of Hyderabad's Dominions. The women lived (and occasionally died) in these 'cages', along with the brothel-keeper and a couple of his assistants or partners, male or female, who helped keep them in line. Any attempt at escape or insubordination, as Akootai would find out, was harshly dealt with.

The 25-year-old Mirza, who hailed from Punjab, was officially a money-lender, as were many of his kind in the city, and this may have been one of the ways he got women in his keeping – in lieu of unpaid debts. Mirza was helped by two women, Gangabai (alias Mariambai) and Gomtibai (alias Sakinabai). The brothel-assistant, of whom there was always usually one (and sometimes the brothel-keeper herself, if a woman), was more often than not, a 'time-expired' prostitute (to use Edwardes' own colourful phrase). No longer able to entice customers through her charms, she kept her younger charges in line, though it must be said that she usually took care of the women and ensured that they came to no harm, either from the attentions of her bawdy customers or from the police, and sometimes from a tyrannical brothel-owner.

Gangabai, a Hindu, was described by the other inmates of the brothel in their deposition as Mirza's wife. Though by her own statement they were never officially married, it was known that she had gone through a *nikah* ceremony with Mirza. Gomtibai was said to be Gangabai's daughter, either biological or adopted. Both women had adopted Muslim names, which suggests they had some deeper connection with Mirza. While the Pathan was ostensibly the boss, the brothel rooms were actually rented out in Gangabai's name, and so they could also be said to be partners and, given their seemingly close relationship, almost a family.

Besides Akootai, there were four other girls in the brothel: Phooli, Paru, Moti, and Jijabai. There was also an older woman named Tarabai (a Bhandari woman who had converted to Islam and also went by the name Halima) who cooked for them.

For almost a week before she was killed, Akootai had complained of pain in her genitals. She had developed venereal sores, which caused a burning sensation, making it difficult for her to carry on her trade. Unable to take the pain and discomfort, she had turned away several customers, which led to verbal altercations with some of them. The women were expected to cater to several men during the course of the day and night, and in her condition Akootai could not do this.

The loss of income did not go down well with Mirza and his two assistants, who assaulted her for turning men away. Instead of calling in a doctor or a *vaid* (traditional healer), they tried to cure the problem of the venereal sores on their own. Gagging and tying Akootai down on her bed, they rubbed lunar caustic, often used for treating gonorrhoea, into her genitals. This caused her intense pain, but she was punched and her genitals pinched when she cried out. The lunar caustic did not provide any relief and Akootai carried on in this state for a few days.

On 19 February, unable to bear the agony anymore, Akootai refused her fourth customer. He complained to Gomtibai, who helpfully suggested that the customer could sodomize Akootai, if he so wished. Akootai protested loudly at this, and the man walked off. Though Akootai's refusal did not cost the brothel anything as the man had already paid and in fact departed without claiming his money, Gomtibai was enraged. She proceeded to give Akootai a severe hiding with a stick. It was this that finally drove the poor woman to despair. She decided to escape from the brothel. A little while later, when Gomtibai went to the toilet, Akootai took what turned out to be a fatal step. Seeing her chance, Akootai asked Tarabai the cook to let her out on the pretext of meeting a customer who was waiting outside. No sooner was the door unlocked than she bolted down the street. But she did not get far. An alarmed Tarabai cried out, and Mirza and two other men, Sulleman Oomar and Walji Narsey, set off in pursuit. Catching up with Akootai some distance away, they dragged her back to the house.

That evening, as the other women stood watching, Akootai was brutally tortured by Mirza, Gomtibai, and Gangabai. This was to be a lesson, not only for Akootai but also to her co-workers, about the perils of attempting to escape their fate. She was beaten with a metal yard-measure[3] and a heavy curry-grinding stone. She was stripped, burnt with lit matches, and scalding hot water was poured on her. Her screams could be heard outside, but no one intervened, which is not surprising given the locality. Denied food and water, Akootai was almost dead by the next morning, her body bruised and a couple of ribs broken.

That afternoon, Gangabai and Gomtibai beat her again, forced her to eat onion peels, and handed her a glass of urine when she asked for water. At some point she lost consciousness, and Gangabai tried to pour liquor into her mouth to revive her. But this did not work, for Akootai had died. Mirza was sent for, and was furious when he saw the woman lying prone. Gangabai, now afraid, lied that Akootai had taken liquor from a customer and had only passed out. Mirza was not fooled. He kicked the body and, realizing that he now had a corpse on his hands, quickly took charge of the situation.

Some yards of cloth were ordered to wrap the body, and Mirza set off to obtain a death memorandum for her burial from the *ramoshi*, a local municipal official. The *ramoshi*, Ganpat Keshaw, duly arrived to register the death, and was unlikely to have been fooled by Mirza's story. However, he did not ask too many questions, and the requisite death memorandum was granted. Gangabai for her part told the *ramoshi* that the dead woman was a pauper, and that she would gladly pay ₹5 as charity towards her burial. Keshaw in his deposition said Gangabai asked Mirza to pay him a few annas for tea (which may have been an attempted bribe) but Mirza did not give him the money.

Mirza now tried to find someone to carry the body away. He approached a group of four coolies standing at a nearby street corner. These men were Marathas, and would have refused to touch the body of someone of the untouchable caste to which Akootai belonged. So Mirza lied, saying the body was that of a Maratha woman, but they still refused to budge and insisted that the body be brought out to them for being wrapped. After a mix of threats and cajolery, the men finally agreed. Bamboo canes, matting and white cloth were bought from a shop nearby, the corpse wrapped and tied up, and the men set off on their unusual errand when they were stopped by the police.

The story, when it came out in the newspapers, evoked horror, revulsion, and sympathy. The women, according to statements made by Akootai's companions, had to sometimes see as many as nine men each day, charging three to four annas per visitor. Any refusal was sure to lead to a beating. All their earnings were handed over to Gomtibai, who allowed them to keep only their clothes and ornaments. Virtual prisoners in the brothel, they were locked into the ground-floor rooms where they received their customers. They all slept in the same room and were accompanied even when they went to the toilet. The girls had some horror stories to relate.

Mirza and Gangabai forced the brothel inmates to drink his urine if they refused a customer. Phooli said she had been made to do this twice. They were assaulted if their earnings fell below expectations. Moti had once had her elbow dislocated after a thrashing and had to go to a bonesetter to get it fixed. When Moti had begun to cry after witnessing Akootai being beaten, Mirza had hit her as well and threatened to take away her ornaments. Strangely, Mirza seemed to have bought ornaments for his brothel workers, and the threat of having them taken away was apparently often used as a threat against the women.

The curry-stone, an unusual if effective object to beat someone with, seemed to have been Mirza's weapon of choice. He often threatened the brothel inmates with it if they refused to fall in line. Even Akootai's cousin Naikoo had been beaten with it a few weeks before the murder when he had apparently gone there searching for his missing wife Bhagubai, who was also at the brothel. Mirza had refused to let Naikoo have her back as he had bought her from another man.

One fact that came out during the police investigation and the subsequent court case was that all the women owed Mirza some money. Phooli was working in the brothel as she had to pay off twenty rupees that she owed Mirza, and had been brought to the brothel by his brother. Paru had been brought to Mirza's brothel from another establishment at Duncan Road by Mirza's brother and she was working there to pay off Mirza who had settled her debt to another man. Moti had been sold to Mirza by a former lover for ₹50. And so it went on and on… there was no end to their misery.

Mirza, Gangabai and Gomtibai were charged with the murder of Akootai. The statements of her co-workers and the police surgeon's deposition could not be denied. The surgeon had found traces of lunar caustic on legs, buttocks, and private parts. During the post-mortem, he said, the contents of the stomach of the deceased had given out a strong smell of onions and garlic. Some of the marks on her body were consistent with beatings that might have inflicted with a yard measure, the police surgeon said. Shown the one that had been found by the police at the brothel, he had no hesitation in concluding that the marks he saw on the corpse could have been caused by that instrument.

The police came in for their share of criticism as well. The public was outraged and the role of the police in the whole affair was also questioned. Surely, these brothels could not have possibly been operating in this fashion without the knowledge and connivance of the men in uniform? And then again, why did they let the Pathans run loose in the city? 'The Pathans are a great nuisance in Bombay and many other parts of India. They are great bullies and are a great terror, particularly in county districts,' the Advocate of India complained on 4 July 1917.

Around the 1920s, Bombay was in the grip of the so-called 'Pathan Menace' as members of that community were notorious for causing law and order problems and often engaged in robbery and other crimes in the city. They swaggered about the streets bullying people, and being moneylenders, many of them used strong-arm methods to collect their debts. They were also said to coerce debtors to sell their wives or other female relatives to brothels, as was amply evident from the Akootai case. In fact, as R. Chandavarkar relates in his book *Imperial Power and Popular Politics*, so feared were the Pathans that owners of shops and other businesses had no choice but to submit to a protection racket whereby Pathan 'watchmen' were employed to 'guard' their property against theft – seemingly the only way to prevent their premises from being looted.

In the same year that Akootai was murdered, the Bombay Police once again got the wrong end of the stick when one of their number – an inspector named Simon Favel, the only Jew in the city's police force – was charged with extorting money from brothel-owners and pimps. Among other transgressions, he also availed of free sexual services from prostitutes by threatening them with deportation. The inquiry against Favel – incredibly a winner of the King's Police Medal and a close friend and confidant of the former Police Commissioner S.M. Edwardes – brought to light the shady nexus between the police and those in the flesh trade, and cannot have done much to instil public confidence in the guardians of the law.

In April 1917, Labshankar Laxmidas, representing the Bombay Humanitarian Fund, petitioned the viceroy to set up a special commission to inquire into the operation of brothels in India, and take such steps as deemed necessary for the protection of 'poor luckless women from the horrors of enforced prostitution – from the clutches of human fiends like Syedkhan and his abettors in Bombay'.[4] Prostitution and its accompanying problems were a headache for the British not just in Bombay but also in other metropolitan cities of colonial India, though Bombay with its notorious 'cages' probably drew more attention than the others. In a sensational case in 1927, Hiralal Agarwalla, a Marwari merchant of Calcutta, was assaulted and killed with a kukri by the cousin of a young Nepalese girl who had allegedly been kept by him as a concubine. The girl, Raj Kumari, was known to be very pretty and had been allegedly sold to the merchant for ₹1,300 by Padma Parshad, a tout from Benares. Kumari claimed to have been abducted from her home in Janakpur by Padma Parshad and said she had escaped from the house of the Marwari merchant who had been harassing and threatening her, but was not provided any assistance by the police. She then sought the assistance of the Gurkha Association of Calcutta, which had in fact asked the city police chief to intervene in the case just before the murder was committed. The affair caused quite a furore in Calcutta. Questions were raised on the age of the girl (some accounts mentioned her age as being only 13 while the police claimed she was about 18) and action was sought against the middleman for procuring a minor girl for immoral purposes. But it could not be proved in court that Kumari had actually been sold to Hiralal, with the defence contending that she was above the age of consent and had been willingly staying with the merchant. In the end, the case against Padma Parshad for trafficking a minor could not be proved and he walked away a free man.[5]

But the law did provide justice to Akootai. Mirza Syed Khan and Gangabai were found guilty of the murder of Akootai and sentenced to death. They were hanged at Umerkhadi Jail within three months of their crime.[6] Their accomplice Gomtibai was given a life sentence. The jury that decided the case also commended Havildar Jagoji's role in bringing Akootai's murderers to book.

Akootai's death could not have been the first murder in a brothel in Bombay, and equally certainly it would not be the last. And in those lanes, where the world's oldest profession is still practised, many more Akootais can be found.

7

Death in the Hills
An Unsolved Murder in Burma

ON THE MORNING OF 17 MAY 1931, A SUNDAY, THE PLEASANT hill-station town of Maymyo (now Pyin Oo Lwin) – in what was then British Burma – woke up to distressing news. One of its most distinguished residents, Col Henry Morshead DSO, had failed to return from his usual ride. The pony he had been riding had trotted into the compound of a local Indian businessman, minus its rider, but with the saddle covered in blood.

As was natural, foul play was suspected, for these were uneasy times for the British in Burma. A peasant uprising of sorts had broken out in the countryside some months ago and a band of rebels had been seen in the jungles around Maymyo a few nights ago. With its English-style houses, set back on well kept lawns bordered by colourful flowerbeds, Maymyo was the summer capital of British Burma. Some 70 kilometres from the heat and dust of Mandalay, it was the closest the English in Burma could get to their island home. So, it was not expected that the troubles in the plains would find their way into the sheltered hills. Nevertheless, there was a feeling of unease and the disappearance of a British official did not seem propitious.

The 48-year-old Henry Treise Morshead was a renowned explorer and fellow of the Royal Geographical Society. A graduate of the Royal Military Academy at Woolwich, he had been commissioned into the Royal Engineers in 1901, before joining the Survey of India in 1906. A keen mountaineer, the hardy Morshead had led the Survey of India's detachment during the Everest expedition in 1921. The next year he was part of the summit team that included the legendary George Leigh Mallory,[1] and while none of the climbers made it to the summit, Morshead lost three fingers to frostbite. Much earlier, in 1913, he had undertaken another adventurous journey when he accompanied the famous Col F.M. Bailey on his exploration of the Tsangpo Gorges. Bailey would later become a household name in England for his escape from Bolshevik Russia, which he detailed in his book *Mission to Tashkent*.

Except for the war years, Morshead served all his life with the Survey of India. In May 1929, he arrived in Maymyo to take over as Director of the Survey of India's Burma Circle. With his wife Evelyn and their five children, he soon settled in a house called Upperford that stood (and still stands) in a large 3-acre compound with its own tennis court. The town and the Survey offices where Henry worked were within easy reach some 3 kilometres away. Fond of the hills and wild country, Morshead was in congenial surroundings and would have found the eucalyptus and pine covered forest paths around the hill station ideal for his daily morning rides. He also tried to pick up the local language, but without much success. In fact, his Burmese lessons ended rather abruptly, with Henry throwing a book at his tutor declaring that he was having no more of it.

In February 1931, Evelyn and the children left for England as the two older boys had to be admitted to school. Henry's sister Ruth had meanwhile arrived to keep house for him and so he was not left alone in the large house. The siblings got on well enough, the weather was cool and pleasant, and Henry had his work to keep him busy. In a few months, the Burmese summer was upon them and Henry undoubtedly enjoyed his early morning ride before getting down to his maps and charts for the day. Early at 6 a.m. on that fateful Sunday, he wrote what turned out to be his last letter to his wife. Half an hour later he set out on his usual morning ride.

The official statement of the commissioner of police, Mandalay Division – published by the *Rangoon Gazette* on Tuesday, 19 May 1931 – detailed the beginnings of what was soon to become a very perplexing affair:

> Shortly after 9 o'clock on the morning of Sunday, 17th May, 1931, the Subdivisional Officer, Maymyo, received a telephone message from Syed Ali of the Maymyo Electric Supply Company to the effect that a riderless pony with blood on its neck and saddle had just come into the compound of his bungalow on Manor House Road from the direction of Elephant Point. He at once collected a dozen policeman and with a Sub-Assistant Surgeon went by car to Mr Syed Ali's house, where he found that though the pony was not in any way injured, it was obvious from the large amount of blood upon it that a serious accident had occurred…

However, this statement is slightly at variance with some of the particulars in the FIR filed at Maymyo Police Station. The copy of the FIR, which Evelyn obtained a year later through a friend in the town, said it was the Syed Ali's *mali* (gardener) who had informed him about the arrival of the riderless pony, and Syed Ali had then called up the subdivisional officer to report the matter.

Harold Oxbury, the subdivisional officer, Maymyo, was then into his very first appointment in the Indian Civil Service. He acted promptly and rushed to Syed Ali's house. Oxbury had first thought that the as-yet-unknown rider had probably met with a riding accident, but changed his mind after seeing the quantity of blood on the saddle. It was apparent that the rider had met with some violence. There also seems to have been some confusion about the actual owner of the pony, and it was not until 11 a.m. that they realized who the rider was.

The ground on which the search was conducted was part of the Reserve Forest and across the road from Henry's house.

The jungle here was fairly thick but not impenetrable. Criss-crossing this piece of ground were several so-called 'rides' – the paths that were maintained for horse or pony rides. Some of these extended several kilometres into the Reserve Forest and had such names as Boundary Ride, Circular Ride, Switchback Ride, describing the nature of the ground traversed by the rider. The pony had been seen coming along Inlya Ride (leading to Inlya village) towards Switchback Ride and Elephant Point, and Oxbury and his policemen searched along these rides but turned up with nothing.

It was now well past noon and Oxbury called the commanding officer of the 20th Burma Rifles for assistance. Soon the area was swarming with troops as a whole battalion of the Burma Rifles along with men from the Governor's Body Guard and the 7th Bengal Mountain Battery turned out to help. A lady, who had been out riding that morning, reported seeing Col Morshead near Elephant Point and heading towards Inlya Ride. Morshead was known to often stray away from the rides and cut through the jungle, and so the ground all around the rides was beaten. Some woodcutters said they had seen a riderless pony along Inlya Ride that morning but knew nothing more. There was a heavy shower of rain that evening, but the searchers persisted and the ground was gone all over again till 9 p.m., when the search was finally called off for the day.

The next day, the search resumed at first light, and at about 7.30 a.m. Captain Rawdon Briggs, Royal Engineers, and a party of Dogras stumbled upon the body in the jungle some 150 yards from Inlya Ride. If there had been any signs of a struggle or drag marks, they had been washed out by the rain. Incidentally, Captain Briggs had been the first member of the English community to visit the Morsheads when they moved into Upperford.

A post-mortem conducted by the Civil Surgeon Major McRobert revealed that Col Morshead had been killed instantly after being shot in the chest at very close range. A second shot fired from a distance had left superficial wounds. His assailant had apparently approached him as he was coming down the ride and shot him in the chest, and then fired again as he was riding away. The body had then been dragged into the bushes and concealed. The police had gone over the ground where the body was found, to try and reconstruct the crime, and this seemed the most likely explanation. A motive was, however, missing, and many theories were doing the rounds. The police made two quick arrests and a reward of ₹1,000 was offered for any information that could lead to the discovery and conviction of the murderer.

The suspects in custody were a Gurkha and a Burman. According to initial reports, the Gurkha had been out shooting with a gun he had borrowed from the latter and had shot Morshead accidentally. On 11 June, three weeks after the murder, the *Rangoon Gazette* carried a story which said the accused Gurkha had 'made a statement' that he had accidentally shot Col Morshead. The colonel had remonstrated with him and tried to snatch away the gun from him when the left barrel was discharged, inflicting a fatal wound. The Gurkha also had some marks on his cheeks – the result, it was said, of being struck by Morshead with his riding crop. The police later accepted the Gurkha's explanation that the marks were caused by a fall.

There was also another fantastic rumour floating around – that Col Morshead had in fact been killed by a tiger! Leonard Aspinall, who was employed by the Bombay Burmah Trading Company at the time, also heard about it in the days immediately after Morshead's body was discovered. This unverified story persisted for many years and Lt Col H. Westland Wright was told about it seven years later when he was appointed to the Survey in Maymyo.

These contradictory and often absurd rumours were syndicated to British newspapers and caused much disquiet in Morshead's family back in England. His brother Owen, who was the King's Librarian at Windsor Castle, wrote to the India Office in Whitehall seeking the official report on the affair from the Government of Burma. The India Office, in its reply on

21 August, said the press reports had been based on unofficial attempts to reconstruct the facts. It was true that a Gurkha and a Burman had been arrested on suspicion solely on the grounds that the Gurkha had been shooting in the area where the body was found, while the Burman had been implicated only because the Gurkha had been using his gun.

However, the police investigation had ruled out the involvement of these men. The police were satisfied that the Gurkha left his village of Inlya at 6.30 a.m. and returned at 9.30 a.m., and that to have visited in this period a place where he satisfied them that he had shot a jungle fowl and the spot where the body of Henry Morshead was discovered (3 kilometres from where the fowl was shot) he would had to have covered at least 12 kilometres. This they considered impossible given the nature of the ground. He was, therefore, released together with the Burman who, being ill, had not left the village on the day in question.

The police had then verified the whereabouts and movements of all the licenced gun-holders in the town on the day of the murder, but this too led nowhere. The authorities had therefore determined that 'the case must remain a mystery,' the report concluded, on a note of resigned finality.

The newspapers in Rangoon and London had a field day, and the headlines were true to journalistic form: 'Col. Morshead Found Dead. After His Pony Had Returned Riderless. Accident or Attack?', 'British Colonel Shot Dead. Mystery Outrage of Burma Jungle', 'D.S.O. Colonel Shot Dead in Jungle', 'Death of Devon Explorer. Tragedy of Burma Jungle'.

The reports were often inaccurate and based as much on facts as on hearsay and innuendo. Could it have been someone that Henry knew well? After all, only a few weeks earlier, Henry's colleague Captain Heaney had been shot at by an employee of the Survey, an Indian by the name of Ahmed Ali who Henry had himself taken on the staff over a year ago on the recommendation of a colleague. He had described the event in his penultimate letter to Evelyn:

> Heaney had not actually been hit. Ali had fired three shots at long range with a scatter gun after being told off for misbehaviour, and one of the pellets went through the top of Heaney's hat. The man has been given 3 years R.I. ... He was a bad fellow... spent all his time messing about with village girls instead of doing his work.[2]

Did any of Henry's employees nurse a grudge against him as well, the papers speculated. The colonel, it seems, had quite a temper. He did throw a book at his Burmese teacher, after all. Behaviour of that sort was not likely to endear him to the locals... someone must have had it for him, and had waited in ambush with a gun... Could Henry have stumbled on to a poacher who panicked and shot him? That, again, was quite possible. Or maybe it was a band of dacoits. The country had been quiet since the so-called 'Pacification of Burma' by the close of the last century when scores of bandits, ruffians, and other undesirables been hunted down, shot and hanged, but banditry had never died away completely in the countryside.

And what of the political angle? Henry was after all a senior civil servant. Was the murder part of a plot against the British at Maymyo? Was it a precursor to an uprising in the little hill-station town? The country had been in an uproar since the so-called Saya San Rebellion began in December 1930 when a faith-healer proclaimed himself the King of Burma and exhorted the masses to overthrow the British. The empire in Burma, while seemingly benign was also quite unjust. To be sure, Burma had prospered under the British and roads, railways, the post and telegraph had certainly made life easier than in the days of King Thebaw. However, the easy-going Burman did not reap much of the benefits of *Pax Britannica*. These were cornered by the Anglo-Indians, the Chinese, and the Indians who had arrived in a flood in the last 50 odd years. Events on the other side of the globe also cast a long shadow. The Great Depression triggered by the Wall Street Crash of 1929 knocked the bottom out of the rice market. Rice was Burma's main export and the peasant in the paddy-growing Tharrawaddy district was hit the hardest. It was here that the rebellion found its impetus. The already-poor peasant was squeezed further when Indian landlords and moneylenders who owned most of the land called in their debts, and resentment against the outsider mounted. There was also a racial element in all this. The foreigners – English, Indian or Chinese – considered themselves superior to the Burman. They took his land and his livelihood, and very often his women. Saya San rode this tide of disaffection, and his cohorts set great swathes of the countryside aflame – attacking villages, government treasuries and police outposts. They lacked modern weapons and armour but were fortified by superstition – wearing charms and amulets that they believed made them impervious to bullets. 'Men advanced upon machine guns chanting formulas; with amulets in their hands they ran upon regular troops. They pointed their fingers at aeroplanes and expected to see them fall,' wrote Maurice Collis in his book, *Trials in Burma*. Collis was the district magistrate of Rangoon in 1929–30, and his first-person account provides an insight into the tensions prevailing in Burma around the time of Morshead's murder.

In the end, the rebellion that began with a noble cause denigrated into banditry. The British knew well how to deal with bandits – they had been doing it for ages in most of their colonies. It took them almost two years, but by the end of 1932, the rebellion had been put down and Saya San sent to the gallows. Over a thousand rebels were killed and nearly double that number sentenced to long terms of imprisonment or transportation for life. The rebellion never did reach Maymyo, though. That was another theory in the Morshead mystery that led nowhere.

There was another angle that seems not to have been thoroughly probed. One of the rumours floating about at the time was that Syed Ali, the man to whose house the pony had trotted up to on the day the murder, was in some way involved. Syed Ali was a person of some consequence in Maymyo. The owner of the Maymyo Bank and the Maymyo Electric Supply Company and a Grandmaster of the local Freemasons Lodge, he was a rich and successful businessman. His residence, Manor House, one of the biggest in Maymyo, was just a little distance away across the road from Henry Morshead's home. How was he involved, if at all? Syed Ali was known to Henry, and found mention in his last letter to Evelyn. Syed and Henry had been 'guests of honour' at the anniversary meeting of the United Club the previous Sunday. It would not be far-fetched to assume that they had a conversation, and so it was natural that the police would question Ali. He was, however, an influential man, and they may have had to tread lightly. One cannot tell for sure if the rumours were true and whether Syed Ali was in fact in some way connected to the murder. What is known is that Syed Ali left Maymyo a few months later, leaving his businesses in the hands of his son and a younger brother.

Another curious point that never seems to have been cleared up concerns the pony that Morshead was riding that day. No one apparently thought it necessary to find out who the actual owner of the pony was, and if they did, the fact was either never made public or deliberately ignored. The statement of the commissioner of police, Mandalay Division, said the owner of the pony was Lt Col Morshead. But this may not have been the case. Kenneth Mason, a friend of Morshead and his junior in the service, wrote in an unpublished memoir that the pony was 'identified as being lent to him'. If so, who was the real owner of the pony and why did it take the police the best part of two hours to realize that the person who had been riding the pony had been Henry Morshead? That, and many other questions, would remain unanswered.

Morshead was laid to rest at the Garrison Church in Maymyo. The great and the good of the town were in attendance, a volley was fired and a bugler sounded the Last Post. A box containing some of his personal effects was sent to England, but never reached the family. The King and Queen sent their condolences to Evelyn through his brother Owen. She was assured that the King would try to secure the maximum possible assistance to the widow and her children. In the end, however, Evelyn was granted only the minimum pension of 80 pounds a year, apparently on the grounds that Henry had not been killed on active service. This would have come as a bitter blow to Evelyn, who was now left alone to bring up five children.

In time, the Morshead murder was forgotten, but not by his family who were never convinced by the official explanation or lack of it. In 1981, his son Ian decided to do a little detective work on his own and flew to Burma to try and solve the five-decade-old mystery. At Maymyo, he visited Upperford where two happy childhood years had been spent, and the memories came rushing back. The house still stood, but the driveway was overgrown and all that was left of the tennis court was a solitary metal post. He visited his father's grave, with the headstone broken and fallen, but still legible. The once-famous 'rides' in the Reserve Forest across the road had now become bullock-cart tracks. He met an 86-year-old English resident who had known his father long ago and had newspaper clippings about the murder (the old man was a collector of odd and unusual stories from the newspapers). He recalled the tragedy, but could not offer any answers.

On the last day of his trip, Ian met a 91-year-old Anglo-Burman named John Fenton, whose statement (it was given in writing) shed some light, however unconvincing, on what might have happened. According to Fenton, there was a 'lady' involved, who was related to Henry. This could only be his sister Ruth, though Fenton did not identify her. Fenton had once seen the lady riding with Syed Ali, who lived in Manor House just across the road from Upperford. There had been rumours that Henry was not happy about his sister going riding with the Indian, and Henry may have exchanged harsh words with Syed Ali. This was all conjecture, of course, but that was what Fenton had heard when he came into Maymyo (he was employed by the Bombay Burmah Trading Company at a place a few kilometres away and visited the town only once in three months). On his next visit, Fenton said, Syed Ali had gone away and it was said that he had been deported back to India. That was all that Fenton could recall – or would reveal.

Fenton's words set Ian thinking. Might Syed Ali have been involved? Did Henry forbid him to talk to Ruth? Ali could very well have planned the murder. Henry had probably been set up. He'd met Syed Ali at the United Club a week before the murder. Ali may well have offered Henry his pony for a ride. Henry's letters had revealed that he sometimes rode and took care of his friends' ponies. The ownership of the pony had never been satisfactorily cleared up, but wasn't it possible that the reason the pony went up to Ali's House was because the Manor House was where he was stabled. Coming up from Elephant Ride, it had passed Upperford and gone on to Syed Ali's house, which it recognized. It was all quite possible, Ian thought. A hired assassin had been probably waiting for Henry somewhere in the jungle. He would have been shown the pony earlier and asked to shoot the rider, whoever it was. Did the Gurkha do it on orders from Syed Ali? He may have planted the alibi about the dead junglefowl a day earlier, and waited for Henry to come along on the lonely forest path that Sunday morning. The marks on the Gurkha's cheeks may well have been inflicted by Henry's riding crop as he raised his gun for a second shot. It all looked quite possible now.

The findings of the police investigation had probably been supressed. The police, in any case, would have found it difficult to get any of the locals to testify against so powerful a man as Syed Ali. And then, if Ruth's name had somehow cropped up in the affair, it would be quite understandable if the deputy superintendent of police in charge of the case (an Englishman) wanted her name kept out of the whole affair. It had probably been decided, at the highest levels, to not probe too deep.

This, after all, may well be the truth. If Syed Ali had indeed been suspected on account of his rumoured association with

Ruth, it is not impossible to believe that the English community in Maymyo would have known about it. Though these things did happen occasionally, the idea of an Englishwoman having a close friendship with a native – close enough to go out riding with him – was scandalous. True to form, the British would have closed ranks and made sure the murkier details of the murder never made it past whispered conversations.

Ian was excited but also somewhat disturbed by the suppositions arising from Fenton's statement. Back in England, he confronted his aunt Ruth, but she denied having ever met Syed Ali. But she did say that Henry did not like him at all. Her brother, she said, used to refer to him as 'that awful man'. If Henry had found Syed so repulsive, would he have accepted an offer to try out the latter's pony? For Ian, there was not much else to go on beyond conjecture.

Ian wrote a book about his father's life and death, titled *The Life and Murder of Henry Morshead* that came out in 1982. While he could never be certain, he seems to have concluded that the matter was hushed up to avoid besmirching Ruth's honour.

In 2019, Christian Gilberti, an American writer based in Myanmar, came across the book, now long out of print, and wrote a blog post about the Morshead murder and its possible connection to the Burmese nationalist movement at that time. He also discovered that Syed Ali's name was Abdul Ali Hamid and that he was a very rich and important man. Important enough to have found a mention in *Who's Who in Burma, 1927*.

Hamid was a Pashtun from Peshawar, who had immigrated to Burma in 1909 and started a number of successful businesses. He was also something of a playboy and was fond of riding and shooting, and he lived in one of the largest houses in Maymyo – Manor House.

Gilberti also found that after the publication of his book, Morshead had visited Lahore in Pakistan to deliver a copy to his cousin Mark Tully, the BBC correspondent. There, while dining at the home of two Pashtun brothers he had met in London,

Ian realized that they were in fact the grandsons of Syed Ali. Morshead even met Ali's son, Rahmat, but did not reveal who he was.

Gilberti's blog post generated a response that helped him get in touch with Henry's grandson Tracy. Ian had passed away some years ago and Tracy was in possession of his notes for the book. Tracy was initially reluctant to talk, but later opened up. He revealed that other members of the family had been upset by Ian's book and the unwanted attention it brought them. Some of them felt that Ian should have at least waited till Ruth was dead before publishing the book. Tracy also confirmed that his father had in fact met Syed Ali's descendants in Lahore, but admitted that some elements about the murder did not add up.

He also had his own theory to account for the official reluctance to talk about the murder: in 1930, following the disturbances unleased by Mahatma's Gandhi's Salt March against British rule in India, the British government was trying to get Gandhi to come to London for negotiations that would continue into 1932. Tracy claimed that Hamid's family had connections to Gandhi's right-hand man, the Pashtun leader Bacha Khan, also known as 'Frontier Gandhi'. 'The last thing they (the British) would want is a senior officer being taken out by someone who was on the negotiating side,' said Tracy.

Tracy did not respond to Gilberti's requests to corroborate his argument, but the latter found it convincing. In the early 1930s, following the recommendations of Simon Commission, the British were preparing for the political separation of Burma and India. Given the fraught climate that existed, the high-profile murder of a British civilian in Burma would have bolstered the argument that the country was not politically ready for separation and raised questions about the safety of British officers in the country. Fears that Indian nationalists were fuelling disturbances in Burma might also have stoked the flames of suspicion against Hamid and necessitated a cover-up, Gilberti wrote. To sum it up in Gilberti's words:

> We may never know the truth about what happened that day in Maymyo as all the interested parties are dead. But the murder of Henry Morshead remains interesting to this day for the light it sheds on British colonial policy in India, the long-standing relationship between India and Burma, and the dynamics of ethnic conflict in modern Myanmar.[3]

That at least rings true. And also this: that the murder of Henry Morshead leaves us with more questions than answers.

8

Sultana
The Life and Legend of India's Favourite *Daku*

ON 20 MAY 1922, A GANG OF DACOITS LAID SIEGE TO THE TINY village of Jalpur in the Bijnor district of what was then the United Provinces (now Uttar Pradesh). They were after the local zamindar, Sibba Singh, who had locked himself up in his fortified *haveli*, the door of which the dacoits tried to break down with axes. Anticipating their arrival, Sibba Singh had hired some Gurkha guards who were well armed, and as they fought back, the sound of gunfire reverberated around the village. The Gurkhas managed to hold off the dacoits for a while, but eventually ran out of ammunition and had to flee, along with Sibba, his granddaughter Omwati Devi and her mother Rampiyari. The dacoits, cheated of their quarry, took their rage out on the two-century-old building, which was set on fire. Sibba and his family, who were sheltered by the locals, had had a lucky escape. For, leading the gang that had come after them was none other than Sultana, the most feared dacoit, or *daku*, of his time. Sultana, is it said, had been given a contract to kill the 85-year-old Sibba Singh and his granddaughter by some of his enemies, as he had no other heir.

This is essentially the story given out by Baljeet Singh, Sibba's great grandson, who still stays in Jalpur.[1] While the exact details of this event are difficult to confirm, it is one of many stirring tales that make up the enduring legend of Sultana Daku, famously called 'India's Robinhood' by none other than Jim Corbett, another legend who made his home in the locality that Sultana ruled over during his brief reign of terror in the early 1920s.

But nearly a century after he was finally caught and hanged for his crimes by the British, his fame endures and stories of his exploits are legion. He does indeed have a 'Robinhood' image. According to local legend, he only took from the rich and gave to the poor, he was fond of children,[2] he was chivalrous and always treated women well, and so on. His admirers outnumbered his detractors, even in his heyday. After all, how could anyone not like a swashbuckling bandit who led the police a merry dance every time they took to the field after him? And Sultana did give the police a good run for a while. Indeed, as his depredations increased, the government had to set up a special task force to bring him to book.

To sift legend from fact in the life of Sultana is not easy. Some facts are known though, mostly from the account written by Corbett in his book *My India*, which seems to offer the most authentic record of some of the bandit's famed exploits. Given his knowledge of the terrain that Sultana operated in, the legendary tiger-hunter's services were sought by Freddy Young, the head of the special task force that was put together to bring Sultana to heel.

Sultana was a member of the so-called 'criminal tribe' of Bhantus in the United Provinces. The Bhantus laid claim to Rajput ancestry and members of the tribe were believed to have fought alongside Maharana Pratap in his battles against the Mughal Emperor Akbar in the sixteenth century. Sultana's full name is said to be Sultan Singh, an overtly Rajput name, which also identifies him as a Hindu. However, it is also said that he was a Muslim, probably because some members of the Bhantu tribe were adherents of the Prophet, but this is all in the realm of conjecture. Over time, the Bhantus' fortunes declined along with that of the great Rajput warrior, and by the 1870s they were classified among the most violent bands of robbers in the United Provinces. With the passing of the Criminal Tribes Act, 1871, they were forcibly transported by the government away from their usual haunts and herded into resettlement colonies in an attempt to get them to take up some occupation and lead honest lives, an effort which did not always meet with success. Later, in the 1900s, this reformative work was taken up by the Salvation Army (also known as the *Mukti Fauj*).

Sultana is said to have been born in a small village or hamlet in Moradabad, and spent part of his childhood in one of the resettlement colonies set up by the British for the Bhantus. Later, he was confined along with other members of the tribe in a Salvation Army camp at Najibabad, from where he decamped to chart out the course of his often violent life. He was then in his early twenties, and may have been involved in some petty crimes earlier. The departure from the Salvation Army camp marked a turning point in his life. After that, there was no looking back, for Sultana then embarked on a serious criminal career that included extortion, armed robbery, and sometimes murder that brought down upon him the wrath of the colonial government, and ended with Sultana swinging on the gallows.

The only known photograph of him, said to be taken in Agra after his arrest, shows a thin-limbed, short, dark man who could have easily been mistaken for a labourer – not the swaggering bandit of legend. Surrounded by a group of policemen and dressed in what looks like home-spun prison garb, his legs in fetters, he belies the image of the dreaded *daku* whose name once struck terror into the hearts of every bania and zamindar in the eastern United Provinces.

Sultana's writ ran over several hundred square kilometres of the eastern United Provinces. His base was Najibabad, not far from where he was born, and within easy reach of the little villages and towns in the fertile and prosperous Bareilly–Muradabad–Bijnor belt. His gang, which on occasion numbered a few hundreds, often hid out in the dense jungles of the Terai and Bhabbar belt, where they were safe from the unwanted attentions of the police force. Sometimes they would also hop over to the nearby dominions of the Nawab of Rampur, where the police could not pursue them without seeking permission from the princely state, which lay outside the territory of British India.

Sultana's activities, which increased in frequency and scope from the beginning of the 1920s and continued for the next three years, alarmed the government enough to set up a Special Dacoity Force to bring him in. In charge of this force was Fredrick S. Young, a 30-something IP officer, who had made a name for himself through his efforts to curb the lawless elements that infested the province. The Scotsman was literally a large man, full of restless energy and enthusiasm, weighing over 127 kgs.

Freddie, as he was known to friends, had passed into the IP in 1909 after clearing the Civil Services examination. In 1913, he was posted as the Assistant Superintendent of Police (ASP) at Gorakhpur. Close by the border with Nepal, the district was notorious for dacoity and a known haven for desperadoes of the worst kind. Freddie showed his mettle early on. In June 1913, within months of taking charge, he led a raid on a house close to the border where a couple of notorious Nepalese dacoits were being harboured by a prostitute. After having thrown a cordon around the house, Freddie with an inspector and a couple of constables broke into the house and rushed at the men, both of whom were armed with pistols. Grappling with one of them, Young managed to hold onto him till the rest of the police party arrived. For this achievement, he was awarded the King's Police Medal for gallantry[3] – an honour that very few men in the IP could claim after just four years of service.

Young also added a bar to his King's Police Medal in a spectacular fashion while foiling a dacoity in 1919. Receiving information that an armed gang would be attempting a dacoity in a village, Young and his men arrived just as the gang were breaking into a house. Never one to show fear, Young boldly rushed into the courtyard at the head of the police party. One of the dacoits charged at him with a spear, and Young would have been impaled by the weapon had he not shot down the man in time.

These exploits made his reputation, and as Sultana's depredations increased, Percy Wyndham, the commissioner of Kumaon, wrote to the government requesting Young's services in setting up and leading a special police force to capture the bandit. Young accepted the challenge with alacrity, but had no illusions about the enormity of the challenge he had taken on. He went about the task with his vaunted energy and efficiency. First, and most importantly, he needed a hand-picked force of trusted men. Young was given a free hand in building up his special force and could take his pick of the best men from the police forces in the adjoining districts. This did not go down very well with some of his colleagues, who had no choice but to surrender their best officers who could have otherwise helped them bag the coveted prize that was Sultana Daku.

Young had realized that to achieve any success against Sultana, he would have to set up an intelligence system that would rival that of his adversary. Sultana had an efficient and far-reaching network of spies and informers, and by a mixture of bribes and threats could obtain information about Young's activities at every step. Patwaris, *tehsildars*, forest guards and police constables were all said to be in his pay, and he could also count on sympathy and assistance from ordinary villagers and townsfolk, for most of whom he was a hero. To quote Corbett:

> "Sultana had a warm corner in his heart for all poor people. It was said of him that, throughout this career as a dacoit, he never robbed a *pice* from a poor man, never refused an appeal for charity, and paid twice the price asked for all he purchased from small shopkeepers." This reputation stood Sultana in good stead and was instrumental in helping him evade the police for a very long time.[4]

Young, for all the might of the *sarkar* behind him, could neither grease palms nor employ strong-arm tactics, though undoubtedly his subordinates on the ground could be counted on to judiciously apply a little pressure to ferret out news about Sultana's plans and whereabouts. Also, at a larger and more personal level, it was Indian vs White Man, and on that score Sultana was holding the better card. Young, a perceptive and sensitive policeman by all accounts, would have been well aware of this.

Young's first attempt to capture Sultana was made when the dacoit was apparently hiding in the jungles of Ramnagar. The forest department, which was then felling a portion of the forests in the area, had employed a large number of labourers, and one of the contractors in charge of providing the labour was prevailed upon by Young to invite Sultana to a *nautch*, to be followed by a feast thereafter. Young and his policemen would lie in wait, and once Sultana and his gang had arrived and the night's proceedings were underway, the police would swoop down upon them.

Needless to say, Sultana's *mukhbars* (informers) soon acquainted him of what was in store if he were to accept the contractor's invitation. However, not one to refuse a challenge, Sultana agreed to attend the *nautch*. True to his word, on the appointed evening, as arrangements for a raucous night got underway, the dacoit chief turned up at the camp with his men. The contractor had spared no expense. The prettiest dancing girls from the district and the best orchestra were engaged. The contractor's rich friends from the neighbouring towns and villages were invited, and cartloads of food and drink transported to the camp in the middle of the forest. All was ready for the trap to be sprung.

But Sultana did not wait for that happy event. On arrival, he informed the contractor that he and his men would first like to partake of the feast before they settled down to enjoy the *nautch*. After having a full meal and gorging themselves on the free drinks, Sultana took the contractor aside and quietly informed him that, much as he regretted it, he would not be able to stay for the dance as he and his men had a long way to travel that night. Outwitted, the contractor could not but agree. It did not do to disagree with Sultana. In the event, Young and his troops, who were slowly tramping towards the site and whose signal to surround the camp was to be a drum-beat that announced the beginning of the dance, could not arrive at the appointed time as the forest guard who was to guide them apparently lost his way. When they finally trudged in, tired and weary, all that greeted them were some bewildered and frightened dancing girls and the friends of the contractor who, not being in on the secret, were quite puzzled by the unexpected turn of events. They could not have been too pleased by the unexpected intrusion of a posse of policemen in the middle of a night that had momentarily seemed so full of delightful possibilities.

His lucky escape from Young's clutches in Ramnagar may have unnerved Sultana, for he decided to duck out of sight and shifted his operations for a while to the Punjab. Unlike the dense forested hills of the Kumaon range, which offered him shelter, the Punjab with its rolling plains did not suit Sultana. After a few months, he was on his way back home. The journey back from the Punjab was fraught with risks as the only way back to his old stomping grounds in the United Provinces was across the Ganges Canal, the bridges of which were heavily guarded as the police had received intelligence of Sultana's movements and police pickets had been placed on all the bridges he was likely to cross. Then, by a stroke of luck, one of his guides informed him about a little-known bridge that was not guarded, and the gang set off. On the way, however, Sultana and his party stopped at a large village where a celebration was underway that night. A rich man's son was getting married in the village, he was informed. Gate-crashing the party, Sultana summoned the headman and the bridegroom's father. Having being told by his informants that the headman had recently purchased a gun, Sultana demanded that the weapon be handed over to him along with ₹10,000 in cash. The headman complied, and Sultana and his men walked out into the night. It was only the next morning that he learnt that one of his men, Pehelwan, had abducted the bride. A furious Sultana, who would not tolerate women being molested, ordered Pehelwan to send the girl back to her family. This was promptly done, the girl also being given a present to make up for the trouble she had been put to.

Back on home ground, Sultana continued his raids, but Young did not let up and slowly the pressure began to build up. In due course, with the help of his informers, Young managed to foil many of the dacoit's plans and arrest several members of his gang. Sultana, however, still managed to keep one step ahead of the police by moving frequently from place to place and not settling down for long in any one locality.

Returning back to the forests around Kaladhungi, he decided upon a raid on the village of Lamachour situated in the Haldwani block of Nainital district. The village headman, his spies had informed him, was playing host to a rich dancing girl from the state of Rampur. The girl was reputed to have a lot of jewellery, and this was the object of the raid.

Sultana and his gang surrounded the house, but not before the girl got away through a back-door and vanished into the night with all her jewellery. Sultana was furious when the headman and his tenants, who had also gathered around, could not disclose the whereabouts of the girl. A beating would loosen the headman's tongue, Sultana reasoned, and he ordered his men to tie up and beat the man. Feudal loyalties run deep in rural India, and one of the headman's tenants objected to his master being treated in this manner. As one of Sultana's men advanced towards the headman, this brave soul, a Nepali, rushed at the dacoit with a length of bamboo, and was promptly shot dead by another gang member. Alarmed that the shot would arouse men from the neighbouring villages, Sultana beat a retreat. But he did not depart empty-handed, taking away a horse that the headman had recently purchased.

This raid was to prove unlucky for Sultana. When the law finally caught up with him, it was for the murder by one of his men of the Nepali tenant from Lamachour that he would be later tried and sent to the gallows.

Following the raid on Lamachour, Young renewed his efforts to capture Sultana, and Corbett was also co-opted to help in the hunt. Tracking Sultana in the dense jungles was not an easy task, and Corbett recounts in *My India* the unsuccessful attempts to capture Sultana. Three months after the Lamachour incident, Corbett, Young, and two other English officers led a 300-strong force of policemen in pursuit of the dacoit who was said to be holed up in a camp deep in the jungles. After a lengthy tramp through scrub jungle and high elephant grass, during the course of which their guides lost their way, the police party arrived at a clearing close to Sultana's hideout. But just as Young was marshalling his troops, an excited young constable fired his musket at a couple of dacoits posted as lookouts on a *machan* high up in nearby tree and gave the game away. The police then charged the camp, only to find that Sultana had decamped. All they got for their trouble was some provisions, a few thousand rounds of ammunition, and some guns.

The police gave chase and in the running gunfight that ensued, a dacoit and a police havildar were shot. Corbett mentions that Young offered the havildar, who had been hit in the chest, the contents of his brandy flask, but the policeman, a high-caste Hindu, refused saying he could not go to his maker with 'wine' on his lips. The dacoit, who had been shot in both legs with a 12-bore musket, had no such qualms and greedily gulped down the contents of Young's flasks. The two men were laid on improvised stretchers and, using relays of runners, rushed to the Najibabad hospital some 20 kilometres away, but could not be saved.

Sultana was now on the run, his gang now reduced to around 40 men. They were still well-armed though and seemed to always have a ready supply of ammunition. Despite all the warnings from the police to the licensed gun-holders and gun-dealers in the surrounding district, the dacoit could always find someone to supply him with arms and ammunition, and the guns that were lost to the police during the raid on the camp were soon replaced.

Young then decided to change tack. With the permission of the government, he offered Sultana a chance to surrender. Sultana agreed to a meeting, and the two men finally faced each other in a jungle clearing at an appointed date and time. Sultana, much to Young's surprise and possibly some delight, offered him a watermelon. Young demanded that Sultana surrender unconditionally, but the dacoit said he would only come in if he was assured that he would not be given the death penalty. This was something Young could not promise – and so the contest between the two adversaries would have to go on for some more time. At this meeting, according to Corbett's account, Sultana warned Young against taking unnecessary risks to capture him. On the day his camp was raided, Sultana told Young, he and ten of his men had watched Young and two other white sahibs coming towards their hiding place, and but for the fact that they had turned back, he would have had no choice but to shoot the three of them. Sultana told the police officer that he had not shot him out of respect and for the manner in which Young had conducted the campaign against him.

A few months after the meeting in the forest clearing, Young made yet another attempt to capture Sultana. This time he was accompanied by Corbett and Wyndham, and one of Wyndham's cousins. Their objective was a cattle-station deep in the Najibabad jungles, where Sultana was said be camping. This time a more elaborate ambush was planned. A force of 300 men would embark at night on country boats, sail down the Ganges for about 32 kilometres, and alighting some distance away from the cattle-station would proceed through the jungle and surround it. This attempt, too, did not initially meet with success. After a nightmarish ride in the boats, the men finally alighted on the bank and tried to make their way through a tangle of dense bush and elephant grass, only to realize after a while that they had in fact not landed on the shore but on an island in the Ganges. It took a while and a lot of hard trekking back and forth in the darkness before they found a place where they could ford the river at a spot where the water was not too deep, and managed to get back on dry land.

By this time, the Europeans were struck by an attack of hay-fever, and the men spent the night in the jungle hungry and tired. One of Young's guides and informers turned up the next morning with the news that that Sultana had in fact left the cattle-station with his gang for a raid towards Haridwar, but that they were expected back by nightfall or early the next day. Corbett and Wyndham left the next morning for Haridwar as the latter, also being the Political Agent of Tehri, was due to meet the ruler of the state in a couple of days.

A day later, early in the morning as Wyndham was preparing to leave and Corbett was arranging some food to take to the men back in the jungle, a runner arrived with astounding news. Young had captured Sultana!

The dacoit leader and five of his men had returned to the cattle-station the previous evening. Having surrounded the station with his men, Young boldly crept into a hut that the men were sleeping in, and seeing a figure covered with a sheet on the only charpoy in the hut, promptly sat down on it. The man under the sheet was the dreaded dacoit, but pinned down by the enormous weight that bore down upon him, Sultana could not offer any resistance. Three other men in the hut were also captured, but two of Sultana's lieutenants, the notorious Pehelwan and another dacoit named Babu, broke out of the police cordon and managed to get away despite being fired upon. Thus, on 14 December 1923, after outwitting the police for nearly three years since his escape from the Najibabad Fort, Sultana was finally brought to book. The dacoit is said to have vowed that he would never be taken alive, and had he been able to reach for his gun, there is no doubt that he would have sold his life dearly.

News of Sultana's arrest evoked sympathy in certain quarters, for the poor in the countryside always saw him as a friend. The rich moneylenders and landlords who were his principal targets no doubt celebrated. Sultana and other members of his gang were tried in Agra, and it is said people came from miles around to see the bandit when he was produced in court in chains and fetters.

While in jail, Sultana sent for Young, for whom he apparently had great regard, and asked the police officer to take care of his child and wife who was even then interred in Najibabad Fort. He also asked him to take care of his dog.[5] According to Corbett, Young agreed, and faithfully carried out his promise.[6] The dog was well taken care of by Young, and was later instrumental in helping him apprehend the two men who had escaped from the cattle-station when Sultana was arrested.

Corbett's account says that Young was in Moradabad for the annual Police Week when an orderly arrived with the news that the two fugitives, Pehelwan and Babu, had been spotted at the Moradabad Railway Station. Young rushed to the station and accosted the two men, who pretended to be on their way from Bareilly to the Punjab. Observing that the train in which they were supposed to have gone had already departed, and the next one was not due until the following day, Young invited them to stay with him for a while at his house, intending to question them further. The men surprisingly agreed, and accompanied him to the bungalow where Young was then staying during the Police Week. While Young had his apprehensions about the identity of the two suspects, Sultana's dog immediately recognized them and flung himself on the two men with obvious signs of delight. Seeing that their cover was blown, the men gave themselves up. These two men, among the last to be rounded up, were said to be responsible for most of the murders committed by Sultana's gang. Most of the Sultana gang were now behind bars, and 120 dacoits were convicted on the basis of evidence of their participation in some 200 dacoities in the province.[7]

Sultana was sentenced to death along with some members of his gang, while a few others were given long terms of imprisonment in the Andaman Islands. He was hanged in Bareilly on 8 July 1924.

According to the *London Gazette* of 3 June 1924, Young was awarded the Companion of the Order of the Indian Empire (CIE) in the Kings Birthday Honours in June 1924. Three sub-inspectors and two head constables were awarded the King's Police Medal for operations against Sultana's gang. Head Constable Gauhar Singh who accompanied Young into the jungle during his negotiations with Sultana was one of them. A constable of the Special Dacoity Force, Mohammad Haidar also distinguished himself during attacks on the gang and once, dashing ahead of his comrades, tackled 11 armed Bhantus single-handedly. He shot one of them while the others took shelter in a sugarcane field, all of whom were arrested when the main body of the police came up.[8]

The Special Dacoity Force continued to operate for seven more years after Sultana's capture as it was never possible to entirely eliminate the menace of dacoity from the region. Among other exploits during 1926–27, they captured several notorious gangs of Kanjar dacoits who operated in the Chambal ravines and areas that encompassed the borders of several princely states. Raids were conducted against the Kanjars in Jaipur, Gwalior, Bharatpur and Dholpur, with the cooperation of the police forces of those states who graciously acknowledged the efforts of Young and his force.[9]

For a while, Young also served as inspector general of police in Jaipur State. He was back in the United Provinces in 1939 as deputy inspector general. In 1942, he was deputed to Sind to help in suppressing the Hur rebellion that had broken out in that province. He also played a conspicuous role in quelling the disturbances which went on for nearly two years, and was awarded a CBE for his efforts in 1944. He retired from the Indian Police in 1945, and then went on to serve the princely state of

Bhopal as inspector general of police. While in Bhopal his health deteriorated, and he died there on 21 December 1948.[10]

While Young is now forgotten in India, Sultana's memory lingers. Nearly a century after his death, Sultana's tale evokes more of sympathy and admiration than dread. His life has been the subject of numerous stage shows, plays, books and movies. The Najibabad Fort, now dilapidated but still standing, draws many sightseers and is more famously known as Sultana's Fort (*Sultana daku ka kila*). The legend of Sultana Daku endures.

9

Deceive and Choke
The Cult of the Strangler

It is a cool evening in the month of magh, *sometime in the early 1820s. The scene: a clearing in a mango grove a few kilometres outside one of the many villages on the dusty, lonely road to Indore in central India. A large and motley group of travellers recline on carpets spread on the ground. The party, composed only of men, appears well-to-do, and around them are pitched some well-appointed tents. In the background, in the gathering dusk, several picketed Arab horses can be seen, which must have cost their owners a small fortune. Also in view are a couple of bullock carts – the beasts now unhitched and tied up alongside, gently chewing the cud after a long day's march.*

An observer, even at a passing glance, can see that the congregation is composed of two disparate groups. The five, slightly portly, sleek-faced men lounging on bolsters, and at their ease after a weary day, are Hindu merchants. Their dozen-odd companions are obviously Mohammedans from Upper India. Tall, stout of build and rather fierce of countenance, the latter are not the sort one would want to pick a quarrel with. Some of them could possibly lay claim to the profession of arms, for tucked away in their cummerbunds are daggers and a couple of swords can be seen propped up against a tent pole. They are admittedly a rough but jolly lot. Their leader, a boisterous fellow who goes by the name of Burhanuddin and deferentially referred to as Jemadar Sahib by the other men, claims to be a former cavalryman of the King of

Oudh and is ostensibly on his way to Bhopal to seek service under the Nawab, who is said to be offering good terms for men who can wield sword, spear or matchlock. The Hindus (banias from Shekhawati in Rajputana), who have been on the road for many days and are making for Indore, are glad to be under his protection. It was fortunate that they had come upon the garrulous Jemadar at a serai that afternoon, and agreed to travel together. The merchants are carrying sacks full of spices bought from Afghan traders back home, and also several bolts of fine quality silk, to be sold at Indore. Two of them have also concealed some diamonds about their person, which they intend to sell in the Sarafa Bazaar, but this they have not told their new-found companions. One could not be too careful these days. The roads in these parts, passing as they did through dense forests, were said to be infested with dacoits and one could not let one's guard down. No doubt, the banias were relieved to have such stout and hearty fellows for company, at least for a few days.

In keeping with their caste restrictions, the two groups have cooked and eaten their evening meals separately. It is now time for some lazy conversation, punctuated by a few pulls at the hookah. The banias refuse to try the hubble-bubble, but the good Jemadar has produced a packet of opium from his cummerbund and offers them to his companions. 'Go on. Give it a try,' he urges, with a naughty wink. A couple of the merchants are tempted and take a pinch of the drug. 'You will soon be seeing the houris,*' says the Jemadar, laughing and slapping his thigh. He really is a merry rogue but, it must be admitted, a boon companion.*

What the merchants have not observed, or seem to have paid heed to, is that seated behind each of them is one of the Jemadar's men. The talk, as is most of often the case with men, revolves around trade, the bad state of the country after the collapse of the Mughal Empire, the growing presence and influence of the English in the country, and then women. The Jemadar, with a twinkle in his eye, offers to provide them the name and address of a very beautiful courtesan he is acquainted with in Indore. 'Go and give her my salaams,*' he says, only half in jest. 'She will take good care of you.'*

'No. No.' The men from Shekhawati protest, a little embarrassed. 'We don't do all that.' 'Oh, you must, you must,' insists the leery Jemadar. 'You must enjoy life when you can. Who

knows what the morrow may bring?' There is much laughter and backslapping all around.

Suddenly, and apparently without reason, the Jemadar claps his hands, calling out for tobacco to no one in particular, 'Tambacu lao!'

Scarcely are the words out of his mouth that long handkerchiefs are whipped out by his men and thrown around the throats of the unwary merchants. A pull and a twist, and the unfortunate banias are in their death throes. All it takes is a few minutes, and five corpses now lie on the ground, tongues protruding. Quickly, and with practiced ease, they are stripped of their clothing and buried in hastily dug graves. One of the stranglers finds the hidden diamonds sewn into a cummerbund, and hands it over to the Jemadar. A few heavy stones are rolled over the graves, for they are shallow and could easily be dug up by jackals. The bullocks are quickly put into their traces, the carts loaded and tents struck, and within half an hour the whole party takes to the road – the Jemadar and his principal lieutenants mounted on their Arab steeds, while the others pile onto the carts. It is a bright moonlit night and they will travel a few kilometres before pitching their tents again to rest for the night – away from the scene of the crime.

***

THE ABOVE SCENE IS FICTIONAL, BUT SOMETHING MUCH LIKE this was played out over and over again for at least a couple of hundred years, if not several centuries, through much of the northern and central part of the Indian subcontinent, until the British put an end to it in the late 1840 and 1850s. These crimes were perpetrated by a class of men who were the scourge of travellers in the early years of British India, and whose infamous description made a very evocative contribution to the English lexicon: thug.

William Henry Sleeman, the English officer credited with putting an end to the menace of thugs, saw them as member of a quasi-religious fraternity, a perverted brotherhood that took great pride in what was to them a preordained task. The Thug Buhram, who by his own admission held the dubious record of being responsible for the extermination of 931 souls, told Sleeman without the slightest trace of compunction that he felt no remorse for his deeds. Indeed, he seemed to almost exult at what he had done, likening it to shikar (hunting). '...Do you not enjoy the thrill of the stalk, the pitting of your cunning against that of an animal, and are you not pleased to see it lying dead at your feet?' he asked the incredulous thug-hunter.[1]

This was what it all seemingly meant to this most infamous class of criminals: a pitting of wits against an unsuspecting foe. And that was largely the modus operandi. Bands of thugs would set out in large gangs, befriend travellers on the road, and having gained their confidence, lure them to some secluded spot and throttle them with a piece of cloth, weighed at one end with a coin or some other piece of metal. Thug expeditions set out every year from their villages and made their way down to the great cities, trading centres, and pilgrim towns of the vast subcontinent, and often came back loaded with the booty taken from their unfortunate victims. It was, in a sense, a part-time vocation. They were family men, too; and a few of them were employed in other professions or had some land under the plough. But once the harvest was collected, and they had their hands free, it was time to go strangling again. They were, first and last, deceivers. In India, to thug someone means to swindle, to cheat.

Philip Meadows Taylor, who dragged the thugs from obscurity to a place in the popular imagination with his best-selling *Confessions of a Thug*, was not the first to harbour suspicions about the cult of stranglers, but it was his book, published to critical acclaim in 1839, that put the deceivers squarely under the spotlight. Taylor had harboured suspicions about the existence of thugs early in his career in 1829, when he was in the service of the Nizam of Hyderabad as the superintendent of bazaars at Bolarum, and later as an assistant superintendent of police in the district. He describes the event in his lesser-known but well-written and mostly out-of-print *The Story of My Life*:

> Returning after an absence of a month through my district, I was met by some very startling revelations. The Police, and chiefly my faithful Bulram Sing, had reported some very unusual occurrences. Dead bodies, evidently strangled, and in no instance recognized, were found by the roadside and no clue could be discovered as to the perpetrators of their death. In two places, jackals or hyenas had rooted up newly made graves, in one of which were found four bodies and in another two, much eaten and disfigured.
>
> The whole country was in alarm, and the villagers had constantly patrolled their roads, but as yet in vain. All we could learn was that sometime before, two bodies of men had passed through the district, purporting to be merchants from the north going southward, but that they appeared quiet and respectable, above suspicion. During these inquiries it transpired that numbers of persons of that part of my district were absent every year from their homes at stated periods. These were for the most part Mussulmans, who carried on a trade with Belgaum, Darwar, and Mysore, bringing back wearing apparel, copper and brass vessels, and the like. Who could these be? Day after day I tried to sift the mystery, but could not. I registered their names and enjoined Bulram Sing to have the parties watched on their return home. But as the monsoon opened that year with much violence, I was obliged, most reluctantly, to go back to my bungalow at Sudasheopet.[2]

Taylor soon moved on to other more pressing concerns, but was again reminded of the unsolved murders a few years later. It was June 1833 and Lt Taylor (having taken up military duties) had just arrived back at his base in Hingolee after subduing a rebellious local chieftain. Sleeman's drive against the thugs was now in full swing and Taylor, recalling the events at Bolarum, volunteered his services. Thugs apprehended by Sleeman in Saugor and Jubbulpore, in central India, had confessed to being part of a widespread network that ran beyond British territory and into the Nizam's Dominions. Thugs in the Deccan were denounced and those living in Hingolee, who had been under suspicion all these years, were now arrested. Taylor readily volunteered to collect evidence from the men held in the districts under his charge.

> Day after day, I recorded tales of murder, which, though horribly monotonous, possessed an intense interest; and as fast as new approvers came in, new mysteries were unravelled and new crimes confessed. Names of Thugs all over the Deccan were registered, and I found one list containing the names of nearly all those I had suspected in my old district.[3]

Some of his camp followers and some men from the artillery also deserted at this time. They, too, had been thugs! This was not a comforting revelation, for these men had been in their midst for years. The thought that they had been living in such close proximity to these murderers made 'many in the station, and especially the ladies, very nervous'.[4]

Gathering evidence was not easy either, and Taylor soon wearied of it. 'We had searched for bodies of murdered people wherever we were told to look by the approvers, and invariably found them, sometimes singly, sometimes whole parties, and the details were so sickening, we resolved to open no more graves.'[5]

Taylor was also a little unhappy at not getting credit for unearthing these gangs of murderers. 'The reader will remember my intense anxiety on this subject in 1829, and my conviction that deadly crime existed, and was only awaiting discovery; now it was all cleared, but I was sore that it had not fallen to my lot to win the fame of the affair,' he noted ruefully.[6] Even so, there was some material gain. While on furlough in London, 10 years later, he was delighted to find that *Confessions of a Thug*, as recounted by the fictional thug Amir Ali, had been well received. The first edition had been sold out, and a second was in the works. Taylor's name however does not ring too many bells in India these days, though his house, Taylor Manzil, still stands in the town of Shorapur in Karnataka.

Sleeman, however, secured his place in history as the unrelenting thug-hunter, and even has a village (Sleemanabad in Madhya Pradesh) named after him. But Sleeman cannot be denied the credit he got, for it was he who relentlessly chipped away at the edifice of Thuggee more than anyone else with the tenacity of a bloodhound.

It was not that the existence of these organized bands of killers had not been suspected earlier. The earliest reference to their presence in India is in Ziauddin Barani's history of Feroz Shah, which says that a thousand thugs had been captured in the vicinity of Delhi, but the Sultan would not allow them to be executed and instead expelled them to the region around Lakhnauti (Lucknow). Thugs were also noted during the reign of Akbar when over 500 were rounded up in the Etawah district. Towards the end of Shah Jahan's reign, Monsieur Thévenot, the French traveller, was aware of the thug menace on the road from Delhi to Agra. 'The cunningest robbers in the world are in that country,' he wrote in 1665. 'They use a certain slip (knot) with a running noose, which they can cast with so much sleight about a man's neck, when they are within reach of him, that they never fail, so that they strangle him in a trice.'[7]

The depredations of the thug gangs also extended to the south of the country, where they were generally termed *Phansigars,* from the Hindi word *phansi,* meaning noose. After the fall of Seringapatam in 1799, officials of the EIC recorded the prevalence of stranglers in the company's territories when about a 100 were caught in the vicinity of Bangalore. In 1810, the bodies of 30 victims of thugs were found in wells in the doab between the Ganges and the Jamuna.[8] In 1807, several thugs were apprehended between Chittoor and Arcot, after having returned from an expedition to Travancore. Most of the thugs in south India were settled around the borders of Mysore, in the Balaghat districts ceded to the EIC by the Nizam of Hyderabad in 1800. They were particularly found around

Chittoor, and the magistrate of the district noted in the records of the Zillah Court in 1809, 'those extraordinary associations of persons called *Phansigars* who take extensive journeys under the disguise of travellers for the purpose of committing murders and robberies.' These *Phansigars*, he added, 'received encouragement and protection from petty Polygars and Headmen of villages, who share in their plunder; and fathers brought up their children to murder and rob, which constituted regular profession, by which many families subsisted from generation to generation.'[9] In 1816, Dr R.C. Sherwood, working in the Madras Presidency, wrote what was probably the most detailed report on thugs until then. The *Phansigars* of south India were 'villains as subtle, rapacious and cruel as any who are to be met with in the records of human depravity.' He seemed to have conducted a fairly detailed study of these criminals, for his report also contained a list of slang terms and phrases used by these men.[10]

By the early nineteenth century, the British were well aware of the threat posed by thugs. One of their own, Lt John Mansell of the 23rd Regiment of Bengal Native Infantry, had disappeared while on his way from Agra on an inspection tour to Etawah in October 1812. Mansell was not riding alone – with him were two sepoys and a horse carrying his personal effects and equipment. They were known to have camped near the village of Sindhouse (now Sanduas in UP) on the second day. A couple of days later, when they failed to turn up at Etawah, a troop of cavalry was sent out to look for them, though no foul play was initially suspected. No trace of them was ever found, but the search party did come across what was left of Mansell's regimental badges and buttons in the ashes of a recent fire. Mansell and his men were armed and it was hard to believe that anyone would waylay an English officer. It was now obvious that Mansell and his men had been murdered. A vigorous investigation would have probably unearthed the truth, but this was not done. Instead, a small punitive expedition was launched against some villages in the vicinity, and some of the inhabitants suspected of having a hand in Mansell's disappearance were handed over for trial to the local authorities. And there the matter ended.[11]

Mansell's superiors do not seem to have given the matter much thought. Indeed, some native soldiers had also occasionally disappeared under similar circumstances, but with the natives you could never tell. They may well have deserted. Bandits were also known to attack and kill unwary or unarmed travellers on the roads. Much of the country was still unsettled and with the EIC's wars of conquest still underway, not much could be done to bring these offenders to book.

It finally took an energetic Lord William Bentinck to come to grips with the problem. In 1829, he directed F.C. Smith, agent general in the Narbada Territories, to put an end to the thug menace which, by this time, centred on the territories of Oudh and central India, extending into the Deccan and parts of south India. Smith had several assistants to help him, the most able of whom was Captain William Sleeman who seems to have taken to the task like a man possessed, but it would take many years of untiring effort. A Thagi and Dakaiti Department was set up in 1835 with Sleeman as general superintendent. In 1839, he was designated as the commissioner. By now, 'Thugee Sleeman', as he was soon to be known, was well into what would become his life's work.

Sleeman was good at police work, and he went about it systematically. When a few thugs were captured, he did not employ strong-arm methods. Instead, he talked to them and tried to learn their ways. It helped that he had a facility for languages and could speak Hindi, Urdu and Persian. He did not have to feign interest, for he was deeply interested in finding all he could about this murderous cult – which seemed to have almost become an obsession.

Sleeman's most famous interlocutor was the thug Jemadar Firangea, thought to be the inspiration for Meadows Taylor's fictional Amir Ali. Firangea had been a soldier, a Jemadar, before he turned Thug, and claimed to have seen service under

General David Ochterlony. Interestingly, Firangea's unusual name was given to him by his mother after she went into labour and delivered a boy following an attack by firangis (Europeans), led by the French adventurer General Perron, on his uncle's village where his mother was staying during her confinement. He was a Hindu and came from a family to whom thuggee was a hereditary profession, but by his own account his wife never knew that he was a thug until Sleeman ordered that Firangea's family be brought to Jubbulpore after his arrest.

Carrying the then substantial reward of ₹500 on his head, Firangea was arrested in December 1830 and brought before Sleeman, who was then on tour in the Saugor district accompanied by his wife. In return for his life, Firangea offered to help Sleeman arrest several gangs of thugs who were due to meet at Jaipur in February and proceed on a thuggee expedition to Gujarat and Khandesh. As proof of his good faith, the thug asked the Englishman to take him to the village of Sehoda near Saugor, and pointed out three places where the bodies of three groups of travellers were buried in a mango grove in the very spot where Sleeman's tent had been pitched.

> A Pundit and six attendants murdered in 1818 lay among the ropes of my sleeping tent, a Havildar and four Siphaees murdered in 1824, lay under my horses, and four Brahman carriers of Ganges water, and a woman murdered soon after the Pundit, lay within my sleeping tent. The sward had grown over the whole and not the slightest sign of its ever having been broken was to be seen.[12]

The thanadar and police from the neighbouring villages were summoned and the ground was dug up. The bodies of the Pundit and his companions were soon found in a condition of great decay, much to the consternation of Sleeman's wife who was accompanying him on the tour.

The lady later declared that she had many horrid dreams after this event, for the bodies of the water-carriers had been interred under the very spot in the tent where she had been sleeping. Sleeman was equally horrified and astonished. Many of these crimes had been committed under his very nose when he was in civil charge of the district of Narsingpore from 1823–24. To him it was inconceivable that all these murders could have been committed in his district without his knowledge.

> No ordinary robbery or theft could be committed without my becoming acquainted with it... and if any man had then told me that a gang of assassins by profession resided in the village of Kundelee, not four hundred yards from my court, and that the extensive groves of the village of Mundesar, only stage from me, on the road to Saugor and Bhopal, was one of the greatest Beles, or places of murder in all India; and that large gangs from Hindostan and Duckun used to rendezvous in these groves, remain in them for many days together every year and carry on their dreadful trade... I would have thought him a fool or a madman; and yet nothing could have been more true.[13]

And as Firangea (and subsequently many others) talked, the thuggee story slowly began to unravel. The scale of this murderous enterprise was mind-boggling, and Sleeman and his men could only wonder how it had continued unchecked and almost unknown all these years. The secrets that spilled out beggared belief: annual expeditions with gangs of sometimes as many as 100 men out thugging; the thousands of victims strangled over several hundred years; the arcane rituals and codes of the thug creed; and all of it punctuated by an utter lack of remorse.

Here is Firangea giving an account of one of his many expeditions to Sleeman:

> We were a gang of about 150 Thugs from Hindostan (the northwestern provinces and Oudh) in the month of January 1829, near Chopra on the bank of the Tuptee River – under Khoseeala, alias Rynwo, executed afterwards at Dholia in Khandeish; Bhujjoo, executed at Saugor in 1832; and Perraud Mussulvu, executed at Indore in 1829 – when seven treasure-

bearers came up, on their way from Bombay to Indore. We followed them, with a select party from all the gangs, on to Dhoree; and thence to the Dhobelee Pass, where they spoke with Dusrut Naig, the officer of the police guard stationed at that pass. While they rested here, one of the seven, without our scouts perceiving it, went in advance towards Godurghat, which is about four cose distant. When they had left the guard we continued to follow; and we were questioned by Dusrut Naig; and we told him that we were government servants, on our way home, on furlough. About half-way between this pass and Godurghat, we came up with the treasure-bearers and strangled them; but to our surprise we found only six, instead of seven. Heera and the others were instantly sent off after the other, but they could not find him; and we hastily threw the bodies into a nullah, and made off with the booty.[14]

Kaem Khan, another thug, had this to say about the murders committed by his gang at Dhosa near Jaipur in his testimony to Sleeman:

We were on our way from Madhorajpoor to Gwalior – a gang of about 40 thugs – in the month of March, ten years ago when we fell in with Bunseelal, the son of Bhujunlal, the Cotwal of Sopur... He had with him two Brahmins, one Rajput Sepahee, and a servant of the Jat caste; and he was going to Rewaree to fetch his bride... They came and took up their quarters in the same serai with us, and we pretended to be going the same road... we went on to Ramgur with them, and thence Bhikka Jemadar went on to select a place for the murder, but he came back without finding one that pleased him; and the day after we went on together to Dhosa... In the afternoon Bhikka went on again to select a Bele (burial spot). He chose one in the bed of a nullah a cose and a half distant; and the five stranglers having being appointed we set out with the boy and his party long before daylight the next morning. On reaching the place appointed, they were persuaded to sit down and rest themselves. The boy sat with one of the Brahmins upon a carpet that we had spread for him; and the other three attendants sat down upon the sand at a little distance from them. A *Shumsheea* (thug tasked with grasping the victim's hands) took his seat by the side of each of them; and the *Bhurtotes* (stranglers) stood each behind his intended victim. The signal was given by Rustam Khan and all five were immediately strangled; the boy himself by Bhikka Jemadar, who is still at large, while his hands were held by his brother Chanda. The bodies were buried in the bed of the nullah.[15]

Zulfikar Jemadar made the following deposition before Sleeman about a thuggee expedition that set off from Chooree near Chupara. The 300-strong party was led by Jemadars from several gangs.

We camped two days near this place (Chooree). The second day, while we were sitting down, after performing the concluding ceremonies of the Moharrum, twenty-seven travelers (they were in fact dacoits) came up, on their way from the Deccan to the west, and lodged in the bazaar. Dhurum Khan brought this intelligence to us; and said they had four tattoos (mules) laden with cash, besides much other rich property.

The next day the above travelers set out for Chupara, where they lodged in the bazaar: We followed them, and encamped outside the town. From Chupara, they proceeded to Lucknadown, and we again followed them, and all lodged in the same bazaar. Bodhoo Jemadar, Mussulman, called himself by the name of Kour Khuluck Singh; and went to the shops were the travelers were put up; opened a conversation with them; and won their confidence by saying the road was very dangerous and we had all better travel together till we could pass through the jungles. They agreed to do so. The next day... about 125 thugs followed the travelers; while the remainder of our party proceeded towards Nutwara... where the detached party was directed to rejoin them after effecting the murder.

When the detached party, with the travelers reached the spot where there are two trees (called Chitureea Peer and Kunkeerea Peer) on which people tie pieces of cloths the whole of the travelers were murdered; sixteen of them were strangled, and eleven were cut down with tulwars. Their bodies were thrown a little off the road; and we came on the booty we obtained from them, and reached Nutwara. The whole of the booty amounted to Rs 13,500.[16]

However, some of the gang leaders were soon captured by a local chieftain (Zulfikar refers to him as the Pandit Manager of Jubbulpore) who Bodhoo Jemadar attempted to bribe with an offer of ₹10,000 to release them. The Pundit accepted but as the thugs were unable to arrange the cash, they were thrown into prison in a fort called the Beaharka Havelee in Jubbulpore. The thugs then tried to escape, and seven jumped over the fort wall. Of these, five made their escape but one had his back broken and another was severely injured in his legs. Both men were recaptured and thrown back into prison.

These men, according to their compatriots, deserved their fate – for they had broken one of the principal commandments of thuggee: not to shed blood. This, many a thug would say, brought them bad luck. Apparently, in the old days, the rules of the cult had been strictly enforced, allowing them to flourish unhindered. It was the breaking of the time-honoured rules of thuggee that led to their downfall, they told Sleeman.

Among these was the killing of women and, according to approvers interviewed by Sleeman, it was the principal reason for the eventual decline and extermination of the cult. Hindu thugs, in particularly, would never kill a woman, and a mixed band of Hindu and Muslim thugs is known to have fallen out over strangling a woman they referred to as the 'Kalee Beebee'.

The approver Punna, who was present at the scene, recalled the event for Sleeman:

She was coming from Hyderabad, and was carried in a dooly, and had twelve followers. She had Rs 4,000 worth of property. The Mussulmans insisted upon killing her; the Hindoos opposed. She was killed with all her followers, and the Hindoos, after a desperate quarrel, consented to share in all but her clothes and ornaments.[17]

Firangea, too, attributed his bad luck to having aided in the murder of a woman the thugs referred to as 'the Mughalanee' nearly a decade before he was captured. In 1921, when returning from an expedition to Jodhpur, his gang had come upon a Muslim lady who was on her way to Agra, accompanied by an old woman mounted on a pony, an armed man servant, and six palanquin bearers. He had not wanted to kill her, had indeed tried to avoid travelling with her, but she seemed to have found him attractive and stuck to him despite several attempts to shake her off, and so sealed her doom. The foul deed was committed by another party of thugs who had joined up with them. There was not much he could do under the circumstances, and he did not feel any pity for her. Once a thug, he told Sleeman, it was very difficult to extinguish the urge to kill. And in the end, it was all ordained. 'It was her fate to die by our hands,' he told Sleeman.

However, Firangea was not entirely immune to female charms. On one occasion, while out with a gang of 150 thugs led by his cousin Aman Soobadhar, they came upon a party traveling from Poona to Kanpur that included a woman who was a maid-servant of the Peshwa Baji Rao.

> We intended to kill her and her followers. But we found her very beautiful, and after having her and her party three days within our grasp, and knowing that they had with them, a lakh and half of rupees worth of property in jewels and other things with them, we let her and all her party go; we had talked to her and felt love towards her, for she was very beautiful.[18]

Keeping these instances in mind, one must dwell briefly here on the origins and tenets of this strange brotherhood.

According to Kim Wagner's authoritative work, *Thuggee: Banditry and the British in Early Nineteenth-Century India*, the thugs traced their origins to the goddess Kali's repeated attempts to kill the demon Raktabija with her sword, when a new demon emerged from each drop of his blood that touched the ground, and soon there was a whole brood of them. Edward Thornton, in his *Illustrations of the History and Practices of the Thugs*, also refers to this although he does not mention the deity by name. The story goes that, frustrated in her attempts to kill the demon, the goddess is believed to have wiped off the sweat from her arms and created two men from it, each of whom were given a length of cloth (a *rumal*, or towel) to strangle the demons without shedding their blood. These two men apparently did Kali's bidding, and the goddess is then supposed to have exhorted them to strangle anyone who was not their brethren – and it is from these two men that all the thugs are said to have descended.[19]

An exotic tale that smacks of the mysterious Orient? Possibly. For there is nothing to substantiate this theory except Sleeman's own words, and it may all well be a myth. Modern-day scholars have questioned Sleeman's version about the origins of Thuggee and there is a school of thought that believes he just made the whole thing up and romanticized it for his own ends. For all we know, Firangea may well have cooked up this story and fed it to a gullible Sleeman to justify his crimes. That these murderous gangs existed is not in doubt, but far from indulging in robbery and murder for quasi-religious reasons, the thugs are now seen by some as having practised their unsavoury profession merely out of economic necessity and a lack of alternative employment.

To get back to our story as Sleeman and his ilk saw it, and which is how it is perpetuated in the popular imagination and literature, certain rules were apparently prescribed for the men who followed this calling. They could not, for example, kill women. Neither could they target religious mendicants or certain classes of people such as oil-pressers, goldsmiths, potters, or musicians. They also had to read the omens before setting out on an expedition, and unless these were propitious, ill luck would befall them. The omens were numerous and make for interesting reading. Among the good ones were a lizard chirping, a crow calling from a tree on the left side, and a noise of a partridge on the right. Conversely, a hare or snake crossing the road before them, a crow sitting on a rock or a dead tree and making a noise, the sound of cats fighting in the daytime, an ass braying, an owl screeching or the sound of a single jackal, or the sight of a leper or a maimed person betokened misfortune.

According to what Firangea told Sleeman, the thugs also underwent an arcane initiation ritual where they swore an oath on a consecrated pickaxe, or *kussee*, to vouchsafe the protection of Kali (or Bhowani, as she was also known to them). They would also eat a piece of coarse sugar, called '*the goor of the tuponee*' – the *tuponee* was the feast made to Kali, and the *goor* apparently acted upon the thug like a lifelong drug, providing an insatiable urge to kill.

'The *goor* of the *tuponee* changes our nature,' Firangea told Sleeman. 'It would change the nature of a horse. Let any man once taste of that *goor*, and he will be a Thug though he know all the trades and have all the wealth in the world... My father made me taste that fatal *goor* when I was yet a mere boy; and if I were to live a thousand years I should never be able to follow any other trade.'[20] In our day, it does seem a little incredible that the Englishman swallowed this amazing tale!

For a long time, according to Firangea, the thugs scrupulously followed Kali's injunctions and were protected by the goddess. But, motivated by greed and heedless of the omens, many thugs began to get reckless. They strangled whoever they could find, as long as they could find a few pieces of copper on their victims. This was frowned upon by Bhowani, who then withdrew her protection, and this had led to their discovery and downfall, some of the thugs told Sleeman.

There is another curious explanation as to why the thugs would only strangle their victims and not shed their blood. This was apparently due to a strange quirk of law during Mughal times when a criminal could not be executed unless the blood of the victim had been shed. A strangler or a poisoner was, therefore, technically immune from capital punishment. At most, a convicted thug would be sentenced to a term of imprisonment or subject to fines or other penalties such as expulsion from a particular territory or forfeiture of property. His head, at all events, would not be upon the block.

And so the thugs thrived and carried on with what would become in some families a hereditary profession. The secrets of their nefarious trade were passed on from one generation to another, the son succeeded the father, and so it went on. In time, there were entire villages of thugs where, at a certain time of the year, the men would set out from their homes to inveigle and strangle.

According to the testimonies of convicted thugs, as recounted in Sleeman's *The Thugs or Phansigars of India*, they often moved in large gangs, occasionally comprising as many as a hundred men. These were often military-style expeditions, with gang leaders being given appellations such as Jemadar or Subedar. Often, several bands from different parts of the country teamed up to go thugging. Over the centuries, they are thought to have murdered a million men, but this is mere conjecture.

Sleeman and his aides kept plugging away. Much of it was routine, if painstaking, police work. A network of informers was developed, thug family trees were compiled, old graves were dug up, and corpses exhumed for evidence that would stand up in the courtroom. Sleeman also managed to compile a dictionary of the Thug language, known as *Ramaseeana*.

The investigations also revealed the existence of a class of men who came to be known as 'river thugs'. These criminals, who were known as *bungoos* or *pungoos*, mostly operated in the riverine areas of Bengal and Bihar, strangling people travelling by boats on the Ganges and throwing their bodies overboard. It was often very difficult to convict these men in the absence of any bodies, and the men took great care to never have any of their victim's possessions that could connect them with their crimes as their boats were frequently boarded and inspected by customs house officers. According to Sleeman, the river thugs resided mainly in the district of Burdwan on the banks of the Hooghly and comprised both 'Mahommuduns and Hindoos of all castes, and they go up the river Ganges as far as Benares, and sometimes even as far as Cawnpore; and they carry on their depredations as well going down as coming up the river.'[21]

The coastal districts of Bengal had always been viewed by the British as prone to crime, with one of the district magistrates of Bakarganj (now in Bangladesh) going as far as to say that the 'whole of the inhabitants of this district are dacoits'.[22]

The river thugs also left their mark in a minor footnote of colonial literature, being featured in Edmund Candler's 'Mecca', a short story about a gang of river thugs preying on travellers setting out on the Haj. The villains in this case ended up hanging for the murder of four men they killed and threw overboard in the waters of the Sunderbans.[23]

When apprehended, thugs were induced to turn approver and betray their comrades. It wasn't easy to convict them, however. Memories had dulled over the space of many years, and often the crimes were decades old and committed miles away from the home of the supposed offender who could not be conclusively identified. An old problem, the bane of the police in India to this day, also reared its head – the witnesses, largely illiterate simple village folk, were suspicious of courts and lawyers, and would not give evidence before a magistrate for fear of being harassed. Another difficulty encountered in bringing the thugs to book was the connivance of local petty chieftains, zamindars and local officials who shared in the thugs' booty and offered them protection.

Captain Vallance found that the thugs operating in the area between Midnapore and Nagpur had for years been protected by a local rajah on the western border of the Puri district. But the rajah was extortionate and so the thugs had moved out of his territory and found shelter in some villages under the protection of the local *serbarakar* or revenue officer, who was well paid for his services. The officer was eventually arrested and brought to trial for colluding with the thugs.[24]

A magistrate in Etawah was told by a zamindar that thugs, who were formerly from Sindhouse but had now settled in the Gwalior territories, were paying protection money to officials from the state, at the rate of twenty-five rupees for each house occupied by thug families. An approver from the state admitted in his deposition that his father, who was a local official, would receive a rupee from every thug house when they returned from an expedition.[25]

Convicting suspected thugs for murders committed in territories ruled over by the numerous princely states also presented a legal conundrum – as these crimes had occurred in places that did not fall within the EIC's possessions, they could not be tried in the Company's courts. But Sleeman's boss F.C. Smith found an easy way out, invoking 'paramount authority' and gave Sleeman the authority to proceed.[26]

It was also very difficult to apply British standard of evidence in the Indian law courts, where every official except the British magistrate was likely to have been bribed or threatened, and witnesses coerced into withdrawing statements or testifying against known thugs who operated from their villages. So, while many thugs were apprehended and convicted, mostly on the often doubtful testimony of approvers, a great many did not pay for their crimes.[27]

However, among those who did were some very stout-hearted and stoical souls who did not quake when led to the gallows. Dr Henry Spry, who was Sleeman's cousin and medical officer in charge of the Saugor Jail in 1830, recorded the conduct of these men, who when faced with death seemed more concerned about being defiled by the touch of the hangman.

> When morning came, numerous hackeries drew up at the gaol door, taking five men in each. They looked dreadfully haggard. As one cart was laden after the other, it was driven away

surrounded by sepoys with fixed bayonets and loaded muskets. The place appointed for the execution was on the north side of the town of Saugor, about a mile and a half from the gaol. 'Ruksat, Doctor Sahib', 'Salaam, Doctor Sahib' – meaning 'Adieu, Doctor Sahib' or 'Compliments to Doctor Sahib' – were the salutations which I received as I rode by the wretched tumbrils which were jolting them to their execution. The gibbets were temporary erections, forming three sides of a square. The upright posts which supported the cross-beams were firmly fixed in stone masonry five feet in height. From each side of these walls footboards were placed, on which the unhappy criminals were to land on reaching the top of the ladder. The cross-beams were each provided with ten running halters equidistant from one another. As each hackery load of malefactors arrived, it was taken to the foot of the respective ladders, and as one by one got out he mounted to the platform or footboard. Their irons were not removed. All this time the air was pierced with the hoarse and hollow shoutings of these wretched men. Each man as he reached the top of the ladder, stepped out on the platform and walked at once to the halter. Without loss of time he tried its strength by weighing his whole body on it. Everyone having by this means proved the strength of his rope with his own hands – for none of them were handcuffed – introduced his head into the noose, drew the knot firmly home immediately behind the right ear, amid terrific cheers, jumped off the board and launched himself into eternity! Thus in the moment of death we see a scrupulous attention to the preservation of caste. To wait to be hung by the hands of a *chamar* (skin curer) was thought too revolting for the endurance. The name would be disgraced for ever and, therefore, rather than admit to this degradation every man hanged himself.[28]

Sleeman himself commented in a letter to the editor of the *Calcutta Gazette* on the equanimity and bravado displayed by some men from Firangea's gang, who were among the first group of thugs to be executed in Jubbulpore in September 1830 for the murder of 35 people on the road between Bhopal and Saugor.

As the sun rose, the eleven men were brought out from the jail decorated with chaplets of flowers and marched up to the front of the drop, where they arranged themselves in a line, each seeming to select the noose or situation that pleased him best, with infinitely more self-possession than men generally select their position in a dance or at a dinner table. When arranged, they lifted up their hands and shouted '*Bindachul Ke Jae, Bhowanee Ke Jae,*' everyone making use of precisely the same invocation, though four were Mohammedans... They took their position on the platform... and taking the noose in both hands, made the same invocation to Bhowanee, after which they placed them over their heads and adjusted them to their necks with the same ease and self-possession that they had first selected them; and some of the younger ones were actually laughing during the operation... Being directed to have their hands tied to their sides that they may not in their agonies seize the rope, and thereby prolonging their sufferings, one of the youngest, a Mohammedan, impatient of the delay, stooped down so as to tighten the rope, either to prevent it breaking with a jerk, or with a view to prevent pain from it, stepped deliberately one leg after the other over the platform and hung himself, precisely as one would step over a rock to take a swim in the sea.[29]

All said and done, the Thagi and Dakaiti Department did achieve a good deal of success. In a ten-year period up to 1835, over 1,500 thugs had been tried, 382 were sentenced to death and 909 to transportation, while 77 received life sentences and 71 others were given various terms of imprisonment.[30]

A majority of thugs who drew sentences of transportation were hustled off to the insalubrious convict settlement of Penang, and later in the 1870s, when it was shut down, to the new penal colony in the even more dreaded Andaman Islands. British officialdom, Sleeman included, seems to have been convinced that being shipped across the 'black water' would serve as a severe deterrent to these men, particularly the Hindu convicts, who risked losing caste if they crossed open water. An unpleasant feature of their incarceration was the tattooing of convicted thugs, apparently to identify them from other inmates in the prisons where they were lodged. A British officer who came across a gang of 97 thugs, shackled in irons and waiting transportation on the Bombay waterfront, noted that all the men had been tattooed on their foreheads with both their names and their offence.[31]

There was some attempt at reform, however. In 1838, a School of Industry was set up in Jubbulpore to teach the approvers and their sons honest trades such as basket-weaving and carpet-making. The hands that choked the life out of so many were apparently quite suited to making high-quality carpets, and an example of their work was even displayed in England at the Great Exhibition of 1851. Another product of the school, an 80 x 40 feet carpet weighing over two tons, was especially woven for Queen Victoria, and is even now displayed at Windsor Castle.[32]

The thugs were also occasionally trotted out for the benefit of western tourists, who were thrilled to see these old rogues stage a strangling act in front of an appreciative audience. Emily and Fanny Eden, sisters of the then Governor-General Lord Auckland, witnessed such a demonstration in Cawnpore in 1837. It nearly went all wrong, Fanny recorded, for as the thugs warmed up to their act, they 'nearly strangled a sepoy in good earnest'.[33]

There was a positive take-away too, for the benefit of future generations of gawkers. One of the most enduring images of the thugs is that by the Venetian photographer Felix Beato who captured images of these retired stranglers re-enacting their crimes for the benefit of the camera, thus ensuring their posterity.[34]

By the end of the 1840s, Sleeman could claim that except for some areas of East Bengal and in the neighbourhood of Midnapore and Nagpur and in Oudh, 'the roads are now from one end of India to the other free from the depredations of the thug gangs'.[35] He did, however, warn the government of the need for ceaseless vigilance to ensure that thuggee never reared its head again. By 1879, the thug menace was thought to be entirely eradicated with only 340 names remaining on the department's register of thugs. Soon, it would be dealing with the other equally dreaded menace of dacoits and poisoners.[36] Sleeman moved on from the Thagi and Dakaiti Department to serve as the Resident at Gwalior from 1843 to 1849, and then at Lucknow from 1849 to 1856, during which he survived three separate attempts on his life. One of these was by a fugitive thug who hid behind a curtain in Sleeman's study, dagger in hand, but meekly gave himself up when confronted by the veteran thug hunter, who seemed to have been warned of danger by a sixth sense, according to his daughter who witnessed this incident.[37]

Sleeman had other interests too, like phrenology, believing as he did that the measurement of skulls could provide hints of possible criminal tendencies in certain ethnic groups. He was also a dinosaur and fossil hunter, and is credited with having unearthed several petrified trees and dinosaur fossil formations near Jabalpur. While he wrote three books on thuggee, his *Rambles and Recollections of an Indian Official*, published in 1893, still remains his most popular work. Sleeman died in 1856 and was buried at sea while on his way home to England to recover his health.

Meadows Taylor, the other Englishman most popularly associated with thuggee, had a troubled life. He lost his wife and two children very early in his career, which was spent entirely in the service of the Nizam of Hyderabad. Though never in the service of the British government, he was honoured with the Order of the Star of India on his retirement from service in 1860 and given a pension. In 1875, his eyesight failing and having contracted jungle fever, he decided to go back to England but died on the way home at Menton in France in May 1876. During his lifetime, he published several books on Indian subjects such as *Tippoo Sultaun – A Tale of the Mysore War*, *Tara – A Mahratta Tale*, *Seeta*, and *A Noble Queen: A Romance of Indian History*, the last published posthumously in 1878.

Ever since the publication of Meadows Taylor's *Confessions*, the thugs have had their place in the popular imagination. Books such as John Masters' *The Deceivers* have only added to their aura, and both Hollywood and Bollywood have not stinted in showcasing their exploits on screen.

The Thug was a uniquely Indian phenomenon, and the image of the strangler with a scarf has lasted for nearly two centuries. However, with some historians and academics beginning to see them in a different light, thuggee is now considered as simply a social problem that was a product of the turbulent times in which it flourished. It has also been argued that thuggee, as seen through Western eyes, was but a figment of the colonial imagination. The truth probably lies somewhere in between. The appellation once applied to the super-stranglers of colonial India is now also employed to describe street hoodlums.

Firangea would surely be turning in his grave.

10

A Never-Ending Headache
Dacoity in the Raj

IF THERE WAS ONE CRIME THAT THE BRITISH COULD NEVER wipe out during their time in India, it was dacoity. The much vaunted Thagi and Dakaiti Department did its best, but it was not enough. From the 1830s, when they officially decided to do something about it, to when they left the subcontinent in 1947, the British could only claim to have achieved limited success in curbing the dacoit menace. There was no real *pax* when *Britannia* departed India. The Indian government, too, struggled with this legacy in the first three decades after gaining independence when a few dacoit gangs still operated with a great deal of impunity in parts of their previous strongholds – the United Provinces (present-day Uttar Pradesh) and the Central Provinces (present-day Madhya Pradesh).

The image of the often cruel, muscular, and moustachioed gun-toting dacoit that has come down to us from novels and the silver-screen is somewhat grounded in fact. Many of these men, as the records bear out, were ruthless desperadoes driven to their calling – sometimes by poverty, often by greed, and occasionally, by revenge. That they were not wanting in courage, albeit of a desperate kind, could not be denied. And so some of their deeds have also acquired the merit of being acts of derring-do, and a few like the famous Sultana (mentioned previously in the book) are still not entirely forgotten. It is a rare human being who does not admire someone who repeatedly cocks a snook at the law.

Eustace Kitts in his *Serious Crime in an Indian Province*, published in 1889, has left us this description of a typical dacoit in what was then known as the North-Western Provinces (NWP) and Oudh.

> These men are all more or less desperate characters, but the success of the gang depends greatly on the merit of its leader. A good dacoit is of no mean order. There is raw fighting material wasted in him, besides considerable skill in organization and attack. He is ruthless and cruel, but he cuts down only those who resist, and tortures only for the betrayal of treasure. Bunnias in a wedding party give him no trouble: they invariably submit, whatever their numbers. They save their skins by arrant cowardice, and stand bleating like sheep with their heads in a circle, while their women are rifled and their carts are pillaged. The dacoit leader will hold his blazing torch to a woman's breast to force her to disclose the treasure hoard; but his object is merely plunder and not wanton or purposeless cruelty. He must be ever on the alert against treachery; and in every expedition he carries his life in his hands.[1]

Dacoity was indeed a fraught occupation. Giving no quarter, the dacoit could rightly expect none, when cornered. But he could fight, and often sold his life dearly, as Kitts tells us:

> Jampa, the Agra desperado, who had broken jail, and Budhu, his comrade were shot in 1887, in the course of a hand-to-hand fight with Lt Ryves, the District Superintendent of Police and his Sub-Inspector Ahmed Hussain; Hulasi Sing, who escaped from the Fategarh Jail, and with him another dacoit leader, Budulla, were shot in 1878; Mangla and Khurgaya, leaders of two bands in the Hamirpur District, were shot on the same day in 1879. Three dacoits were killed by the Agra police in a hand to hand fight in 1881, and the Rana of Dholpur killed four in 1884.[2]

The law did not have an easy time bringing them to book, for the crime was endemic throughout much of the country. It did, however, see dacoits as a separate class of criminals, with the Indian Penal Code defining 'dacoity' as robbery committed by five or more persons. It also stipulates that when any number of persons agree together to commit a dacoity or theft or any of a number of other offences, and any overt act is done in pursuance of this common purpose, they shall all be punishable for thus conspiring to commit the offence.

And there were a great number of such offences, many of them committed by roving bands of men belonging to certain classes and castes, that the police termed 'criminal tribes' attributing to them an innate propensity to commit unlawful acts.[3] These men led a roving, itinerant life, and while not all of them used violence, it was not unknown for large bands of these vagrants to indulge in armed robberies. In 1881, of the 67 arrests made in cases relating to dacoity in the NWP, 34 of the men came from one or other of the so-called criminal tribes. In 1886, of the 39 cases tried, these men were offenders in 22 cases.[4] Moreover, one half of the minor land dacoities and large robberies committed in the NWP in 1881 were attributed to members of vagrant criminal tribes.[5]

Among the most notorious, according to Kitts, were the Sanseas and Kanjars. A gang of 15 Sanseas waylaid a 30-strong bridal party in Bulandshahr in 1878, and made away with the bride's jewellery, apparently meeting no resistance. The next year, another band committed five dacoities in three nights in the vicinity of Shahjanpur. Two years later, another gang was involved in 16 dacoities in Moradabad and Bijnor.[6]

Their activities also extended to the south of the country, into the Nizam's dominions. In 1837, a band of Sanseas attacked a sahukar's shop at the cantonment in Bolarum, some distance away from Hyderabad. A scout was first sent ahead to reconnoitre, and the venture being deemed worthwhile, a gang of 24 men under Rungeela Jemadar set out a little after dusk. A dacoit who participated in the raid (the scout) narrated what happened next to a police officer after being arrested 10 years later:

> ... [A]bout half-past seven or nearly 8 o'clock, we proceeded in straggling order towards the shop about to be attacked, and which we reached without being challenged by anyone. The sentry posted near the shop did not appear to suspect or notice us; and the moment our mussal (torch) was lighted, he was speared by Baraham Shah and Kistniah, while others commenced breaking in the doors of the inner room, the outer partition of the shop having been found open. Three bankers, who we found writing their accounts in the outer shop, rushed into the house and disappeared. The axe of the shop yield to one blow from the axe of Rungelah, and, on throwing down the planks of which it was formed, we found the box which I had seen on a former occasion, unlocked and open. Of this we took 16 bags full of money, leaving four which we were obliged to relinquish, as we were pressed for time, and had not sufficient men at hand to remove them.[7]

The whole place now being in an uproar, the dacoits quickly drew off, chased by a crowd of people and a few soldiers from the cantonments. However, the pursuers gave up after a while as the gang struck off across some rice fields and made their escape. A little distance from Bolarum, a couple of their bags broke and the money fell to the ground. Nearly ₹1,500 were thus lost, but the gang got away unmolested with ₹14,500 and some silver horse-furniture worth about ₹1,500.[8]

The Kanjars, says Kitts, specialized in attacking camel carts; on one occasion plundering seven of them on the Mathura road in 1879. Their depredations continued until escorts were provided for the carts. In 1879, they were also charged with attacking a party of Bengali ladies who were visiting the holy shrines at Mathura. These men frequented the Agra district but would sometimes commit raids in other districts as well.[9]

Among the most notorious of the tribes that took to dacoity were the Budhuks, who resided mainly in the Sitapur and Kheri districts, close to the Nepal border. They could be counted upon to put up a good fight when opposed, and Shuja-ud-Daula, the Nawab of Oudh, had once attempted to reform them by making soldiers out of them. Some 1,200 of them were enrolled into a corps, but the exercise was not a success. Their criminal propensities, which they could not shake off, and their continued depredations soon earned them the epithet 'the Wolf Regiment'. They were also not amenable to discipline and always inclined to mutinous acts, and were soon disbanded.

The Budhuks living in the eastern part of the Terai were originally agriculturists but took to dacoity during the time of Shuja-ud-daulah. They lived in small colonies and were protected by the local zamindars to whom they gave 25 per cent of their booty from their thieving expeditions. In 1826–27, Fredrick Currie, the magistrate of Gorukhpore had set up a corps of Irregular Cavalry to hunt them down but only succeeded in driving them out to Rohilcund, the doab, Rajputana and Gwalior.

While a change of scene did halt them in their tracks for a while, they could not be put down for any appreciable length of time. Between 1818 and 1834, the Budhuks of the Oudh Terai region were known to have committed 118 dacoities, in which 172 men were killed, 682 wounded, and property worth nearly ₹11.5 lakh looted. And although 457 dacoits were arrested during this period, only 186 could be convicted, and the actual number of the dacoities carried out by them were known to be far higher than that stated in the records.[10]

Some of their stirring deeds are worth recounting:

In 1818, a gang of Budhuks set off to intercept a party of treasure bearers from Benares that was escorted by 60 armed policemen. Disguised as bird catchers, the Budhuks got on their trail, and aided by information from their scouts who had been sent on ahead, learnt that the treasure would be lodged at the *Chobee Ka Serai* between Allahabad and Kanpur on a certain night. Arriving at the serai after dark, the dacoits scaled the walls of the serai and boldly attacked the police escort and made off with the treasure. This daring enterprise, which left eight policemen dead and 17 wounded, netted them ₹76,000 in cash.[11]

In another daring attack in 1822, a gang of some 40 Budhuk dacoits armed with swords, matchlocks and spears, ambushed a party of treasure bearers going from the native collector's treasury at Badruana to Gorukhpore. The attack was launched on a deserted jungle path at dawn. The naik leading the escort was killed along with two of the sepoys. The dacoits made off with ₹12,000, and despite being chased could not be brought to book.[12]

Among the most famous Budhuk dacoits was Bukshee, who was known to be involved in several daring attacks. In November 1830, Bukshee and his gang set off from Oudh disguised as Ganges water carriers, on the trail of a party of treasure bearers going from Mirzapur to Farrukhabad, and crossing the Ganges in boats, they ambushed the party at around midnight, wounding six or seven men of the escort. Breaking open the treasure boxes, they made off with 25 bags – each containing ₹1,000.

The next year, Bukshee and his gang, again in the guise of Ganges water carriers attacked a merchant shop in Mirzapur. It was late in the evening and the gang, carrying flaming torches, burst into the shop, terrifying the people inside and slashing and stabbing whoever stood in their path, and said to have decamped with ₹40,000 or ₹50,000. Safely back in their homes, the money was divided between all those who took part in the raid – Bukshee receiving one-fifth of the loot, apart from his proper share, as had been agreed upon between the bandits beforehand, because he needed the extra cash to bail out his parents who were being held in Lucknow jail for the last 12 years. In the event, he never could get his parents out, as the money was claimed by his wives of whom he had several![13]

'Thuggee Sleeman' had also tried to bring them to book, but wasn't very successful. Hutton sums up their notoriety by quoting the following proverb in his book: 'Once a Budhuk, always a Budhuk, and all Budhuks are dacoits.'[14]

Another tribe which resorted to dacoity were the Haburas, who frequented the Aligarh district. While their women and children lived in small huts made of leaves and grass, the men went to do their 'business' in the Bulandshahr and Budaon districts. On 3 February 1877, a gang of Haburas plundered three grain-laden boats that had been tied up for the night at the Gangaoli Canal Bridge. Pelting the boats with a shower of stones, they rushed upon the boatmen, using their lathis freely, and walked off with all the grain, while also depriving their victims of their cooking pots, clothes and cash. The next year they attacked and robbed a group of pilgrims on their way to bathe at Ramghat.[15]

Other tribes that indulged in dacoities, according to Kitts, were Aheriyas, Baheliyas, Beriyas, and Badhaks. In January 1879, a band of Aheriyas, who were traditionally fowlers by profession, robbed some carts returning from the bazaar at Hathras, and followed this up the next month with an attack on an octroi post. In November 1884, they made a brazen raid on the house of a Borah merchant in the Aligarh district. The merchant was beaten up and his womenfolk stripped of ornaments. An alarm was raised and the police who followed the Aheriyas to their huts were also attacked.[16]

The dacoits, according to Hutton, did not possess the sense of 'honour' (warped, as it may seem to us) that was supposed to exist among thieves in such a high degree as the thugs. Anyone with anything worth looting was fair game, and they were seemingly not too bothered by their conscience or scruples. For the most part, dacoity was a means to an end. Money, or loot, was the primary motive. Some of them even gloried in their calling, referring to it as a *'padshahi kam'* (imperial business).

A Budhuk dacoit, when asked if he would mend his ways if released after a decade behind bars, replied with a laugh:

> No, no; that would never do. Why should I become an honest man – work all day in the sun, rain and all weathers, and earn – what? Some five or six pice a day! We dacoits lead very

> comfortable and agreeable lives. When from home, which is generally during the cold season, we march some 14 or 16 miles a day for perhaps a couple of months, or four, at the outside – commit a dacoity and bring home money sufficient to keep us comfortable for a year, or perhaps two. When at home we amuse ourselves by shooting, or visiting our friends, or in any way most agreeable – eat when we please, sleep when we please. Can what you call an honest man do that?[17]

Often, when caught, it was not hard for a dacoit to bribe his way out. In Oudh, before its annexation by the British, dacoits were sent to Lucknow for trial and imprisonment, and greasing the right palms at the Nawab's court to obtain a remission was not unknown.

Sleeman's diary of his Oudh tour in 1849–50 records that in the village of Palee, near Shahabad, resided 'Bulbhuder Sing, a notorious robber, who was lately sent as a felon to Lucknow. After six months' confinement he bribed his way out, got possession of his estate… and has been ever since diligently employed in converting it into a den of robbers.'[18]

But the dacoit could also expect rough and summary justice when apprehended. During the course of his tour, Sleeman saw a man hung up by his heels on a mango tree by the roadside. The man, he was told, was one of a notorious gang of dacoits, and had been caught and strung up after an attack on a nearby brahmin village.[19]

While most dacoities took place on terra firma, the rivers and inland waterways were not immune to attacks by these gangs. A major river dacoity occurred in January 1878 in the Faizabad district where a gang of 15 men attacked a boat coming from Chapra which was loaded with grain. A couple of months later, villagers in the Farrukhabad district cast off a grain-laden boat from its moorings, took it across to the opposite bank, and looted it. The next year, a brahmin who was transporting some grain down the Kairali river in two dugouts was attacked by 10 men while he slept.[20]

The riverine and coastal areas of Bengal seemed to have been especially prone to lawlessness and dacoity, with Henry Beveridge, the district magistrate of Bakargunj (now in Bangladesh), lamenting that the 'general moral character of the inhabitants is at the lowest pitch of infamy'. His five years in the district had driven him to the conclusion that 'there is no species of fraud or villainy the higher classes will not be guilty of, and to these crimes in the lower classes may be added murder, robbery, theft, wounding & c., on the slightest occasion'.[21]

It was not to be wondered then that the terrible Bengal Cyclone of 31 October 1876, which devastated large parts of the coastal districts of Bakargunj, Noakhali, and Chittagong, was followed by an increase in cases of dacoity and looting. Many criminals had been released or managed to escape from jail on the night of the storm and these men quickly set about grabbing what they could. The inadequate response of the British administration that left many people destitute also pushed numerous otherwise honest citizens into committing robberies. For many, it was often simply a question of filling one's belly as much of the standing crop was destroyed and the warehouses and granaries inundated. Reginald Porch, the collector of Noakhali, was warned by an alarmed government to take the most stringent measures to suppress dacoity. A report on the criminal administration in Bengal for 1877–78 noted that Bakargunj topped the districts in the province for cases of murder, riots, and dacoities. When called to account for this rampant lawlessness, the divisional commissioner of Dacca, Frederick Peacock, attributed the high number of dacoities to a rise in the price of food since the cyclone. Not satisfied with this reply, lieutenant governor of Bengal Ashley Eden, sought an explanation from the deputy inspector general of police who, in keeping with time-honoured bureaucratese, replied that he found no real increase in criminal activity in the district and that the number of dacoities had shown an increase purely due to a change in the way that these incidents were categorized![22]

The Thagi and Dakaiti Department, in its heyday in the 1840 and 1850s, did try very hard to bring these criminal elements to book, with no real results. The methods that were employed to curb thuggee met with limited success when applied to the problem of dacoity. This was one menace that could not be completely wiped out in the subcontinent.

In 1863, with the provincial police now in charge of investigating almost all manners of crime, the department was not left with much work and became a kind of central intelligence gathering agency for the government of India. The main work of the department was now in the princely states, and faced with the question of jurisdiction there was not much the police could do. Dacoits committing offences in the territory of British India had only to hop over to a neighbouring princely state to have the police stop chasing them. It was then left to the Resident or the Agent to the governor-general in that state to take things forward to apprehend and prosecute criminals. While this was not a major problem with the big states, obtaining the cooperation of minor princes and petty chieftains (who were often hand in glove with these criminals) was often very difficult.[23] A lot of things could go wrong between the time a dacoit was caught and finally made to stand trial. The old problem of bullying and buying off witnesses could never be entirely done away with.

Thus, in March 1867, we find Charles Hervey – who had been Sleeman's assistant in the old days, and later general superintendent of the department – cautioning his assistant in Indore, with regard to the case of two men who had been arrested for an opium dacoity. Aware of the likelihood of bribes being offered and evidence tampered with, Hervey wrote, 'Pray therefore examine every witness yourself personally. Keep every document concerned with the case in your own box, under lock and key.'[24]

By the late 1870s, the Thagi and Dakaiti Department's role had increasingly become that of a centralized intelligence agency. In 1877, the department was reconstructed and the general superintendent was tasked with collecting secret and political intelligence. Minor changes were effected in its structure and function in 1893 and 1896, but by 1904 it had more or less come to an end, with the responsibility of dealing with violent crime like dacoities and gang robberies now solely resting with the local police departments.

Dacoity refused to die down however, particularly in the United Provinces, and the Special Dacoity Force was set up in 1922, mainly to bring in the gang of Bhantu dacoits led by Sultana.

The force, which was composed of men of the police forces of the United Provinces and the princely state of Gwalior, had some hard fights to their credit. In April 1930, after a chase of some 56 kilometres, they overtook the notorious Doongar Sahai gang that had committed a dacoity in the Gwalior state. There were only five men in the advance party when they made contact with the dacoits, who promptly opened fire. The police fought back but could not prevent the dacoits from escaping into the nearby ravines. The same gang had been encountered just over six months earlier in the Nandpura ravines of Gwalior, but had given the police the slip. In May 1930, the Doongar gang was intercepted yet again in the ravines just a few kilometres from their headquarters. The police, though outnumbered by the dacoits of whom there were nearly 30, went into the attack. Constable Sharafuddin of the United Provinces Police was shot dead by a dacoit, thought to be Doongar himself, as the small police party fought back. Reinforcements were called in, but despite being hotly pursued, the gang managed to get away, though Doongar had to leave behind his pony and four camels laden with loot.

In another of their many daring exploits, four constables of the Special Dacoity Force engaged a gang led by the notorious dacoit Shama in a night-time shoot-out. The police seized the sentries that the dacoits had placed around their position, but the rest of the gang rallied to the attack, and the small police party was pinned down. One of the constables was killed, but the beleaguered policemen kept up a steady fire, until daylight revealed that the dacoits had melted away. Left behind were the dead bodies of Shama and his lieutenant Balwanta, five weapons, 300 rounds of ammunition, and seven ponies.[25]

Another feather in the Special Dacoity Force's cap was its success against the Chambal Kanjar dacoits. Deputy Superintendent of Police Freddy Young, who made his name with the capture of Sultana, began his campaign against the Kanjars in 1926. Several raids were conducted with mixed results. Large-scale military-style operations were also launched against the Kanjars, aided by the forces of Gwalior, Dholpur, Bharatpur, and Jaipur, the states most affected by their depredations. In March 1927, after a joint raid with the Gwalior State Police, many members of the gang were captured after a brisk fight on the bed of the Chambal River, and a considerable amount of loot was recovered.[26]

Occasionally, the supposedly gentler sex also took to dacoity. Among the most notorious of these was a woman who went by the name of Tumbolin, the wife of a dacoit leader who had been executed by the British. Taking over the reins of the gang, which operated mostly in central India in the 1850s, she quickly proceeded to make a name for herself with some very daring raids. One of these was on the military cantonment of Sholapur to rob the treasure chest kept there. The gang, having penetrated the cantonment in the guise of wandering minstrels, decided upon a night attack. Two sentries guarding the treasure were speared and the chest was broken open, but found to be empty. However, the alarm was raised and the dacoits had to beat a hasty retreat. One of their number was shot, but Tumbolin and the rest of the gang managed to get away. Her depredations continued unchecked, and ten years after the Sholapur incident, Tumbolin's gang ventured into Poona to rob the house of a wealthy Marwari merchant. The dacoits succeeded in breaking into the house and got away with the contents of his strong room. They were, however, pursued and two of the men, including Tumbolin's right-hand man Himtya, were captured. The lady managed to escape though, and no one ever claimed the large reward that was put upon her head. Eventually, Tumbolin retired to end her days peacefully among her own kind in the dense jungles of Oudh.[27]

Despite the menace of dacoity remaining largely out of control, one province where the police managed to seriously check the menace of dacoits was Sind, which fell within the Bombay Presidency. In the first two decades of the twentieth century, the Sind Police could boast that they 'did not allow dacoity'. And so they well might, for the annual number of dacoities in the province was a mere 10–20 – a trifling number, considering that the populace was composed of people known to be warlike and disposed to fight when provoked. A strict vigil over these people was however needed as even the slightest leniency could result in the problem surfacing again. In 1914, when troop trains carrying soldiers for embarkation at the port passed through Sind, a rumour went about that the British were leaving India, leading to minor outbreaks of dacoity in the province. However, the energetic Sind Police quickly rounded up the concerned offenders and peace was restored.

The pacification of the Sind, then known as the Unhappy Valley, had begun early after General Charles Napier conquered it in 1842. The province was known to be plagued by dacoits and an Irregular Cavalry Corps was formed to hunt them down. Napier then organized a police force along the lines of the Royal Irish Constabulary. He made them a separate and self-contained organization under their own superior officers, whose sole duty was to supervise them and ensure that they had adequate means to deal with crime. So successful was this system that the province was almost free from dacoity and robbery in the second half of the nineteenth century. Sir George Clark, governor of Bombay, during a visit to Sind in 1847, was so impressed by their performance that he decided to organize the police of the Deccan along the same lines.[28]

One reason the Sind Police achieved signal success in controlling dacoity was the unstinting support and assistance they received from the large landowners whose interests were aligned with the British. Another remarkable fact that enabled the police to apprehend the dacoits was the assistance they obtained from the famous Sind trackers, who could track them down in the harsh and inhospitable desert-like terrain that covered much of the province.

On 6 August 1926, a gang of dacoits raided the village of Kartal in the Sukkur district in the night and made off with booty worth ₹5,000. The police, accompanied by the trackers from the village, were soon on their trail, and a few hours and several kilometres later managed to come upon the dacoits as they were sitting down to share the loot. The police party was unfortunately unarmed and a head constable had been sent back to the house of a local zamindar to obtain firearms. Riding up to them, a lone mounted policeman by the name of Sobdar Khan challenged the dacoits armed with nothing but a cane. The dacoits refused to surrender but agreed to give up the property they had looted. This was not acceptable to the policeman who then rode into their midst and tried to seize one of them. He was promptly attacked with axes, pulled down from his horse, and struck on the head. A few Baluchi peasants who were with the tracking party joined in and a fierce fight ensued. Two of the dacoits were killed and two others so badly injured that they were unable to escape. Eventually, the entire gang was rounded up, but the gallant Sobdar Khan died of his wounds. On the recommendation of his British officers, his widow was granted a pension.[29]

The North-West Frontier Province was also known for the lawless propensities of its inhabitants. Bands of tribal marauders from the mountains would periodically descend on villages in the plains to loot and pillage, and officials would be kidnapped for ransom. This was a recurring problem on the frontier and the government – on the principle of setting one thief to catch another – recruited militias and levies from the tribal areas to bring these desperadoes to heel, with limited success. The most prized possession for a man on the frontier was a government-issue rifle and isolated military or police outposts would often be attacked to get at rifles that the men were carrying. It was drilled into soldiers and policemen on the frontier that come what may, they were not to lose their rifles in a firefight. The menace of these armed gangs, who gave no quarter and expected none, could never be entirely eliminated, right up to the end of British rule in India.

'Dacoity presents a most formidable problem to the Indian Police,' wrote J.C. Curry in the 1930s.[30] Despite all the government's efforts, the dacoit menace was still prevalent in much of British India and the Indian princely states when the end of the empire was just over a decade away. Not much seemed to have changed in over a century, and the typical dacoity, Curry informs us, was committed at night 'by a gang of some 30 ruffians who hold up a small village or one or two houses therein, ransack their objective, beat a more or less hurried retreat with the loot'.[31]

These men were usually armed with axes, spears or swords, often with firearms, and quite likely to murder anyone who offered resistance. In most cases, no resistance was offered but sometimes the victims put up a fight, and police reports contain many accounts of dacoits being beaten off or captured by the villagers, despite some of them suffering casualties.

Prosecution in cases of dacoity carried out by several large gangs who often combined to carry out raids was not an easy job and called for an immense amount of labour on the part of the district police, who were often not equipped to make a professional job of it. Sometimes, it involved producing as many as 50 to 100 accused before the court, and calling in about 400 witnesses.

According to Curry, there were three major difficulties in bringing dacoits to book. The first was the wide expanse of territory in which these gangs operated, and the nature of the terrain. The second was the difficulty in obtaining accurate information. The records, he says, 'are full of stories of the horrible fate of suspected informants at the hands of desperate men: of village watchmen bound hand and foot and thrown into rivers, or slowly roasted alive, or hideously mutilated'.[32] This led to the third difficulty: producing evidence sufficient enough to satisfy the courts and secure a conviction. 'The elaborate laws of evidence and the strict legal procedure of our Courts render it difficult to bring offenders to justice and keep crime under control,' Curry concluded.[33]

Little wonder then that even when the British left India in 1947, the dacoit problem had not been solved. Among the last of the famous dacoits of British India was Daku Man Singh. Born in 1896, he had been sentenced to life imprisonment in 1929 for attacking the relative of a man who had tried to get his father Bihari Singh implicated in a case of robbery, at the instigation of some men in his village. The resulting feud saw two of Man Singh's four sons being killed while the other two turned fugitive and took to the ravines. When Man Singh walked out of Agra Central Jail in 1939, he was, not surprisingly, a man with a grudge against society. For the next 15 years, he unleashed a reign of terror in the Chambal valley that was to stop only after he was gunned down in an encounter in 1955. It took a Special Armed Force of picked Gurkha and Garhwali troops to finally kill him.

During his time, according to Taroon Coomar Bhaduri, author of *Chambal: The Valley of Terror*, Man Singh committed 185 murders, 1,102 dacoities, and collected over ₹50 lakh as ransom from relatives of kidnapped persons. The police, in the course of 80 encounters with the famed dacoit since 1954, lost 32 men while Man Singh's gang suffered 15 casualties.[34]

As the government of Independent India was soon to discover, much like the British came to realize in well over a century of combating these reckless desperadoes, dacoits died hard.

11

Unpalatable Crimes
The Menace of the Professional Poisoner

BY THE 1860S, WITH THE THUGS LARGELY ACCOUNTED FOR, the Thagi and Dakaiti Department turned its attention to the activities of professional poisoners. The crime of poisoning in India was an ancient one, with roots going back into the realm of mythology. The Hindu god Krishna, when an infant, was the victim of a failed poisoning attempt by the demon Putana who suckled the toddler by applying poison to her breasts.

The fear of being poisoned sat heavy on the crowns of Indian rulers as well. Babur, the founder of the Mughal dynasty in India, survived a poisoning attempt by the mother of Sultan Ibrahim Lodi, who got the emperor's food taster to spike his meal. Indeed, monarchs worldwide employed food tasters to thwart just this possibility, but did not always succeed.[1]

Among the most notorious cases of poisoning in British India was that of the alleged attempt on the life of Col Phayre, the British Resident of Baroda, in 1875, which cost the Gaekwar his crown. In the last century, the notorious Agra Double Murder case, that saw an Anglo-Indian woman and her paramour make repeated attempts to poison their respective spouses with arsenic, showed that such crimes were not the preserve of natives alone.

The most commonly used poison in India was *datura* (*datura fastuosa/alba*). A kind of 'poor man's poison,' the deadly plant grows wild by the wayside and was therefore easily procurable. When consumed in small quantities, it had the advantage of stupefying and incapacitating the victim long enough for the poisoner to make his getaway with whatever valuables he could lay his hands on, and avoiding a possible murder charge if apprehended.

A really vile poisoner could also resort to another time-tested method of getting rid of an enemy – powdered glass. A few glass bangles and a mortar and pestle were all that was needed. When mixed well in a bowl of pudding or gravy, it was not easy to detect, and assured an agonizing and painful death for the victim. Other options in the Indian poisoner's pharmacopoeia were opium and arsenic, the former quite easily procurable and even otherwise consumed by many of the natives to deaden the senses after a day of toil.

Much like the thugs, poisoners often moved in large gangs across the country to ply their evil trade, and their depredations extended to every part of India.

> People of all castes and callings take to this trade, some casually, others for life... they assume all manner of disguises... and the habits of cooking, eating and sleeping on the side of the road, and smoking with strangers of seemingly the same caste, greatly facilitate their designs upon travelers... Sometimes, an old man or woman will manage the thing alone, by gaining the confidence of the travellers and getting near the cooking pots while they go aside; or when employed to bring the flour for the meal from the bazar. The poison is put into the flour or the pot, as opportunity offers.[2]

Quite a few poisoners were actually practicing thugs who had slightly altered their job profile, and were sometimes known as *datura thugs* or *daturiahs*. The pure *rumal*-wielding thug of yore would have not stooped to the use of poison, but as time went by and the rules began to be broken, the thug sometimes turned into a poisoner to achieve his ends.

However, unlike the thug who was traditionally most active in and around the upper and North-Western Provinces and central India, the poisoner covered a much wider field. As a report compiled by Major E.R.C. Bradford for the year 1875 shows, the latter plied their trade right across the subcontinent from Sind in the west to Bengal in the east, and from Punjab in upper India all the way down to Madras in the south. Only in British Burma, says the report, were the 'crimes of thuggee and systematic poisoning' unknown. The highest number of poisoning cases in 1875 was recorded in Punjab (67), followed by Bengal (59) and the North-Western Provinces (51), claiming 24, 18, and 17 lives, respectively. The province of Assam had only two recorded cases, with one fatality. Bombay (the entire province including native states and Sind) reported 49 cases of poisoning that led to 20 deaths.[3]

These numbers may not reflect the situation of the ground, for these are only the officially recorded cases. In crimes like poisoning, given the ease of execution and difficulty of detection, it is often not easy to get the correct picture.

Lt Col Dalmahoy, the deputy inspector-general of police for the North-Western Provinces, writing in 1875 conceded that 'our returns cannot be considered an accurate statement of the number of cases that occurred, as there is no doubt that the crime is to a very great extent not reported to the police'.[4]

The concealment of poisoning was an old problem. William Sleeman, during his rambles in Oudh in the late 1930s, came across an old fakir living alone in a hut close to a roadside shrine near Moradabad. The man's 10-year-old son had been poisoned by a family of *daturiahs* for the sake of a blanket that had been put out to dry in the sun. The poisoners – a man and his wife, accompanied by two children – had arrived at the shrine, and being allowed to cook their meal there, had offered the fakir a little flour with which he made two rotis. The fakir's son being very hungry had a roti and a half, while he had only the leftover half. Soon they fell into a stupor and the man woke up hours later, incoherent and in a daze. His son, though unconscious was still breathing, but died soon after. Their guests had vanished. The fakir, however, did not reveal all this to the police, telling them instead that the boy had been attacked and killed by wolves, who were known to frequent the locality. This, Sleeman found, was done under pressure from the leading men of the village who were anxious to avoid any trouble with the law. The poison used in this case was *datura*. Sleeman describes the modus operandi of the poisoners:

> It (datura) is sometimes given in the hookah to be smoked, and at others in food. When they require to poison children as well as grown-up people, or women who do not smoke, they mix up the poison in food. The intention is almost always to destroy life as 'dead men tell no tales'; but the poisoned people sometimes recover, as in the present case, and lead to the detection of the poisoners.[5]

However, even in cases where the victims survived, it was not easy to trace the poisoners, and even when they did, convictions were not easy to obtain, for 'very few (victims) will undertake to prosecute them through the several courts of the magistrate, the sessions, and that of the last instant in a distant district, to which the proceedings must be sent for final orders'.[6]

Poisoning, according to Sleeman, was 'among the greatest evils with which the country is at this time affected' and he seems to have despaired of ever bringing this evil trade to an end. 'The members of one party may sometimes be punished, but the conviction is accidental, for the system which has enabled us to put down the thug associations cannot be applied, with any fair prospects of success, to the suppression of these pests to society.'[7]

The career of Sharafuddin, a notorious poisoner from Punjab who was involved in at least 69 cases, illustrates how these men could ply their deadly trade for years together without being apprehended.

Sharafuddin was the son of a butcher in the village of Kaithan in the Hoshiarpur district. Always something of a wastrel and ne'er-do-well, he became a professional gambler in his teens, a career choice that did not sit well with his father who disowned him in 1861, when he was about 18 years of age. Sharafu, as he was known, then enlisted in the Bareilly Police, who could not have known much about his antecedents. However, he had a violent disposition which soon landed him in the district jail for having cut off the nose of a girl he had abducted. Serving a 15 months' sentence in the Bareilly Jail, he soon made the acquaintance of Tikka Ram, the head of a gang of professional poisoners. Tikka Ram was believed to have converted to Islam and was known by several aliases – Babu Khan, Lal Mohammed, and Laljee. On their release, Tikka Ram and Sharafu moved to Aligarh in the North-Western Provinces, where they were involved in several cases of poisoning. Tikka Ram was soon caught, but Sharafu got away. Incredibly, he managed to get a job with the police again, this time in Agra, but was soon dismissed. He then went back to his native village, and commenced afresh with a 14-strong gang. Assuming various disguises, the gang poisoned and robbed several people travelling on the Grand Trunk Road from Oudh to their homes in the Punjab. Sharafuddin, who had picked up the Purbiah dialect from Tikka Ram while in jail, would pass himself off as a native of Oudh and befriend men coming from that province with their wages. An invitation to a meal would follow and the victims, their minds dulled by a generous helping of country spirits, would soon be dining on food laced with opium or *datura*. Very shortly, their victims would be lying insensible if not dead, and the gang would take off with whatever valuables they could lay their hands on. They carried on thus for a five-year spell from 1867, confounding all efforts to nab them, and leaving behind a trail of corpses that on post-mortem revealed the presence of *datura*.

In 1872, Sharafu's luck ran out when he was denounced by his former mentor Tikka Ram's wife to the Jullunder Police. Making a quick getaway disguised as a *Darwesh* (a Sufi mendicant), he was always one step ahead of his pursuers, moving from Patiala to Delhi and then to Alwar and Jaipur. In Jaipur, he set himself up as a professor of alchemy and claimed to be able to cure diseases by means of charms that he sold to an unsuspecting public. He had, by this time, collected a new gang of seven men and the poisonings resumed, but he was careful not to go back to his home province.

By now, John Paul Warburton of the Punjab Police was hot on his trail. The 'Controller of Devils', as Warburton was famously known in the Punjab, had compiled a dossier on Sharafuddin with the help of Tikka Ram and his wife Mussamat Zahuran, with whom Sharafu had lived for some time. A credible description of the poisoner was put out and a reward of ₹500 offered for information leading to his arrest.

In 1874, Sharafu's gang was suspected of poisoning two travellers in a garden near the Rai Police Station in Delhi district, and a reward of ₹1,000 was offered for his arrest, but he still could not be found.

Finally, in 1879, Warburton received word from Tikka Ram that his former protégé was now lodged in Agra Central Jail for a crime committed under another alias. Sharafu was now sporting a different look, having shaved off his beard, and leaving only a short tuft of hair, or *chotti,* on his head. However, he was positively identified by other marks on his person, and finally admitted to being the much-sought-after poisoner. A lengthy court case followed, with the usual problems of forgetful witnesses and often insufficient evidence, but a conviction was finally obtained and Sharafu was hanged in January 1881.[8]

Another professional poisoner was Radha Ballabh of Mathura. When arrested in Agra in 1877, he confessed to a good many crimes in the district, including two serious cases in which five men were killed, but could not be robbed as the poisoners had been disturbed in their work and had to make a quick getaway. On one occasion, wanting money to spend on Holi festivities,

Ballabh and his accomplice Megha, posing as a well-to-do merchant and his servant, hired a cart and cartman at Ferozepur. On the way, four of his men joined the party. Drugging the cartman, they sold the cart and bullocks to some traders who habitually bought cattle from known poisoners.[9]

These itinerant poisoners also gave a bad name to the wandering bands of ascetics, or bairagis, who were frequently found on the roads of India, simply because a professional poisoner found it to be the most convenient disguise.

Dressed as holy men, professional poisoners would take the roads to the country's many pilgrim towns, befriending fellow travellers and winning their confidence before poisoning them and moving on to the next town. As these men had no fixed abode, catching up with them and their crimes was almost impossible.

'These ascetic devotees do not even spare their own castemen,' lamented Eustace Kitts in his 1889 book *Serious Crime in an Indian Province*, citing a few cases:

> Two Bairagis of Basti in 1887 drugged another, who had come to them as a spiritual disciple, and stole his purse containing Rs 33... A Bairagi in the Azamgarh district in 1883 drugged and robbed a party of pilgrims on their way to Ajudhiya; another Bhagwandas by name, in January 1884, drugged a couple of Bairagis at Muttra; another Bairagi at the same city drugged and robbed an old woman on a pilgrimage to the Putrakhund.[10]

Among those most vulnerable to poisoning on the road were the itinerant Powindahs from Afghanistan. These men were traders who made annual trips from their homes in the mountains to the cities in the plains of India, leading caravans of camels loaded with grain, dry fruits, clothes, shawls and fur. They were often targeted while homeward bound, with pockets full of cash. The 'Kabulis,' as they were generally called, would congregate at certain locations on their return journey, where professional poisoners also lay in wait. While otherwise sharp businessmen and skilled bargainers, they would fall prey to blandishments and sweet talk, and consume the *datura*-laced food offered to them by the poisoners. In Bombay, where they were known to collect, the Kabulis would frequently end up in the hospital with symptoms of food poisoning, but often survived due to their healthy constitutions.[11]

S.T. Hollis, while serving as assistant superintendent of police in the CID in Meerut in 1909, was told by his boss to keep a sharp lookout for poisoners ahead of the *Kumbh Mela* that year. The body of a man had been recently discovered under a tree on the road to Begumabad in the Meerut district. There was no suspicion of a poisoner at work until a week later, when a man named Murari Lal was drugged and left for dead in Muzaffarnagar. Fortunately, the man had been quickly admitted to a hospital, but had not recovered enough to make a statement. A few days later, another man was found dead near a camping ground in the Saharanpur district. The police were now almost certain that a professional poisoner was working on the pilgrim roads to Haridwar. There were still no leads, however, till a week later when Hollis was informed that the victim in the Muzaffarnagar case had now completely recovered and could identify the poisoner.

Murari Lal, who had stopped at a camping site on the road to Haridwar, was preparing to cook his evening meal when a sadhu invited him to share his food, offering him some chapattis and curry. Finding the curry, in which he had dipped his chapatti, to have an odd taste, he had thrown it away when the sadhu turned his head to get some cow dung cakes for the fire, but continued to eat the chapattis. Soon he was drowsy, and lay down to sleep. He woke up many hours later in a hospital, only to find that a bangle he had on his right wrist, a ring, and ₹30 in cash were missing.

Murari Lal was able to give Hollis a description of the sadhu: The man was tall and well built, with a shaven head, round face and protruding teeth, and had a round burn mark on the inside of his left wrist. Like most holy men, he was clad in saffron robes and a white pagri, and on his wrist was a string of amber beads. While most sadhus dressed alike in saffron garb, Hollis was reasonably confident that, given the detailed description, they could probably identify him. Murari Lal had recovered well enough to travel and willingly agreed to accompany the police to Haridwar to try and spot the fake sadhu among the hundreds that thronged the city.

It was decided that the best chance of spotting their target was to keep a watch at the entrance to the bathing ghats, where Murari Lal would be posted in the guise of a constable. The superintendent of police in charge of the Mela, an old friend of Hollis, agreed to the plan and Murari Lal took up his post accordingly, with a police team led by Inspector Mahadeo Prasad of the Meerut Police standing by some distance away. After a 16-hour-long wait, Murari Lal finally spotted the suspect. The police did not move in immediately, but watched him perform his ablutions, and then followed him to a pilgrim encampment a mile away, where the suspect entered a small tent. The police then rushed into the tent and the sadhu was arrested on a charge of attempted murder, which he stoutly denied, despite Murari Lal identifying him by the burn scar on his wrist. Hollis, who was also present, ordered the constables to search the man and his belongings, but nothing incriminating was found. Inspector Prasad then suggested that the floor of the tent be dug up. This was done and up came a box containing a large amount of jewellery and ₹300 in cash. Among the jewellery was Murari Lal's ring and bangle, which he identified. Also in the box was something that did not escape Mahadeo Prasad's practiced eye – dried seeds of the datura plant.

While the evidence was incriminating enough, the sadhu was uncooperative and refused to give his name. His fingerprints were then taken and sent to the Central Fingerprint Bureau in Delhi. Their report revealed that the fake sadhu was in fact a professional poisoner named Bishen Lal, who had already served a 7-year prison term for attempted murder by poisoning. This time, though, he was sentenced to life.[12]

Women, too, took to the trade. In the Ghazipur district in 1878, four women and a boy were drugged by two old women. In 1881, a woman from Bareilly drugged and robbed her nephew's family in their house. She repeated this at the house of yet another relative at Budaon, but was caught along with a male confederate while selling the victim's ornaments. Another old woman was convicted in 1880 for killing two men with poisoned sherbet in Benares, and another similar case in 1879. In Mainpuri, an old woman and her son befriended a young man from Agra and offered to find him a wife. They set off for Shikohabad, the young man also being accompanied by three of his friends. The hopeful suitor was carrying ₹100 and some clothes for his expected bride. On the way, however, they were poisoned by the old woman who vanished leaving behind their dead bodies. The old woman was probably also involved in three similar cases in Agra and Mathura districts in 1882, where men were inveigled by marriage proposals by an old woman who was accompanied by a boy.[13]

Young boys were suspected of being taught the trade by these women, and they began their training early. A 12-year-old boy was arrested in May 1885 for drugging a party of men travelling with the agent of the Raja of Mohsan. This was not his first offence though, having been in the dock for the same offence on four earlier occasions. Another boy was held a few months later for drugging three pilgrims from Gaya, who survived to tell the tale. The same boy had been charged with a similar offence a year ago, but was let off as the victims, worried about the long legal procedures, changed their story, attributing their delirium to having being out in the hot sun.[14]

Young boys from thug families also sometimes went back to their family trade, despite the attempts made to reform them at Sleeman's School of Industry at Jabalpur, though now they used *datura* to rob their victims instead of the customary scarf. Mr Upham, an engineer working for the GIPR near Sleemanabad in the Central Provinces, escaped a poisoning attempt by two such boys employed as table servants at his house. He had seen them crushing some green pods and putting them into his cooking pot, but presumed they were herbs. Upham survived – he only had a light meal as he was not hungry, which caused him some uneasiness. The pods, when shown to his doctor, were immediately identified as being of the *datura* plant and both youths were arrested.[15]

While the recorded instances of poisoning were greater in the northern parts of India, the south was by no means immune. The yearly report of the inspector general of police, in 1875, notes the following among the 23 recorded in the Madras Presidency for that year:

Two cases occurred in the Kistna District. Some bandymen (sic) were drugged with datura and robbed by a Telugu traveller, who joined them, and in the second case, a chuckler[16] going to buy leather was drugged and robbed...

There were two cases in Bellary, the traveller and pretended sorcerer administered poison in betel nut to a person suspected of theft; the man died – corrosive sublimate and arsenic were found in his stomach and the drugger was charged... and sentenced to three years rigorous imprisonment.

There were two cases in Kurnool by the same person. In April, one Nagareddy hired a cart, drugged the *bandyman*,[17] and sold the cart and bullocks. In September he repeated this experiment in another part of the district, but this time he was caught and convicted in both cases...

Two cases occurred in Tanjore. In one case, some travellers by rail to Nagapatam were, on arrival, invited to a house by a fellow traveler, treated to food with datura in it, and robbed. In the other, a *bandyman* driving his cart and bullocks from South Arcot took food in a *chuttrum* [resting place for travellers]; someone must have dropped datura into it unseen, for the bandyman became insensible, his cart and bullocks disappeared, and no trace could be found of the drugger.[18]

Given the near immunity from detection and punishment, it is not surprising that these men did not mend their ways. Pardoned and released from Barabanki Jail on the occasion of the proclamation of Queen Victoria as Empress of India in 1877, it did not take long for the notorious poisoner Sheoparshan, who had been earlier convicted in two cases, to go back to his old calling. In May 1878, he poisoned two women in the city of Ayodhya, robbing them of ₹23; a month later, he robbed a man in Gonda of ₹45 after giving him a spiked drink.[19]

When it came to professional poisoners, the police were up against a class of criminals who seemingly showed no remorse and no tendency to reform. 'It would appear from a perusal of the different cases, that once an individual takes to poisoning as a profession he or she never gives it up,' wrote Lt Col Dalmahoy, deputy inspector general of police for the North-Western Provinces, in his report for 1875. 'They may be imprisoned time after time for the offence – it matters not for what period – no sooner are they out of jail than they are back to the old trade.'[20]

Dalmahoy had reason to be pessimistic despite many of the offenders being arrested, as his detailed reported reveals:

> In both the Muzaffarnagar cases the police acted promptly and with intelligence; in the old woman an important capture was made; by her own confession she has been at the trade for 30 years; but I am sorry to say we have not been able to get any information out of her, she stoutly denies having any accomplices... In the Bareilly case, Ellahi Buksh a regular old professional was arrested by a chowkidar; he committed three cases last year and was once before in jail for seven years for poisoning: he has now got transportation for life... I believe the poisoner in the Muttra case to be an old offender, but beyond that he drugged some people in Bindrabun in 1874, there were no cases proved against him; he has now received only three years imprisonment... Pir Buksh is a very old offender; several cases have been brought home to him, and for a similar offence, he, on a former occasion, got 10 years; he has now been transported for

life... Mussamat Purbutti, Rajputin, the culprit in the Benares case; is also an old offender; in fact she had only just come out of the Agra Jail, where she had been for five years for poisoning, when she committed this case: she has now been transported for life.[21]

While the crime of poisoning could not be entirely eradicated, improvements in toxicology and chemical analysis that led to quicker detection, and legislation to restrict the sale and purchase of poisons in the bazaars (for use in traditional medicine) may have served as a deterrent to the professional poisoner. Certainly, poisoning was not as bad a problem in the early twentieth century as it was in the mid-1800s, thought it still reared its head in the police reports.

In the 1900s, the expansion of the railway network opened up a new field for the professional poisoner to practise his trade. Detection and apprehension of the perpetrator in cases of poisoning on the railways was even more difficult as the offender could be kilometres away in another part of the country by the time the victim was discovered.

Datura, however, still continued to be the poisoner's favourite. 'Many of the reported cases of *datura*-poisoning occur within railway limits, and are committed for the purpose of facilitating robbery,' wrote S.M. Edwardes in 1924.[22] Six such cases were reported in the Rajputana Agency in 1920, including one in which an 8-year-old boy was given poisoned sweetmeats. In the following year, the Railway Police in the United Provinces arrested and convicted seven professional poisoners, of whom one had five previous convictions for poisoning.[23]

While the poisoner may not have been as destructive as the dacoit, his shadow has always loomed disproportionately large on the Indian criminal scene. Given the sneaky and underhand nature of his enterprise, the professional poisoner plying his trade on road or rail was always a greater source of dread to the traveller.

His legacy still remains with us: how often have you been reminded not to accept anything to eat from a stranger?

12

Crooks on the Line
The Railway Thieves

IN 1915, RAI BAHADUR M. PAUPA RAO NAIDU, A MUCH DECORATED officer of the Madras Police, had the satisfaction of seeing in print the fourth edition of his remarkable work, *The History of the Railway Thieves, with Illustrations and Hints on Detection*.[1] The book, published by Higginbotham's of Madras, was part of 'The Criminal Tribes of India' series, and focused on the activities of a set of people the author described as 'railway thieves'. The classification was rather broad and may not necessarily have been accurate considering that Naidu, following the established practice of the day, seems to have held that crime on the railways was practised by some of the so-called 'criminal tribes' who made a living by preying on people travelling by rail across the Indian subcontinent.

Naidu wrote four such handbooks on these supposedly habitual criminals, including one on 'Professional Poisoners and Coiners' – a rather unique achievement considering that such 'guides' were usually brought out by British officials, either serving or retired from the Indian Police. The handbooks were intended as a means to help identify criminals in each of the Indian provinces by their habits, methods of operation, and even their physical features, for they were often profusely illustrated with photographs of representative members of each tribe, presumably to serve as a quick reference identikit to help apprehend such characters if one came across them. While this system was fraught with possibilities of misuse and the miscarriage of justice, in all fairness it could be said that there wasn't much the police could do to identify these offenders before the advent of fingerprinting and the widespread use of photography enabled detailed files to be kept on such criminals.

Joining the Madras Police in 1888, Naidu had been employed with both the Special Branch and the Criminal Intelligence Department, and was a recipient of the prestigious King's Police Medal. His long years of service had inevitably brought him in contact with the criminal fraternity of the day, leading him to conclude that certain tribes and classes were involved or specialized in particular fields of crime. Among those that chose the railways as their field of endeavour, Naidu included in his book the Bhamptas of the Deccan, the Kepmaries or Koravars, and the Takku Waddars or Ghantichors of south India, the Bharwars who frequented parts of both the United Provinces and the central India, and the Mallahs, Ahirs, and Aheriyas of the United Provinces. Then there was a category of freelancers who were mainly pickpockets but did not belong to a particular tribe or caste, operating solo and depending largely on their wits and sleight of hand for survival.

While they were by no means the only ones, the aforementioned classes of people were recorded as having resorted largely to crime on the railways in colonial India and, hence, answered to the simple, if necessarily inaccurate, description of 'railway thieves' and provided the title for Naidu's work. The book, though dull in parts, still makes for interesting reading, offering insights into the lives of these itinerant bands of men and women for whom the coming of the Iron Road opened new avenues of mobility and employment, though admittedly of a dubious nature.

The rollout of the railways in India with the GIPR first run from Bori Bunder to Thana in April 1853 also served to widen the field of criminal enterprise in the subcontinent. No longer would a malefactor have to depend entirely on *tonga*, *dak-gharry*, or his two feet to make a quick getaway. With the expenditure of a few pice or annas, he could now be kilometres away from the scene of his crimes in a matter of hours, with the law none the wiser. The introduction of smaller branch lines and connections to the princely states, some of which had their own railway lines, also provided the added advantage of quickly hopping across the border of British India into princely state territory from where it was difficult to extract an offender without a lengthy and time-consuming legal process.

For the habitual criminal, therefore, the railway was a blessing. The crowds congregating on and outside the platforms, the packed trains, and the general air of bustle and confusion at any Indian railway station were such that would delight any pickpocket. For other professional criminals and fugitives, too, the chaos of the railway provided an easy refuge from the reach of the law.

This was a fact well known to the authorities, who admitted as much. A committee of inquiry whose findings were published in the Railway Police Report of 1882 said it had 'reason to believe that the railways is undoubtedly largely used by the criminal classes, both as a field of operation and as offering facilities for the commission of crime and evasion of pursuit'.[2]

The report also listed the usual suspects, who also find a place in Naidu's handbook, noting that:

> ...the Sasiahs, the Bowreahs, and Harbourahs of the Northern Districts, the Dullerahs of Rohilcund, the Burwars of Gonda, the Awudiahs from Lucknow, the Sanoriahs from Lalitpur and Central Provinces, the Bomptias from Bombay, all tribes living by crime and traveling to the furthest parts of India, have been satisfactorily shown to use the Railways...[3]

The so-called railway thieves, however, did not necessarily resort to crime on the railways alone, and over several decades had also changed their area and methods of operations. Writing in 1889, Eustace Kitts in *Serious Crime in an Indian Province* says that the Bauris in the 1850s were 'a tribe of desperate dacoits' who made the whole of upper India from Gujarat to Calcutta their hunting ground and were notorious as cart- and tent-robbers on the Grand Trunk Road. Attempts were made to reform, and many were employed as watchmen, but these efforts were not always successful.[4] The Sonorias still exist and resort to robbing third-class travellers, Kitts writes, citing Railway Police returns.[5] While they may not have always confined their activities to the railways, the mobility provided by this new and faster means of transport allowed these men to ply their nefarious trade with a greater degree of freedom from arrest and prosecution.

Crime on the railways took many forms, from pickpocketing on the trains and platforms, drugging travellers and depriving them of their possessions to pilfering fruits and liquor bottles from crates, removing the nuts and bolts from axle boxes or simply throwing out the contents of moving goods trains to be collected by accomplices waiting by the tracks. 'When trains go slow (and they sometimes go very slowly indeed) a train thief will jump on a goods train, open the wagon doors, throw out the bags and bales, and then jump off again.'[6] While this called for a degree of daring and skill, it was not infrequent. In 1878, there were 36 such cases, and seven of them occurred within one month between Moghalserai and Buxar, while similar cases were also reported on the lines between Agra and Cawnpore and between Allahabad and Satna.

Among the most common crimes on trains was robbing travellers while they slept. The Bhamptas of the Deccan were quite adept at this, Naidu informs us. Indeed, 'their criminal propensities have acquired such a notoriety that in northern India the word Bhampta has become a bye-word for a thief, no matter to which class of thieves the particular individual belonged'.[7]

Their modus operandi was, in fact, deviously simple and is best described in Naidu's own words:

> They look out for passengers having bags which seem likely to contain anything valuable, and they follow such persons into the same carriage, and sitting near, endeavour to enter into conversation... After a time, when it begins to get dark... one of the Bhamptas, on the pretext of making them more comfortable, lies down on the floor, and covers himself with a large cloth under the pretext of going to sleep, while his confederate, stretching his legs on to the opposite seat, spreads out his cloth, thus more or less screening the man beneath. This latter, when all appears quiet, begins manipulating the bag he has spotted under the seat, to feel with his hands if anything valuable is there, and if he cannot succeed in getting his hand into the bag, he takes from his mouth a small curved knife which all Bhamptas carry concealed between their gum and upper lip, and with that he rips the seam of the bag and takes out what he finds. If the curved knife is not sharp enough to cut the canvas, he uses the other knife he has with him and if the article spotted be a tin or wooden box he makes use of a chisel in forcing it open, generally at the lock, and transfers the contents to his bag or bundle or passes up what he has stolen to his confederate, and at the next station the two get out together, or get into another carriage.[8]

At Narayangunj in Bengal in 1905, a gang of these men extracted money from the middle one of three boxes that had been lashed together and placed under the seat. One side of the box was removed, the cash taken out and the side replaced. In another instance, the hasps of a steel trunk were cut noiselessly without being detected.[9]

Thefts like these were not easy to pull off by any means, and certainly called for a great deal of skill and daring, and required quite a bit of practice. The passenger would wake up to their loss, but not wanting to look a fool would often avoid lodging a complaint.

The Bhamptas had earlier only targeted fairs and festivals in large villages and towns and operated only by day, but with the opening of the railways, extended their beat to the trains, 'because they discovered that darkness favoured their designs on the persons and property of travellers; it may be said that all successful thefts in trains are committed by them only during the night.' With the extension of the railway network, Naidu warned, 'they are also increasing in number every day, and spreading in all parts of India, committing their depredations'.[10]

The Bhamptas studied railway timetables and were well up in their knowledge of trains. In Bengal, they had a reputation for specializing in thefts on running trains from which they would toss out heavy trunks and then jump out of the carriage before the alarm was raised. To a Bhampta also goes the credit of stealing a travelling bag belonging to the governor of Bengal from a saloon car of the Southern Mahratta Railway.[11]

They were known to travel widely and in Bengal were reported to be operating in places such as Ranaghat, Kushtea, Saidpur, Dacca, Howrah, Ranigunj, and on the Dacca–Mymensingh Railway. Their women, too, lent a hand, committing thefts from ladies' compartments. During 1908–10, a gang of about 30 Bhamptas committed several robberies on the East Indian Railway, Bengal–Nagpur Railway, and the Eastern Bengal State Railway. During this period, they were found to have remitted back to their families more than 200 money orders to the tune of ₹8,000.[12]

The Bhamptas did well out of their chosen profession, and Naidu lists individuals, some in their 70s and 80s, who led and financed these gangs, advancing loans to the men for the maintenance of their families while they trawled the various railway lines and took a cut out of the proceeds of these expeditions.[13]

According to Naidu, the Koravars, who mostly came from the Madras Presidency but were familiar with all the languages of southern India where they operated, were noted for thieving on the railways, stealing canvas or carpet bags, bundles or small boxes from platforms, waiting rooms and sometimes from railway carriages. The Koravars would carry a decent-looking canvas bag or bundle and place it next to another similar-looking bag belonging to a passenger, and at a favourable opportunity walk away with the latter's bag, leaving his own behind. By the time the switch was discovered, it was often too late as the thief would have already boarded a train and moved off or simply left the platform. On occasion, when deemed worthwhile, the target would be followed into the railway compartment and his bag extracted in a similar manner while the passenger dozed off or was otherwise distracted. They would then get off at the nearest station or hide himself in the latrine till he could alight safely from the train. At times, they would also cut open bags, break open trunks or boxes or throw them on the line, to be retrieved later by their accomplices. For the most part, however, they confined their activities to theft on the platforms. They also kept in step with the times, as Naidu found, and had progressed from carrying canvas or cloth bags and bundles to steel trunks and 'put on more gentlemanly apparel as a safer mask to their villainy'.[14]

The Koravars, who as a class comprise several clans and sub-clans, had not always been railway thieves. Frederick Mullaly, in his *Notes on Criminal Tribes of the Madras Presidency* published in 1892, writes that 'highway dacoity on parties returning from weekly markets is a very favourable mode of crime' for the Koravars. They were also expert burglars who broke into houses by drilling into the walls, and were always willing to put up a fight if detected.[15]

They were easily identified, writes Mullaly, with the women wearing 'necklaces of shells and cowries interspersed with beads of all colours in several rows hanging low down on the bosom; brass bangles of various shapes from the wrist to the elbow.' The men, he says, were dirty and unkempt and kept their hair long and tied in a knot at the top of their head. A cloth around the loins and a bag called the 'vadi sanchi' made of striped cloth were all they usually had.[16]

Attempts had been made to reform them and direct their energies to honest pursuits, but did not meet with any notable success. They preferred a nomadic life and as hardly any of them had the slightest degree of education, 'it will be a long time before they can be persuaded to give up their criminal habits'.[17]

Apart from these, among the criminal classes mentioned in Naidu's book are the curiously named Ghantichors, who along with the Takku Waddars and Donga Dasaries carried out their depredations in the Bombay and Madras Presidencies, the area around Mysore, the Northern Circars, and the Nizam's Dominions, but were not strictly railway thieves. Roving as they did across a wide swathe of territory, these gangs, which included various caste groups and subgroups comprising men and women and children, would have found the railways to be a congenial adjunct for their criminal activities. Moving about in large bands, they were notorious for house-breaking, and committing robberies and dacoities and, unlike the 'pure' railway thieves, were known to use violence when challenged. The Ghantichors would often go about in the guise of religious mendicants, their forehead smeared with caste-marks, and carrying a *garuda-stambham* (lamp post), a gong of bell metal, a small drum called a *jagata*, and a tuft of peacock feathers.[18]

The Donga Dasaries, or Gudu Dasaries as they were also known, adopted a similar ruse wandering around as holy men or bairagis, all the while keeping an eye out for houses that could be easily burgled. Using an implement called a 'Kuchi–Kol', they would drill through the walls, and making a hole sufficiently large enough to allow a man to put his arm in to draw the bolt of the door, and having thus gained entry, decamp with whatever valuables they found within. To the casual observer, the Kuchi-Kol seemed to be a musical instrument, somewhat resembling a 'veena'. A closer examination would, however, reveal that it was composed of two parts capable of being separated from each other, one of the halves encasing a sharp iron tool about 12 to 15 inches in length, octagon shaped, and tipped with steel.[19]

The railways, not surprisingly, were also plagued by the commonplace nuisance of pickpockets. The Railway Police

Report of 1882 revealed that almost all the lines suffered from them their attentions. Professional thieves and pickpockets from Agra, Muttra, and Delhi, and from the districts near Gwalior, Jhansi, and Indore were found to be active on the Rajputana–Malwa Railway, while on the Sind, Punjab, and Delhi Railway thefts by pickpockets were 'most numerous'. The latter was used by 'bad characters of Calcutta or by migratory gangs of pickpockets and pilferers who are found all over the country.'[20]

Among the railway pickpockets were men of 'all castes and creeds from Brahmins down to outcastes,' who were for the most part 'street Arabs, who having while quite young, fallen into evil habits and associations, having been abandoned or neglected by their parents, relations and friends'.[21] These men did not belong to any particular criminal tribe and were not part of any large gangs, except when they set out on thieving expeditions to distant fairs and festivals at religious shrines.

Their methods of concealment were often ingenious. Some of these men wore shoes called 'chadvas', which were used to hide small articles, while others concealed stolen property in their anus or swallowed small jewels or coins 'which were afterwards recovered from their evacuations'.[22] Sometimes, a sharp piece of glass was hidden in the mouth under the upper lip and used for cutting necklaces. They also set up shop on platforms, offering small knives and scissors for sale, which when the opportunity presented itself were used to cut open knots, packets, and bundles.

Naidu also noted the growing menace of juvenile thieves in southern India in 1914. Most of these boys came from Kumbakonam and were involved in stealing neck or wrist ornaments, removing trunks or bags, and making away with coats suspended from hat-pegs in second- and first-class compartments.[23]

Some thieves underwent a painful ordeal to help them conceal small valuables on their person. Naidu's description of the unusual process of creating an artificial cavity in the throat is worth a careful read:

> A lead bullet with a hole bored through its centre is fastened by a silk cord. The bullet is lowered into the throat on the left side, and the patient has to recline on his left side for several weeks. To obviate any chance of the bullet being accidently swallowed, the silk cord is fastened on the outside round the patient's neck. The lead corrodes the surrounding tissues and the natural cavity becomes enlarged. After about six weeks, the lead bullet is drawn up and a gold bullet is let down; the tissues then heal quickly and the gold bullet keeps the cavity from filling up and smooths any rough surface that may have formed. When the cavity is fully developed it is capable of secreting small but valuable articles such as rings, women's nose rings, sovereigns, etc.[24]

Needless to say, Naidu adds, only a few stout-hearted souls went through this painful and tedious process.

There were other reckless souls, too, who while travelling in third-class compartments, would walk along the footboard to the first- and second-class carriages when the train was in motion and remove handbags and other small items through the windows, or if the opportunity occurred, enter a carriage and carry away luggage or throw it down to an accomplice waiting along the line. In one such case in the Madras Presidency, a missionary's bag was stolen from a second-class carriage. It was later found, emptied of its contents, in the first-class carriage next to it. The accused in this case was, however, caught by the Railway Police and turned out to be a dismissed fireman from the same railway![25]

In January 1911, a man named Thakur Lal, who also went by the aliases Mohammed Hussain and Inder, entered the brake van of a train at Chapra dressed as an assistant station master and made away with several articles belonging to the guard. When he was later arrested, it was recalled that he had earlier been seen in the uniform of a guard at Manji Ghat. With half-a-dozen convictions in Benares, Gorkahpur, Saran, and Azamgarh, he was at the age of 27, an accomplished railway thief.[26]

It was hard to keep tabs on such men, and while the introduction of fingerprinting enabled the arrest and conviction of many habitual criminals, the sentences in most cases were not onerous and in a few years they would be back at work on the railway platforms.

Further, the railway thief was no respecter of social class or nationality. Anyone carrying anything worth stealing was fair game, as Mr H. Shugio, an advisor to the Japanese-British Exhibition of 1910, found to his cost when travelling first class from Arrah to Dinapore on the East Indian Railway. Arriving at his destination, Mr Shugio, who had fallen asleep in the train, made the mortifying discovery that his handbag containing promissory notes, cash, and jewellery to the value of nearly ₹3,000 were missing. Neither the offer of a substantial reward nor the most energetic efforts of the police helped flush out the offender. The stolen property was never recovered.[27]

While most crimes on the railway only involved loss of property, the ugly spectre of violent crime did make an occasional appearance. In July 1913, a military police clerk named Ganjam Singh travelling from Howrah to Jullandar was murdered in the train and his body was thrown out at Hathras Junction in the United Provinces. He was suspected to have been drugged and murdered by his companions, who were never traced.[28]

In February, 1919, a Punjabi Mussalman entered a third-class compartment of the Quetta Mail at Karachi and, on being denied a seat near the window, stabbed one of the passengers with a large knife and then threw him out of the window. Another man who intervened was also attacked, but ran into the lavatory and after smashing a window pane jumped out of the train. A general melee then developed as other passengers waded into the fight and in the free-for-all one man was killed and eight others severely injured.[29]

The fairer sex, too, was not immune to violence on the railway, though such incidents were not commonplace. Naidu mentions an incident that occurred in 1903 on the North-Western Railway in Sind, when a lady travelling first class was molested and thrown out of the running train. She survived with minor injuries, but her attacker was not brought to justice despite the reward of ₹1,000 being offered for information leading to the arrest of the culprit. In another such case, a lady travelling in a second-class carriage grappled with the thief only to be thrown out of the window. She too survived, and had the satisfaction of seeing her attacker arrested and convicted.[30]

Musammat Kando, who was travelling from Hathras to Delhi on 4 April 1914, was somewhat luckier in that she avoided injury or worse. Hardly had the train pulled out of Khurja station, when a young man wearing European clothes entered the compartment, and throwing her to the ground snatched her necklace and jumped out of the train.[31]

In another notorious case in 1917, a Ms Jackson was attacked in her first-class carriage on the Oudh and Rohilcund Railway. She fought off her attacker and yanked the communication cord (which did not work!) but the man got away. While no arrest was made, a salutary outcome of the case was the decision by some railway companies to do away with the continuous footboards that ran the entire length of the train, which made it easy for thieves to move from one carriage to another without detection.[32]

Interestingly, but then not surprisingly, another class of people who robbed or defrauded their employer were the railway staff themselves. In Naidu's opinion, over half of all railway thefts were committed by servants of the railway! An astonishing charge, for which he does not provide any specific numerical proof, but declares 'that with little or no scruples of conscience they prove treacherous to the trust reposed in them by their officers and the public notwithstanding the decent salaries paid to them'.[33] While Naidu's claim may be a little over the top, the little army of booking-office clerks, parcel- and luggage-room staff, porters, tally-clerks, yardmen, and guards employed by the railways certainly had enough opportunities for enriching themselves, and a few undoubtedly did succumb to temptation and dip their fingers in the till.

For example, in 1896 and 1897, five guards operating from Bangalore committed a series of thefts from boxes or parcels that were marked for distant locations, escaping detention for quite a while. The guards would get into the luggage van at night, open the boxes at their ease, and help themselves to whatever took their fancy before repacking them. On one occasion, these men, who called themselves 'the Golden Gang,' pilfered 10 of 19 boxes belonging to the Nawab of Amroha, stealing goods worth about ₹3,000. A Special Railway Police Inspector from Lucknow, who was deputed to investigate the affair, suspected it to be the work of railway employees on the Guntakal–Bangalore line and asked Naidu to look into the case. A trap was accordingly laid for the men, who were apprehended at Bangalore and a cartload of stolen booty was recovered from them.

On another occasion, a guard was arrested for stealing part of a consignment of high-quality cigars that passed through the Agra Fort station. A few days later, he unwittingly offered a couple of them to the station master and his assistant who were out airing themselves on the platform. On being casually questioned as to the origin of the valuable cigars, he hesitated a moment before replying that he had got them from a friend in Calcutta. This aroused the officials' suspicions, and enquires were discreetly instituted about the guard and his wife. The guard's house was searched and many valuable items worth several thousand rupees were recovered. The guard was convicted but his wife managed to give the police the slip.[34]

Those tasked with preventing crime on the railway were also sometimes found to be involved. In November 1919, a parcel containing '37 Brahmin Ladies Saries' dispatched by a cloth merchant went missing at the Olavakkot (now Palakkad) Junction of the South Indian Railway. When it failed to reach its destination, a complaint was lodged but the railway officials at Olavakkot took no immediate steps to trace the package, and no complaint was made to the police. Over six months later, two constables of the Railway Police who were on duty when the crime was committed were arrested. One of them subsequently committed suicide by placing his head on the rails when a goods train was passing over the tracks during the night.[35]

The effrontery of some railway servants knew no bounds. In the infamous 'Croton Case', the station master at Nidadavole on the East Coast Railway sent an order to the Horticultural Gardens of Bangalore under a fictitious name for various kinds of flowering and croton plants. When these arrived at the station, he informed the consignor that the consignee could not be traced and then proceeded to plant the crotons on the station platform. The Horticulture Garden officials could only ask that the plants be auctioned at the earliest, which he did, buying them up under a false name. He apparently did this as he wanted to win the prize that was offered by the East Coast Railway to its station masters for beautifying their platforms! The man was subsequently charged and convicted in another case of theft and dismissed.[36]

Cases of fine wine, tins of condensed milk, bags of grain, baskets of fruit, parcels containing silk sarees, shirts and other apparel, even the very nuts and bolts that held the rails together were not spared the attentions of crooked railway staff. Seemingly, goods sent by rail seldom reached their destinations intact. The representative of the Tata Iron and Steel Co. complained that scarcely one per cent of the consignments of fruit, fish, and vegetables sent to its industrial colony at Jamshedpur arrived safely! The Mysore Chamber of Commerce said one-half of every consignment of coal was pilfered by women who openly carried it away in baskets. The Indian Tea Association lost 20 per cent of the rice it had ordered for the use of its garden coolies. In fact, it was only on a complaint by the Upper India Chamber of Commerce that a committee was appointed by the Home Department to enquire into the workings of the Railway Police administration in India.[37]

The Railway Police Committee Report of 1921 was not in the least edifying and the depositions made before its members made for very dismal reading. Theft and pilferage of materials dispatched by rail were on the increase, facilitated by the railway staff with the connivance of their superiors; thefts from goods sheds and transhipments were up nearly 67 per cent in 1919 over 1915. The railways themselves were not spared. The East India Railway lost nearly a quarter of million gallons of mineral oil to theft in 1920 while 600 maunds of coal were being stolen every day from the depot at Asansol. Security was lax, and the quality of watchmen employed was poor. These men were often recruited from the menial classes, associated with bad characters and assisted them in committing thefts. In Bombay and Madras, the committee heard, many of the watchmen were ex-convicts or dismissed railway employees. Railway station staff, too, were not above committing frauds and petty thefts, and some even stole oil from the lamps, leaving the stations in darkness. The Railway Police were not of much help and the quality of the staff 'left much to be desired'. Indeed, many witnesses told the committee, the Railway Police was 'a dumping ground for inefficients'.[38]

The Committee's recommendations were summarized in 24 points and included measures such as the institution of a properly supervised watch-and-ward system, improving the protection of goods wagons by riveting or other means, provision of more lighting at station yards and goods sheds, employing greater precautions for consignments of fruit- and liquor, and the provision of moveable cages to secure parcels at railway stations. To safeguard passengers on night trains, it recommended the provision of door bolts on all first and second-class carriages (not ladies' compartments alone), and also the employment of a suitable number of police guards in uniform on all trains. Looking at the larger picture though, it also recommended the setting up of a special detective and investigating agency for the railway police in each province with special training to be provided for all ranks. It also called for a Central Bureau of Investigation and Advice to be created under the Home Department, to be headed by an officer of the rank of inspector-general of police, to coordinate and advise the central and provincial governments and the Railway Board on matters connected with railway police administration.

While the recommendations were accepted and steps put in place to implement them, they were not always successful. S.M. Edwardes, writing in 1924, asserted that attempts to check theft from railway premises and running trains 'failed to check effectively this class of crime, which is committed daily with impunity.' In Punjab, armed observation patrols on night trains fought off bands of well-organized gangs that turned out with axes, lathis and hammers to loot goods trains.[39]

It may be that they were just an incorrigible lot, or perhaps the railways provided easy pickings and were a temptation that was hard to resist, but the 'railway thieves' were never entirely supressed, and their descendants, not any more defined by tribe or caste, are still with us long after the British departed our shores. The photos of wanted men on the notice boards of railway platforms in most of India's large cities are testimony to the fact that the railway thieves continue to ply their trade, just as they did in Naidu's heyday over a century ago.

Acknowledgements

I HAVE SEVERAL PEOPLE TO THANK FOR CONTRIBUTING TO THIS book. First off, Harish Nambiar – author, colleague and friend from my *Indian Express* days – who suggested I sound out literary agent Kanishka Gupta about my idea for this book, while scouting for a publisher. Kanishka embraced the project with enthusiasm, as did then Hachette India's Publisher Poulomi Chatterjee, who unfortunately moved on just after I completed the first draft of my manuscript. My sincere thanks to Poulomi for her interest in the book, and the feedback she provided in the early stages. Commissioning Editor Swarnima Narayan also worked hard on the book, and her valuable inputs on improving its contents along with insights into publishing that she provided as we went along are deeply appreciated. A jumbo-sized thank you to Hachette India's Managing Director Thomas Abraham who, during the course of a very interesting conversation on books and collecting, suggested we bring out the book in hardback – something I had always wanted! Thanks also to Gavin Morris for designing the lovely cover and Parul Sharma for the edits. The Hachette team has been superlative. I cannot thank them enough.

Many thanks are also due to author and fellow journalist Dhaval Kulkarni, who very generously shared his insights and research on the Bawla Murder Case. Mumbai police historian Deepak Rao tendered useful advice and regaled me with some fine stories on the so-called Pathan menace and other aspects of crime in colonial-era Mumbai. Thank you for some incredible stories, Rao*saheb*! Thanks also to Harveer Dabas and Baljeet Singh for inputs on the life of Sultana Daku. Baljeetji also provided me a rare photograph of Freddy Young which we were unfortunately not able to use. Dr Amol Divkar also helped with suggestions on avenues for research. Former Reuters colleague and friend Shreejay Sinha, and the staff at the National Archives of India also deserve my heartfelt thanks for assistance in locating documents related to the Akootai murder case.

To one of my very few friends in Bangalore, Dr. P. Vishnu Kamath, former professor of chemistry at Bangalore University, I owe a great debt for periodically bullying me into completing the manuscript, and for being a valuable sounding board on various issues. Friends from the old journalism days – Santosh Nair, Sandeep Unnithan, Niharika Bisaria, Manisha Rathore and Padmaja Parulkar-Kesnur – also encouraged me to keep at it. Former Reuters colleague and friend Aniruddha Basu also did his bit to cheer me up with the occasional free peg or pint at the exclusive Bangalore Club!

I am nothing without my family. To my mother Subhadra and father Karunakaran Nair, for their boundless faith in an often wayward son, I am eternally grateful. Sadly, they are not here to see this book. Thankfully, I have been blessed with the best of siblings in my brother Suresh and sister Suja, and also with in-laws whose support has never been lacking.

My 11-year-old daughter Arunima deserves kudos for the ceaseless chatter that enlivened the writing of this book, and helped fill out the long and often dreary pandemic days. Last, but not the least, my greatest thanks go to my wife Asha whose infinite patience and good cheer saw me through some very difficult days.

Endnotes

Chapter 1

1. T.H. Thornton, *General Sir Richard Meade and the Feudatory States of Central and Southern India*, United States: Palala Press, 2015. 179.

2. H.L. Adam, *The Indian Criminal,* London: John Milne, 1909. 226–227.

3. Ibid, 228.

4. Ibid, 229–230.

5. Philip W. Sergeant, *The Ruler of Baroda*, London: John Murray, 1928. 13–14; Adam, The Indian Criminal. 231.; Manu S. Pillai, 'Gold Cannons and a Poison Plot', Mint Lounge, 18 October 2019. Web. July 2022.

6. Thornton, General Sir Richard Meade, 164.

7. Ibid, 165–166.

8. Ibid, 167.

9. John Gunther, *Inside Asia*, New York and London: Harper and Brothers, 1942. 469.

10. Ibid.

11. Rosie Llewellyn-Jones, *The Great Uprising in India 1857–58*, Delhi: Supernova Publishers, 2010. 66–95.

12. Charles Chenevix Trench, *Viceroy's Agent*, London: Jonathan Cape, 1987. 210–11.

13. Caroline Keen, *An Imperial Crisis in British India: The Manipur Uprising of 1891*, India: Bloomsbury Publishing, 2020. 164.

14. Shaharyar Muhammad Khan, *Bhopal Connections: Vignettes of Royal Rule*, India: Roli Books, 2017. 44.

15. In later years, Dadabhai achieved the distinction of becoming the first Indian Member of Parliament in the British House of Commons and, following a distinguished career in public life, came to be venerated as the Grand Old Man of India.

16. Thornton, *General Sir Richard Meade*, 177–78.

17. Kate Colquhoun, *Mr Briggs' Hat: A Sensational Account of Britain's First Railway Murder*, United Kingdom: Little, Brown Book Group, 2011. 200.

18. Details of the Commission's proceedings in subsequent paragraphs have been largely taken from *The Great Baroda Case: Being a Full Report of the Proceedings of the Trial and Deposition of His Highness Mulhar Rao Gaekwar of Baroda for Instigating an Attempt to Poison the British Resident at his Court* reprinted by Nabu Press, 2012.

19. Adam, *The Indian Criminal*, 243–44.

20. Thornton, *General Sir Richard Meade*, 203.

21. Philip W. Sergeant, *The Ruler of Baroda*, London: John Murray, 1928. 20.

22. Ibid, 20–21.

Chapter 2

1. The description of the events on Malabar Hill is largely based on the works of K.L. Gauba, D. Kulkarni, and the Bombay High Court Records held at the National Archives of India. Kulkarni's book on the case is by far the most comprehensive and authoritative to date.

2. Mumtaz's story is pieced together from the accounts of D. Kulkarni, P.B. Vachha, and Bombay High Court Records, from the National Archives of India.

3. K.L. Gauba, *Famous Trials for Love and Murder*, Delhi: Hind Pocket Books, 1967. 140.

4. Details of the trial in subsequent pages are largely sourced from Bombay High Court Records, Bawla Murder Case available at the National Archives of India and online at abhilek-patal.in.

5. From the testimony of Lt Saegert in Bombay High Court's Records of the Bawla Murder Case.; *Emperor Vs Shafi Ahmed Nabi Ahmed*, 22 of 1925, Bombay High Court. National Archives of India. File No: Home/Political/NA-1925/F114/II. 37.

6. Ibid, 40.

7. Gauba, Famous Trials of Love, 150–152.

8. Pratiek Dhadha and Akshay Chavan, 'Maharajas of Indore', *The Diamond Talk*, 23 Aug 2021. Web. April 2022. <https://thediamondtalk.in/maharajas-of-indore/>.

9. Charles Chenevix Trench, *Viceroy's Agent*, London: Jonathan Cape, 1987. 174–176.

10. John Gunther, *Inside Asia*, New York and London: Harper and Brothers, 1942. 476.

Chapter 3

1. Cecil Walsh, *The Agra Double Murder*, Delhi: Speaking Tiger, 2017. 10.

2. Ibid, 9.

3. Molly Whittington-Egan, *Khaki Mischief: The Agra Murder Case*, London: Souvenir Press, 1990. 112–113.

4. Ibid, 126.

5. Ibid, 134–135.

6. Ibid, 141.

7. Ibid.

8. Ibid, 242–243.

Chapter 4

1. Dr (Sir) Nil Ratan Sircar was a renowned medical practitioner, philanthropist and entrepreneur of pre-Independence Bengal. One of the founders of the Indian Medical Association, he was knighted for his services to medicine in 1918. His alma mater, Campbell Medical School, was renamed Nil Ratan Sircar Medical College and Hospital in his honour in 1950.

2. *Benoyendra Chandra Pandey v. Emperor*, on 10 January, 1936, *Indian Kanoon*, n.d. Web. May 2022. https://indiankanoon.org/doc/1586771//doc/1586771/

Chapter 5

1. George Hext's story is largely based on the book *The Punjab Mail Murder* by Roger Perkins, the only work I have found on the subject,

and from *The Roll of Honour* by K.C. Ghosh. The papers relating to the case are in the National Archives of India. NAI-Home-Pol/File No 4/22/1931).

2. Kali Charan Ghosh, *Roll of Honour*, Calcutta: Vidya Bharti, 1960. 504–505. https://ia600701.us.archive.org/15/items/dli.bengal.10689.12784/10689.12784.pdf

3. Report on the Police Administration of the Central Provinces and Berar for the Calendar Year 1931, 13–14. https://dspace.gipe.ac.in/xmlui/bitstream/handle/10973/28563/GIPE-010373-08.pdf?sequence=3&isAllowed=y

4. Roger Perkins, *The Punjab Mail Murder*, Chippenham: Picton Publishing, 1986. 43.

5. Ibid.

6. Ibid, 44.

7. Ibid.

8. Ghosh, *Roll of Honour*. 506.

Chapter 6

1. In his deposition, he gave his name as Mirauzel Syedkhan, but seems to have been known by the name Syed Mirza, which is also used in other documents. I have used the name Mirza throughout.

2. This reconstruction of Akootai's life is largely based on documents for the case (King-Emperor vs Miroza (sic) Syedkhan and others), National Archives of India: Home Department, 1917A, Police A, December 128-130; High Court of Judicature Bombay, 2nd sessions, 1917, case no 13) Also, Ashwini Tambe's *Codes of Misconduct: Regulating Prostitution in Late Colonial India* provided insights into the lives of Akootai and other brothel workers in colonial Bombay.

3. A yard-measure was a carpenter's measuring tool of that length made of wood or metal, often brass. Some models were made in two or three sections and could be folded for ease of carrying.

4. Proceedings of the Home Department, 1917A, Dec 128-130. National Archives of India].

5. Sandy Chang, 'Colonial Haunting: Prostitution and the Politics of Sex Trafficking in British India 1913-1939', Thesis, University of British Columbia, 2012. 32–36.

6. Ibid.

Chapter 7

1. George Leigh Mallory never achieved the distinction of having conquered Mt. Everest, but he made it to the pantheon of mountaineering giants when he disappeared along with his climbing partner Andrew Irvine on the north-east ridge some 800 feet from the summit during their 1924 attempt. His body was only found in 1999. Irvine's body was never discovered.

2. Ian Morsehead, *The Life and Murder of Henry Morshead*, Cambridge: The Oleander Press, 1982. 148. This book is the primary source I have consulted for writing this account of Morshead's murder.

3. Christian Gilberti, 'Unearthing the Truth Behind a Colonial Murder in Maymyo', Frontier Myanmar, 4 October 2019. Web. May 2022. <https://www.frontiermyanmar.net/en/unearthing-the-truth-behind-a-colonial-murder-in-maymyo/>

Chapter 8

1. Harveer Dabas, 'How the Legend of Sultana Daku Refuses to leave this Bijnor Castle', *Times of India*, 10 Sept 2017. Web. April 2022.

2. It was said that Sultana had been told by an astrologer that he could only be captured when he was seated on the ground with a child on his lap.

3. *London Gazette*, 2 Jan 1914.

4. Jim Corbett, *My India*, Delhi: Oxford University Press, 1996. 101.

5. The dog was apparently named 'Raibahadur' to show the dacoit's contempt for Indian officials who received titles from the British. Sultana also had a horse, supposedly named 'Chetak' after Maharana Pratap's famous steed. What became of the horse is not known.

6. Among the many tales that make up the legend of Sultana is one that claims that Young in fact sent Sultana's son to England to be educated and the young man later came back home and served as an officer with the Indian Police. However, there is nothing in the written record to substantiate this.

7. Percival Griffiths, *To Guard My People: The History of the Indian Police*, London: Ernest Benn Ltd, 1971. 408.

8. J.C. Curry, *The Indian Police*, London: Faber & Faber, 1932. 218.; Supplement to *London Gazette*, 3 June 1924. 4421.

9. Curry, The Indian Police, 216–217.
10. Griffiths, To Guard My People. 409.

Chapter 9

1. James L. Sleeman, *Thug; Or, A Million Murders*, India: Pilgrims Book Pvt Ltd, Delhi, 1998. 3.
2. *The Story of My Life: Meadows Taylor*, His Daughter (ed.), India: Asian Educational Services, 1986. 61–62.
3. Ibid, 80.
4. Ibid.
5. Ibid.
6. Ibid.
7. Sleeman, Thug, 20.
8. Ibid, 19–20.
9. Edward Thornton, *Illustrations of the History and Practices of the Thugs*, New Delhi: Asian Educational Services, 2000. 271.
10. Kim Wagner, *Thuggee: Banditry and the British in Early Nineteenth-Century India*, New Delhi: Primus Books, 2014. 203, 143.
11. Ibid, preface.
12. W.H. Sleeman, *The Thugs or Phansigars of India*, Philadelphia: Carey and Hart, 839. 95–96.
13. Ibid, 97–98.
14. Thornton, Illustrations, 163–164.
15. Ibid, 191–192.
16. Ibid, 205–206.
17. Sleeman, Thugs or Phansigars, 154.
18. Ibid, 146.
19. Wagner, Thuggee, 144–147.; Thornton, Illustrations, 55–57.
20. Sleeman, Thugs or Phansigars, 199–200.
21. Ibid, 102–104.
22. Henry Beveridge, *The District of Bakargunj: Its History and Statistics*, 1876, qtd. in Benjamin Kingsbury, *An Imperial Disaster: The Bengal Cyclone of 1876*, Delhi: Speaking Tiger, 2018. 69.
23. Saros Cowasjee, *Stories from the Raj*, London: Bodley Head, 1982. 155–180.

24. Percival Griffiths, *To Guard My People*, London: Ernest Benn, 1971. 126.

25. Ibid. 126–127.

26. Wagner, Thuggee, 214.

27. Griffiths, To Guard My People, 127.

28. Mala Sen, *India's Bandit Queen*, Britain: Harvill, 1991. 119–120.

29. Mike Dash, *Thug: The True Story of India's Murderous Cult*, London: Granta Publications, 2005. 256–257.

30. Wagner, Thuggee, 228.

31. Dash, Thug, 269.

32. Ibid, 274.

33. Ibid, 265.

34. Ibid.

35. Griffiths, To Guard My People, 132.

36. Ibid.

37. Dash, Thug, 279.

Chapter 10

1. Eustace J. Kitts, *Serious Crime in an Indian Province*, Bombay: Education Society's Press, 1889. 19–20.

2. Ibid, 20.

3. The Criminal Tribes Act enacted by the British in 1871 held that certain classes and castes of people were inherently criminal by nature or profession, and gave the colonial police wide powers to arrest them and monitor their movements. Thus, many classes of people who had no fixed occupation or place of residence and led nomadic lives came to be unjustly branded as 'criminal'. The Act was repealed in 1952, but the colonial legacy has survived and the descendants of these tribes or castes still face discrimination and harassment.

4. Kitts, Serious Crime, 27.

5. Ibid, 33.

6. Ibid, 27–28.

7. James Hutton, *A Popular Account of the Thugs and Dacoits: The Hereditary Garrotters and Gang Robbers of India*, London: William H. Allen & Co., 1857. 156–157.

8. Ibid.

9. Kitts, Serious Crime, 28.

10. Hutton, Thugs and Dacoits, 122.

11. Ibid, 106–107.

12. Ibid, 110–112.

13. Ibid, 123–127.

14. Ibid, 104.

15. Kitts, Serious Crime, 30.

16. Ibid, 31.

17. James Hutton, *A Popular Account of the Thugs and Dacoits: The Hereditary Garrotters and Gang-Robbers of India*, London: William H. Allen & Co., 1857. 159–160.

18. P.D. Reeves ed., *Sleeman in Oudh: An Abridgement of W.H. Sleeman's 'A Journey Through the Kingdom of Oude 1848–50*, United Kingdom: Cambridge University Press, 1971. 210–211.

19. Ibid, 71.

20. Kitts, Serious Crime, 33.

21. Henry Beveridge, *The District of Bakargunj: Its History and Statistics*, London, 1876, qtd in Benjamin Kingsbury, *An Imperial Disaster*, Delhi: Speaking Tiger Publications, 2018. 69.

22. Kingsbury, An Imperial Disaster, 149–151.

23. Percival Griffiths, *To Guard My People: The History of the Indian Police*, London: Ernest Benn Ltd., 1971. 133

24. Ibid, 135.

25. J.C. Curry, *The Indian Police*, London: Faber & Faber, 1932. 213–214.

26. Ibid, 216.

27. Arthur Griffiths, *Oriental Prisons*, London: The Grolier Society, 1900. 117–120.

28. Curry, The Indian Police, 32.

29. Ibid, 211.

30. Ibid, 220.

31. Ibid, 206.

32. Ibid, 220.

33. Ibid, 221.

34. Taroon Coomar Bhaduri, *Chambal: The Valley of Terror*, Delhi: Vikas Pub. House, 1972. 39.

Chapter 11

1. Ira Mukhoty, 'The First Betrayal Through Poisoned Food Changed the Mughals' Dynamics with Food and Drink', *The Hindu*, 18 Nov 2017. Web. May 2022.

2. W.H. Sleeman, *Rambles and Reflections of an Indian Official*, Vol. 1, New Delhi: Asian Educational Services, 1995. 105.

3. E.R.C Bradford, *Statements of the Crime of Poisoning in British Territory for the year 1875, compiled by Major E.R.C Bradford, C.S.I., General Superintendent of Operations for the Suppression of Thuggee and Dacoity*, Simla: Government Central Branch Press, 1877.

4. Ibid, 62.

5. Sleeman, Rambles and Reflections, 101–104.

6. Ibid, 105.

7. Ibid, 105–106.

8. G.D. Martineau, *Controller of Devils: A Life of John Paul Warburton, CIE, of the Punjab Police*. 28–32.

9. Eustace J. Kitts, *Serious Crime in an Indian Province*, Bombay: Education Society's Press, 1889. 4.

10. Ibid, 5–6.

11. Arthur Griffiths, *Oriental Prisons*, London: The Grolier Society, 1900. 102.

12. S.T. Hollis, *No Ten Commandments: Life in the Indian Police*, London: Hutchison, 1954. 114–119.

13. Kitts, Serious Crime, 6–7.

14. Ibid.

15. Griffiths, Oriental Poisons, 103–104.

16. Shoemaker.

17. Cart driver; derived from bandy or vandy, meaning cart in Tamil and Malayalam.

18. Bradford, Statements of the Crime, 68.

19. Kitts, Serious Crime, 4–5.

20. Bradford, Statements of the Crime, 62–63.

21. Ibid.

22. S.M. Edwardes, *Crime in India*, London: Oxford University Press, 1924. 40

23. Ibid, 39–40.

Chapter 12

1. The first edition came out in 1904.
2. *Report on Railway Police*, File No. Progs Nos. 1&2. No. 1, Home Department Proceedings, Police Branch, Calcutta, 12 June 1882, National Archives of India, quoted from C.S.R. Shankar, 'Misusing the Railway: Theft, obstruction and Modernity in Railways of Colonial India, c. 1876–1922', *Academia*, n.d. Web. May 2022.
3. Ibid.
4. Eustace J. Kitts, *Serious Crime in an Indian Province*, Bombay: Education Society's Press, 1889. 78–79.
5. Ibid, 85.
6. Ibid, 65.
7. M. Pauparao Naidu, *History of the Railway Thieves in India*, New Delhi: Vintage Books, 1996. 4.
8. Ibid, 11.
9. F.C. Daly, *Manual of Criminal Classes Operating in Bengal*, Calcutta: Bengal Secretariat Press, 1915. 51.
10. Naidu, Railway Thieves, 9.
11. Daly, Manual of Criminal Classes, 51.
12. Ibid. 53
13. Naidu, Railway Thieves, 8.
14. Ibid, 54.
15. Frederick S. Mullaly, *Notes on Criminal Tribes of the Madras Presidency*, Government Press, 1892. 53–56.
16. Ibid, 61.
17. Ibid, 66.
18. Naidu, Railway Thieves, 140.
19. Mullaly, Criminal Tribes, 9.
20. *Report on Railway Police*, File No. Progs Nos. 1&2. No. 1, Home Department Proceedings, Police Branch, Calcutta, 12 June 1882, National Archives of India, quoted from C.S.R. Shankar, 'Misusing the Railway: Theft, obstruction and Modernity in Railways of Colonial India, c. 1876–1922', *Academia*, n.d. Web. May 2022
21. Naidu, Railway Thieves, 145.
22. Ibid, 146–147.
23. Ibid, 163.

24. Ibid, 169–170.

25. Ibid, 148–149.

26. Ibid, 158.

27. Naidu, Railway Thieves, 158.; Bibek Debroy, Sanjay Chadha and Vidya Krishnamurthy, *Indian Railways: The Weaving of a Nation al Tapestry*, Noida: Penguin Random House India, 2017. 208–209.

28. Naidu, Railway Thieves, 161.

29. 'Affray in a Train', *The Hindu*, 21 February 1919. Web. May 2022. <https://www.thehindu.com/archives/from-the-archives-feb-21-1919-affray-in-a-train/article26322860.ece>

30. Naidu, Railway Thieves, 149.

31. Ibid, 162–163.

32. Shankar, Misusing the Railway.

33. Naidu, Railway Thieves, 173

34. Ibid, 178–179.

35. 'A Sensational Railway Theft', *The Hindu*, 7 May 1919. Web. May 2022.

36. Naidu, Railway Thieves, 188–189.

37. *Report of the Railway Police Committee*, Government Monotype Press, 1921. 3–4. Web. May 2022. <https://ia803407.us.archive.org/26/items/dli.ministry.21379/0994.pdf>

38. Ibid.

39. S.M. Edwardes, *Crime in India*, London: Oxford University Press, 1924. 57–58.

Other Works Consulted

Chapter 1

Charles Allen and Sharada Dwivedi, *Lives of the Indian Prince*, London: Century Publishing Co, 1984.

Terence Creagh Coen, *The Indian Political Service*, London: Chatto & Windus, 1971.

S.M. Edwardes, *The Bombay City Police: A Historical Sketch 1672-1916*, London: Humphrey Milford, Oxford University Press, 1923.

Mulhar Rao Gaekwar, *The Great Baroda Case: Being a Full Report of the Proceedings of the Trial and Deposition of His Highness Mulhar Rao Gaekwar of Baroda for Instigating an Attempt to Poison the British Resident at his Court*, reprint, India: Nabu Press, 2012.

Arthur Griffiths, *Oriental Prisons*, London: The Grolier Society, 1900.

Sunil Raman and Rohit Agarwal, *Delhi Durbar 1911: The Complete Story*, Delhi: Roli Books, 2012.

Louis Rousselet, *India and its Native Princes*, Delhi: Niyogi Books, 2011.

Judith Rowbotham, 'Miscarriage of Justice? Post-colonial Reflections on the Trial of the Maharajah of Baroda 1875', *Liverpool Law Review*, Vol. 28:377–403, 2007.

P.B. Vachha, *Famous Judges, Lawyers and Cases of Bombay*, Gurgaon: Universal Law Publishing Co., 2011.

The Trial and Deposition of Mulhar Rao Gaekwar of Baroda, Bombay: Bombay Gazette Steam Press, 1875.

V.K. Chavda, *Sayaji Rao Gaekwad*, New Delhi: National Book Trust India, 1972

Chapter 2

'Bawla Murder Case-1925', *Bombay High Court*, n.d. Web. May 2022. <https://bombayhighcourt.nic.in/libweb/historicalcases/cases/BAWLA_MURDER_CASE-1925.html>

S. Dutt, *True Stories of Strange Murders in India*, India: Vikas Publications, 1972.

Angma D. Jhala, *Courtly Women in Late Imperial India*, London & New York: Routledge, 2008.

———, 'Troubles in Indore, the Maharaja's Women: Loving Dangerously', *Courtly Indian Women in Late Imperial India*, London: Pickering and Chatto, 2008.

———, 'The Malabar Hill Murder Trial of 1925: Sovereignty, Law and Politics in Colonial Princely India', *The Indian Economic and Social History Review*, Vol. 46(3):373–400, 2009.

Dhaval Kulkarni, *The Bawla Murder Case: Love, Lust and Crime in Colonial India*, Gurgaon: HarperCollins Publishers, 2021.

P.B. Vachha, *Famous Judges, Lawyers and Cases of Bombay*, Gurgaon: Universal Law Publishing Co., 2011.

Coralie Younger, *Wicked Women of the Raj*, Noida: Harper Collins Publishers India, 2006.

Chapter 3

David Burton, *The Raj at Table*, Delhi: Rupa & Co., 1995.

John Emsley, *The Elements of Murder: A History of Poison*, Oxford: Oxford University Press, 2005.

K.L. Gauba, *Famous Trials for Love and Murder*, Delhi: Hind Pocket Books, 1967.

Chapter 4

A.K. Biswas, 'Crime Under Cover of Pandemic. Plague in Pakur Raj Fratricide', *Mainstream*, Vol. LVIII(38), 5 September 2020. Web. May 2022.

S. Dutt, *True Stories of Strange Murders in India*, Delhi: Vikas Publications, 1972.

S.M. Edwardes, *Crime in India*, London: Oxford University Press, 1924.

K.L. Gauba, *Famous Trials for Love and Murder*, Delhi: Hind Pocket Books, 1967.

Arthur Cunningham Lothian, *Kingdoms of Yesterday*, London: John Murray, 1951.

Rudrajit Paul, 'Bacteria as a Murder Weapon: A Tale from Colonial Calcutta', *Bengal Physician Journal*, Vol. 6(2):37–39, 2019.

S. Rajagopalan, *Famous Murder Trials*, India: N.M. Tripathi, 1968.

Supratim Sarkar, *Murder in the City: Twelve Incredible Case Files of the Kolkata Police*, translated by Swati Sengupta, Delhi: Speaking Tiger Publishing, 2018.

Chapter 5

Rajendra B. Aklekar, *A Short History of Indian Railways*, India: Rupa Publications, 2019.

Manoshi Bhattacharya, *Chittagong: Summer of 1930*, Noida: HarperCollins Publishers India, 2012.

———, *Chittagong: Eye of the Tiger*, Noida: HarperCollins Publishers India, 2014.

Bibek Debroy, Sanjay Chadha and Vidya Krishnamurthy, *Indian Railways: The Weaving of a National Tapestry*, Noida: Penguin Random House India, 2017.

Ian Talbot and Tahir Kamran, *Lahore in the Time of the Raj*, Noida: Penguin Random House India, 2016.

Chris Moffat, *India's Revolutionary Inheritance: Politics and the Promise of Bhagat Singh*, United Kingdom: Cambridge University Press, 2019.

Chapter 6

S.M. Edwardes, *The Bombay City Police: A Historical Sketch 1672–1916*, London: Humphrey Milford, Oxford University Press, 1923.

———, *Crime in India*, London: Oxford University Press, 1924.

R. Chandavarkar, *Imperial Power and Popular Politics*, United Kingdom: Cambridge University Press, 1998.

Michael Kirwan Joyce, *An Exposure of the Haunts of Infamy and Dens of Vice in Bombay*, India: The Bombay Gazette Press, 1854.

Samuel T. Sheppard, *Bombay Place-Names and Street-Names*, India: Indus Source Books, 2019.

Ashwini Tambe, *Codes of Misconduct: Regulating Prostitution in Late Colonial Bombay*, Delhi: Zubaan, 2009.

Chapter 7

David Breashears and Audrey Salkeld, *Last Climb: The Legendary Everest Expeditions of George Mallory*, Washington: National Geographic Society, 1999.
Burma: Insight Guides, 2nd ed., Hong Kong: Apa Productions (HK) Ltd., 1982.
Maurice Collis, *Trials in Burma*, London: Penguin Books, 1945.
Wade Davis, *Into the Silence: The Great War, Mallory and the Conquest of Everest*, London: The Bodley Head, 2011.
Nicholas Greenwood, *Shades of Gold and Green: Anecdotes of Colonial Burmah, 1886–1948*, India: Asian Educational Services, 1998.
Emma Larkin, *Finding George Orwell in Burma*, New York: Penguin Press, 2005.
'Murder and Mystery in Myanmar', *Thamine*, 9 March 2019. Web. May 2022. <https://thamine.blog/2019/03/09/murder-and-mystery-at-maymyo/>
Robert Slater, *Guns Through Arcady, Burma and the Burma Road*, Sydney/London: Angus and Robertson, 1941.
Shway Yoe, *The Burman: His Life and Notions*, London: MacMillian & Co, 1910.

Chapter 8

Taroon Coomar Bhaduri, *Chambal: The Valley of Terror*, Delhi: Vikas Publishing House, 1972.
S.M. Edwardes, *Crime in India*, London: Oxford University Press, 1924.
Mala Sen, *India's Bandit Queen*, Britain: Harvill, 1991.

Chapter 9

S.M. Edwardes, *Crime in India*, London: Oxford University Press, 1924.
Arthur Griffiths, *Oriental Prisons*, London: The Grolier Society, 1900.

- James Hutton, *A Popular Account of the Thugs and Dacoits: The Hereditary Garrotters and Gang-Robbers of India*, London: William H. Allen & Co., 1857.
- Eustace J. Kitts, *Serious Crime in an Indian Province*, Bombay: Education Society's Press, 1889.
- George McMunn, *The Religions and Hidden Cults of India*, London: Samson Low, Marston & Co., 1931.
- P.D. Reeves (ed.), *Sleeman in Oudh: An Abridgement of W.H. Sleeman's 'A Journey Through the Kingdom of Oude 1848–50*, United Kingdom: Cambridge University Press, 1971.
- Kevin Rushby, *Children of Kali: Through India in Search of Bandits, the Thug Cult and the British Raj*, London: Constable, 2002.
- W.H. Sleeman, *Rambles and Reflections of an Indian Official*, New Delhi: Asian Educational Services, 1995.
- Philip Meadows Taylor, *Confessions of a Thug*, London: Folio Society, 1974.

Chapter 10

- E.R.C Bradford, *Statements of the Crime of Poisoning in British Territory for the year 1875, compiled by Major E.R.C Bradford, C.S.I., General Superintendent of Operations for the Suppression of Thuggee and Dacoity*, Simla: Government Central Branch Press, 1877.
- S.M. Edwardes, *Crime in India*, London: Oxford University Press, 1924.
- W.H. Sleeman, *Rambles and Reflections of an Indian Official*, New Delhi: Asian Educational Services, 1995.

Chapter 11

- William Crooke, *Things Indian: Being Discursive Notes on Various Subjects Connected with India*, India: Niyogi Books, 2012.
- John Emsley, *The Elements of Murder: A History of Poison*, Oxford: Oxford University Press, 2005.
- G.D. Martineau, *Controller of Devils: A Life of John Paul Warburton, CIE, of the Punjab Police*. Dorset: Lyme Regis.

Chapter 12

Rajendra B. Aklekar, *A Short History of Indian Railways*, India: Rupa Publications, 2019.

J.C. Curry, *The Indian Police*, London: Faber & Faber, 1932.

Percival Griffiths, *To Guard My People: The History of the Indian Police*, London: Ernest Benn, 1971.

E. J. Gunthrope, *Notes on Criminal Tribes Residing in or Frequenting the Bombay Presidency, Berar and the Central Provinces*, Bombay: Times of India Steam Press, 1882.